Studies in Diplomacy

General Editor: G. R. Leicester

MW01132652

The series was launch scholarship on the theory and practice of international diplomacy, including its legal regulation. The interests of the series thus embrace such diplomatic functions as signalling, negotiation and consular work, and methods such as summitry and the multilateral conference. Whilst it has a sharp focus on diplomacy at the expense of foreign policy, therefore, the series has no prejudice as to historical period or approach. It also aims to include manuals on protocol and other aspects of diplomatic practice which will be of immediate, day-to-day relevance to professional diplomats. A final ambition is to reprint inaccessible classic works on diplomacy.

Titles include:

G. R. Berridge, Maurice Keens-Soper and T. G. Otte
DIPLOMATIC THEORY FROM MACHIAVELLI TO KISSINGER

Herman J. Cohen
INTERVENING IN AFRICA
Superpower Peacemaking in a Troubled Continent

Andrew F. Cooper (*editor*)
NICHE DIPLOMACY
Middle Powers after the Cold War

David H. Dunn (*editor*)
DIPLOMACY AT THE HIGHEST LEVEL
The Evolution of International Summitry

Brian Hocking (*editor*)
FOREIGN MINISTRIES
Change and Adaptation

Michael Hughes
DIPLOMACY BEFORE THE RUSSIAN REVOLUTION
Britain, Russia and the Old Diplomacy, 1894–1917

Donna Lee
MIDDLE POWERS AND COMMERCIAL DIPLOMACY
British Influence at the Kennedy Trade Round

Jan Melissen (*editor*)
INNOVATION IN DIPLOMATIC PRACTICE

Peter Neville
APPEASING HITLER
The Diplomacy of Sir Nevile Henderson, 1937–39

M. J. Peterson
RECOGNITION OF GOVERNMENTS
Legal Doctrine and State Practice, 1815–1995

Gary D. Rawnsley
RADIO DIPLOMACY AND PROPAGANDA
The BBC and VOA in International Politics, 1956–64

TAIWAN'S INFORMAL DIPLOMACY AND PROPAGANDA

Studies in Diplomacy
Series Standing Order ISBN 0-333-71495-4
(*outside North America only*)

You can receive future titles in this series as they are published by placing a standing order. Please contact your bookseller or, in case of difficulty, write to us at the address below with your name and address, the title of the series and the ISBN quoted above.

Customer Services Department, Macmillan Distribution Ltd, Houndmills, Basingstoke, Hampshire RG21 6XS, England

Diplomatic Theory from Machiavelli to Kissinger

G. R. Berridge

Maurice Keens-Soper

and

T. G. Otte

First published 2001 by
PALGRAVE
Houndmills, Basingstoke, Hampshire RG21 6XS and
175 Fifth Avenue, New York, N.Y. 10010
Companies and representatives throughout the world

PALGRAVE is the new global academic imprint of
St. Martin's Press LLC Scholarly and Reference Division and
Palgrave Publishers Ltd (formerly Macmillan Press Ltd).

ISBN 0–333–75365–8 hardback
ISBN 0–333–75366–6 paperback

This book is printed on paper suitable for recycling and made from fully managed and sustained forest sources.

A catalogue record for this book is available from the British Library.

Library of Congress Cataloging-in-Publication Data
Diplomatic theory from Machiavelli to Kissinger / [edited by]
G.R. Berridge, Maurice Keens-Soper, T.G. Otte.
    p. cm. — (Studies in diplomacy)
    Includes bibliographical references and index.
    ISBN 0–333–75365–8 (hbk.) — ISBN 0–333–75366–6 (pbk.)
    1. Diplomacy—Philosophy. 2. Diplomats. I. Berridge, Geoff.
    II. Keens-Soper, H. M. A. III. Otte, Thomas G., 1967– IV. Series.
    JZ1305 .D57 2000
    327.1'01—dc21
                                                              00–048350

10   9   8   7   6   5   4   3   2   1
10   09 08 07 06 05 04 03 02 01

Transferred to digital printing in 2006.

Contents

Preface

There is a long tradition in the Department of Politics at the University of Leicester of teaching political theory through the 'political classics', and three collections of essays providing guidance to these texts have been published by members of the Department or persons at one time associated with it. It was natural, therefore, when diplomatic theory subsequently began to be taught in the Department as well, that thought should turn to producing a guide to the 'diplomatic classics'. These however proved more difficult to identify, and it has been necessary, therefore, as a rule, to make the diplomatic *oeuvre* of selected authors, rather than single texts, the organizing principle of this particular collection. However, the very scarcity of diplomatic classics and the consequent need to sift through many works for valuable reflections on diplomacy, perhaps makes a book of this sort especially valuable. It is our hope that it will not only stimulate interest in diplomatic theory but for the first time provide an accessible text for courses on this subject.

I am responsible for the Introduction to this volume but it has benefited greatly from the suggestions of Maurice Keens-Soper and T. G. Otte, the member of our trio who, I am bound to note with regret, is not associated with the University of Leicester. The Introduction explains the focus of the book, indicates the character of diplomatic theory, and highlights some of the major themes which emerge from the subsequent chapters. The chapters themselves are ordered chronologically and each is rounded off with suggestions for further reading.

G. R. Berridge
Leicester

Acknowledgements

G. R. Berridge would like to express his great appreciation to Wayne Shannon for commenting on his Machiavelli chapter, to Richard Langhorne and Monteagle Stearns for their helpful observations on the chapter on Richelieu, and to Anne Rafique for her expert copy-editing of the whole book. In connection with his chapter on Nicolson, T. G. Otte would like to say that he is greatly indebted to Nigel Nicolson, Sir Harold's surviving son and literary executor, for his kind hospitality and the generosity with which he made available to him his father's papers. Without these benefactions the process of writing this chapter would have been a great deal less enjoyable. Extracts from his father's papers are quoted with his kind permission. T. G. Otte would also like to record his thanks to Mrs Ileana Troiano, the daughter of Viorel Tilea, who kindly allowed him access to her father's correspondence with Harold Nicolson. The advice on titles given by John Young for the 'historical background' section of the 'Further reading' at the end of the Kissinger chapter is also acknowledged with gratitude.

Introduction

Diplomacy is the term given to the official channels of communication employed by the members of a system of states. [1] In the modern world system these are to be found chiefly in a network of diplomats and consuls who enjoy the protection of special legal rules and are permanently resident abroad, some at the seats of international organizations. This network first came into being in the Italian peninsula in the second half of the fifteenth century and reached its full expression in Europe in the two and a half centuries that followed the Congress of Münster and Osnabrück (1644–8). From the end of the First World War until well after the end of the Second, the diplomacy of this system was subjected to unprecedented criticism: it was said to be the handmaiden of war, or imperialism – or both. Nevertheless, it withstood its detractors and, at the height of the Cold War, was strengthened by the successful codification of the customary international law governing its procedures. [2]

Diplomacy turns chiefly on regular and regularized negotiation, [3] and its advent was a moment of profound historical importance. For so long as power continues to be dispersed among a plurality of states, negotiation will remain essential to the difference between peace and war. It is only negotiation, in other words, that can produce the advantages obtainable from the cooperative pursuit of common interests; and it is only this activity that can prevent violence from being employed to settle remaining arguments over conflicting ones. When war breaks out nevertheless, it is also negotiation that remains indispensable if the worst excesses of fighting are to be limited and if, in addition, a mutually tolerable peace is eventually to be achieved. In orchestrating and moderating the dialogue between states, diplomacy thus serves as a bulwark against international chaos; in this way it may be understood as a more fragile counterpart, operating within a system based upon states, to the domestic order or 'political system' of the state itself.

Although diplomacy thus conceived is the theme of this collection of essays, something further needs to be said about 'diplomatic theory'. As with other forms of theorizing, including the political theory of the state, diplomatic theory is reflective in character, permanently indebted to historical reasoning, and unfailingly ethical in inspiration. The moral element is perhaps nowhere better illustrated than by the question: must diplomats always keep their promises to foreign governments? However, even the claim of Martin Wight that diplomacy is 'the master-institution of international relations'[4] is an argument not solely – or even chiefly – about its varying impact on everyday international events, but about its value and the consequent wisdom of upholding it.

Diplomatic theory appeared at the same time as diplomacy began to assume its distinctively modern form in the late fifteenth century, though it is not surprising that at this stage it was weak and stunted in growth. In the course of analysing many treatises on the ambassador produced in the period from the late fifteenth until the early sixteenth century, Behrens[5] observed repeated emphasis on the following lines of questioning: What is an ambassador? What class of person and manner of entourage should be sent on different kinds of mission to princes of varying standing? Is a hierarchy of official classes of diplomat desirable and, if so, what form should it take? On what grounds are the privileges and immunities of diplomats justified? For what purposes do embassies exist? By what principles should an ambassador regulate his conduct; in particular, must he always be honest?[6] Above all, were the newly emerging resident embassies a good thing or not?[7] Though the answers to these questions were seldom extensively considered and often lacking cogency, we can at least see that the questions themselves were good ones. Most have remained points of departure for diplomatic theory until the present time.

In those days most of the writing on diplomacy was the work of either diplomats such as Ermolao Barbaro, jurists like Alberico Gentili, or some typified by Grotius who were both. As a result, and also in obedience to the fashionable 'mirror of princes' tradition, until the late seventeenth century discussion of diplomacy tended to revolve around 'the perfect ambassador' and his complex legal standing at a foreign court. In the aftermath of the Congress of Münster and Osnabrück however, when it became clear that the rulers of Europe had a common interest in regulating their frequently bellicose 'foreign' relations, diplomatic theory acquired a more explicit *political* flavour. This occurred when attention came to centre on the part played by the combined and continuous activities of numerous embassies representing the constituent parts of the loose association of 'Europe'. This is particularly evident in Wicquefort's encyclopaedic analysis, which adds to the usual account of the 'law of nations' relating to diplomatic immunity a refreshing emphasis on the regime of work daily engaged in by ambassadors and other envoys. The new angle of interest was however given most trenchant expression in the more succinct and accessible treatment provided by Callières. It is Callières, writing at the time of the Congress of Ryswick (1697), who first and most tellingly explains diplomacy by reference to the business of a multiplicity of states, and who is persuaded of its indispensable usefulness – amounting to necessity – to the European states-system.

As with Wicquefort and Callières, the other seven accounts of diplomacy have been chosen for the understanding they bring to some of the enduring questions raised by this distinctive activity. Separately and in combination, the consideration of these 'classic texts' is rewarding for both philosophical and historical reasons. However, the authors collected together in this book have also been chosen to illustrate the evolution of diplomatic theory. It is for that reason that each century since the Renaissance has its representative. We have additionally kept in mind the limited use of producing interpretative essays on texts no longer easily obtainable. Hence all of the main titles to which the following chapters refer are currently in print or available in a well-stocked university library. Where not originally written in English, all are currently available in translation.

Some of the questions which preoccupied those who reflected on diplomacy in the early modern period have already been mentioned. It remains to ponder for a moment longer the main themes emerging from this account of diplomatic theory which have persisted until the present day. Perhaps the most dominant one centres on the recognition that even the most powerful states are unable to achieve or maintain their ends solely or securely by force. As a result, diplomacy is seen as a valuable 'means' or 'instrument' of foreign policy. Indeed, it is frequently noted that a diplomatic service that is well resourced and above all well staffed can give a state a significant increment of power and influence. Machiavelli, though acutely aware that 'pure diplomacy' was not enough, expresses this point of view in his admiration for the money spent on express messengers by the Duke Valentino. Richelieu considered diplomacy of such vital importance in furthering the interests of France that he thought it should be 'continuous'. Kissinger was similarly so persuaded of the productiveness of diplomacy that although National Security Advisor and then Secretary of State as well, he never hesitated to keep to himself the kernel and detail of important negotiations.

Once accepted, the claim that well conducted diplomacy confers important advantages leads on to related themes. Among these is the argument that finds in diplomacy no 'true end or purpose' such as the pursuit of peace, though this had been an important element in mediaeval thought.[8] The embodiment of an entirely neutral instrument, diplomats must support the foreign policy of their state no matter what its content. If an envoy is instructed to negotiate an aggressive alliance, so be it. A second theme is found in the claim that negotiation should wait for 'the right season', a precept suggested by Guicciardini almost five centuries before it was rediscovered and glossed by peace research institutes in Scandinavia and elsewhere. Like others, he also stressed the need to conduct negotiations in secrecy, on pain of forfeiting the trust and ability to compromise without which they are stifled. Thirdly, diplomats need not keep their promises to foreign governments if this does not serve the interests of their own state. However, as Machiavelli made shockingly plain, the ability to break one's word goes hand in glove with the advantages of preserving a reputation for trustworthiness. Fourthly, and with the caveat that Grotius himself stood out against this view, opinion came to accept the merits of continuous diplomacy; of permanent rather than sporadic negotiations conducted with wartime enemies as well as peacetime friends. And lastly, while lobbying, gleaning information and negotiating agreements are staple functions of the ambassador, his representational tasks are of more than trivial ceremonial importance. To re-present a state in the company of one's host and protector is to give dignified expression to the independence claimed by those in whose sovereign name he acts.

Alongside the foregoing, it is necessary to keep in mind that continuing strain of thought which takes for granted the necessity *for* diplomacy and dwells instead on the requirements *of* diplomacy. Among those who served in what Nicolson called the 'French system' of diplomacy, one can detect a lingering fascination with the attributes of the 'ideal diplomatist'. Added to this, and following in the wake of Callières, is a burgeoning interest in the need for diplomacy to be better organized and made more professional. This is accompanied by entrenchment of the view (already noticeable in Grotius) that the privileges and immunities which international law ascribes to its practitioners are justified by the impossibility of conducting effective diplomacy without their safeguard. [9]

There is lastly a need at least to acknowledge the important theme in diplomatic theory which treats diplomacy as an independent – or at least distinctive and at times additionally separate – influence in foreign affairs. A corollary of the theme of professionalization, this is the claim detectable in Callières, through Satow to Nicolson, though somewhat lost sight of in Kissinger, [10] that diplomacy is not simply lobbying, bargaining and eavesdropping. Instead, it is accomplishing these tasks *in such a way* that the moderating and thereby civilizing effect of diplomacy on the general conduct of states is maximized. Honest dealing must therefore be maintained even though this may bring no immediate or tangible gains. The maintenance of peace – though not at any price – must be a high priority. Protocol must be studied and carefully followed, not merely to prevent arguments over status and correct procedure from distracting attention from more serious matters, but so that it can help cushion and mollify relations between states. In short, this is the claim that diplomacy is a civilizing as well as a civilized activity.

Even though differences of standpoint among the contributors to this book will be apparent, the chapters are broadly similar in composition. Each begins with a biographical sketch of the author in question and includes a summary of his diplomatic experience. Mention is next made of his most important writings, some of which are then singled out for more thorough examination. We shall be amply rewarded if the effect of these essays is to lead those interested in diplomacy and its theoretical formulation to renewed interest in the authors concerned.

Notes

1. That is, a dispensation in which the members retain sovereignty but act – with more or less enthusiasm – as if they are part of one body.
2. The Vienna Convention on Diplomatic Relations (1961) and the Vienna Convention on Consular Relations (1963).
3. Until Edmund Burke invented the term 'diplomacy' in the late eighteenth century, 'negotiation' was the word normally employed to describe the work of ambassadors.
4. Martin Wight, *Power Politics*, ed. by Hedley Bull and Carsten Holbraad (Leicester, 1978), p. 113.
5. B. Behrens, 'Treatises on the ambassador written in the fifteenth and early sixteenth centuries', *English Historical Review*, vol. 51, 1936, pp. 616–27.
6. See also Garrett Mattingly, *Renaissance Diplomacy* (Harmondsworth, 1965), p. 209ff.

7. Mattingly notes this, too, pointing out that some writers believed that residents were responsible for the moral debasement of diplomacy, *Renaissance Diplomacy*, p. 210.
8. Mattingly, *Renaissance Diplomacy*, p. 103.
9. This later came to be known as the functional theory of diplomatic privileges and immunities.
10. Despite his own concern with the role of diplomacy in a revolutionary international environment.

1
Machiavelli

G. R. Berridge

Niccolò Machiavelli, who was born in the republic of Florence in 1469, is a towering figure in political theory but not known at all for his reflections on diplomacy. This is not surprising since, in a direct way, they were meagre. Nevertheless, he reached his maturity in the very years in which diplomacy was being transformed by the invention and spread of the resident embassy among the turbulent city states of Italy, and he died in 1527, by which time this most significant institution was well entrenched beyond the Alps. For such a man at such a time it would be rash indeed to overlook anything that he might have had to say, directly or indirectly, about diplomacy. In any case, Machiavelli was, as Meinecke reminds us, 'the first person to discover the real nature of *raison d'état*, [1] and on the face of it this doctrine had considerable implications for the methods of the ambassador. It is for this reason that in his account of 'the Italian system' of diplomacy Harold Nicolson lays particular emphasis on Machiavelli's writings, both for what they reveal and for the influence on diplomacy which they are alleged to have had. [2] It seems worth adding, too, that his general method, that is to say, the uncompromising 'realism' which marked in his work such a break with classical political philosophy, was the method imitated almost two centuries later by Abraham de Wicquefort, author of the greatest manual on diplomatic practice of the *ancien régime* (see Chapter 5). The Dutchman openly admired the Florentine and recommended his works despite the risk that 'people will perhaps be scandaliz'd'. [3] These reasons are the justification for beginning this book with Machiavelli.

Machiavelli's Diplomatic Career

It was not only the circumstances of his time that gave Machiavelli a most remarkable opportunity to observe the conduct of diplomacy. He came of a family which, though in modest circumstances, had been important in the politics of Florence for more than two centuries [4] and in 1498, at the age of only 29, he was appointed second chancellor of the republic, despite apparently having no previous administrative experience. [5] The second chancery dealt mainly with correspondence about Florence's own territories but a month after assuming this office Machiavelli was also made secretary to the Ten of War. This was the influential subcommittee of the Florentine government – the *signoria* – charged with conducting its foreign affairs, and it was in its service that Machiavelli came to diplomacy, only four years after the French invasion had plunged the peninsula into turmoil.

The first chancellor, Marcello Adriani, was also a professor at the university and 'more interested in Greek poetry than Italian politics'. [6] As a result, Machiavelli played a more important role in the affairs of the Ten of War than his formal position might suggest. All of the correspondence passed over his table and he was required to write many papers, especially instructions to ambassadors. [7] After 1506 he was also virtually the republic's defence minister. [8] Of most interest for our purposes, however, Machiavelli was frequently required to travel abroad on behalf of the Ten, not only within Italy but as far afield as France and Germany. His biographer, Ridolfi, describes his various roles in this regard: 'Sometimes...they [secretaries or chancellors] were entrusted with commissions and even embassies, when to save expense or because of the nature of the business or for some other reason they [the *signoria*] did not wish to send a real ambassador. The chancellors sent on such missions were not called ambassadors or orators, but envoys (*mandatari*). They were not sent to negotiate peace treaties or alliances but to observe and report, or to negotiate matters of moderate importance where speed was essential, or to prepare the way for duly elected ambassadors, or sometimes to accompany, assist, advise or supervise them.' [9] It is, however, Hale who draws the most significant conclusion, pointing out that, in contrast to the ambassadors, it was the *mandatari* 'who saw the seamy side of international relations most clearly'. [10]

Thus the 'Florentine Secretary', as Machiavelli was known and liked to be known, was for a significant part of his career actually a diplomat, even though for temperamental reasons he appears not to have reached the highest professional standards, either as observer or negotiator; [11]

nor was he ever a resident, at least not for more than six months. Machiavelli was employed on two diplomatic missions within Italy in the first half of 1499 but he did not undertake his first foreign mission until July 1500, when he went to the allied court of Louis XII of France, where he remained for almost half a year. In June 1502 Machiavelli provided 'discreet reinforcement' [12] to the Bishop of Volterra, Francesco Soderini, on a mission to Urbino, recently seized by Cesare Borgia, who had just been created duke of the Romagna by his father, Pope Alexander VI. The 'Duke Valentino', who was at this juncture at the height of his power, was attempting to carve out a territory for himself in this anarchic region bordering Florence, which he was clearly resolved to 'protect'. Machiavelli next visited the dangerous duke alone, arriving at his court at Imola on 7 October 1502 and remaining there for almost four months, prevaricating on the pretext of waiting for a sign from the French and watching Borgia closely, not least when he took his savage revenge on the Vitelli and the Orsini. [13] Thereafter, Machiavelli was sent on important missions to Rome (October–December 1503, August–October 1506), to France (January–February 1504, June–October 1510), and Germany (1507–8). He undertook his last diplomatic missions prior to the collapse of the Florentine republic in September 1511, [14] when he was sent to Milan and then back to France once more in order to petition Louis to suspend the convocation of the schismatic francophile cardinals who were so complicating Florence's relations with Rome. [15]

Machiavelli remained in office until 1512, when the Florentine republic paid the price of not being on the winning side when the Spanish forces invited into Italy by the pope succeeded in driving out the French. The Medici returned to the city, the republic was dissolved, and on 7 November Machiavelli was dismissed and sent into internal exile. In the following year worse was to come. Accused of conspiring against the new regime, he was tortured and imprisoned but shortly afterwards released into obscure unemployment under a general amnesty declared to celebrate the election of a Medici pope.

The Relevant Writings

The only point in his writings at which Machiavelli gives direct and sustained attention to the manner as opposed to the circumstances in which diplomacy should be conducted is in the letter of 1522 subsequently entitled 'Advice to Raffaello Girolami when he went as Ambassador to the Emperor'. [16] It is true that there is a vast collection of his diplomatic papers, which are usually known as the *Legations*, though hereafter they will be styled the *Missions* since this is the title employed in the translation on which I have generally relied.[17] However, the *Missions* were until recently accessible only with difficulty to the English reader and are not easy to distil for theoretical significance.[18] I shall certainly draw on them for this chapter but otherwise it is advisable to rely chiefly on *The Prince*[19] and, more especially, on the much longer and more important work called *The Discourses on the First Ten Books of Titus Livy* (hereafter *The Discourses*).[20] His last great work, *The History of Florence*, is also very useful. These books, among others, were the fruits of the enforced leisure experienced by Machiavelli after his removal from office and tell us a great deal about his views on diplomacy.

Diplomacy, Force and Republican Expansion

Machiavelli's focus was the state – especially the republican state – and the requirements for its stability. However, this led him to consider the relations *between* states as well, since the external environment contained enemies who could extinguish the liberties of the state altogether, while the foreign policy which it adopted to cope with external threats had implications for its internal politics which were not much less momentous.

On the face of it, argued Machiavelli, it might be supposed that the best external posture for a state to adopt was to make itself sufficiently strong in arms to deter any predatory attack but not so strong as to provoke a pre-emptive one. It might also be supposed, he suggested, that the last possibility would be further discouraged by constitutional avowal, supported by convincing practical demonstration, that it had no expansionist designs on its neighbours. Unfortunately, says Machiavelli of this 'middle way' between great weakness and great strength, in the real world where 'all human affairs are ever in a state of flux', this is not likely to work: 'necessity' will often lead states to follow policies of which 'reason' disapproves. Necessity may, for example, lead a state to expand – perhaps for 'defensive' reasons – even though it is not constituted for this policy, with consequences inevitably dire. On the other hand, if the middle course produces a prolonged peace this will in the end be no better, since it will 'either render it [the state] effeminate or give rise to factions'.[21]

In consequence of these considerations, Machiavelli concluded that 'one ought, in constituting a republic, to consider the possibility of its playing a more honourable role'. This required a state whose constitution divided power between nobles and people, armed and welcomed the expansion of the latter, and thus made a policy of imperialism realistic should this be required. [22] In the process, friction between nobles and people, though having its inconveniences, would stimulate 'legislation favourable to liberty', [23] while reliance on citizen soldiers rather than mercenaries would create better citizens as well as better soldiers. [24] His model, of course, was the ancient Roman republic and its great empire, an empire which was created via hegemony rather than by confederation or naked dominion. [25] Where did diplomacy [26] fit into this theory?

Machiavelli's fundamental assumption was actually that skill in the art of war was more important to the state than anything, including skill in diplomacy, because of his belief that 'sound laws' follow 'sound arms'. [27] Nevertheless, states did not always have sufficient military strength to achieve their aims, and it was out of this necessity that diplomacy was born: 'what princes have to do at the outset of their careers,' Machiavelli tells us, 'republics also must do until such time as they become powerful and can rely on force alone.' [28] Whether republics or principalities, if they were as weak in arms and as ineptly led in the field as the average Italian state of the fifteenth century, it was unavoidable that they should place particular reliance on 'deceptions, . . . tricks and schemes'. [29] Notwithstanding the suggestion that states which grow to be great powers can rely on force alone, it is obvious that Machiavelli believed that diplomacy remained important for a prince who wishes 'to do great things' even after he has acquired large armies, [30] because prudence dictated the avoidance of military overstretch. Thus, we are informed, 'the Romans never had two very big wars going on at the same time'; instead, it was their policy to select one military target at a time 'and industriously to foster tranquillity among the rest'. [31]

Human Nature, Good Faith and Diplomacy

If Machiavelli urged the constant need for diplomacy, his professional experience and historical reading had led him to a second view which was, in the circumstances, an encouraging one: it was an activity to which men (and women) [32] were peculiarly amenable. [33] Observing how they really behaved rather than dwelling on how they ought to behave, he concluded, says Mattingly, that men were 'selfish, . . . cowardly, greedy, and, above all, gullible and stupid'. [34] In this connection it is instructive to recall Machiavelli's famous play, *Mandragola*, the 'glory' of which, as Lord Macaulay points out, [35] is Messer Nicia, the simpleton who despite his learned profession is gulled by a young gentleman, a devious hanger-on and a venal friar into encouraging his beautiful wife to share her bed with the gentleman by whom she is so admired. [36]

On the inter-state plane, the baseness and gullibility of the denizens of princely courts made them as vulnerable as Messer Nicia to the gilded tongue and full purse of a skilful diplomat, whether it was his purpose to encourage them in a line of action congenial to the interests of his own prince or obtain sensitive information. In two despatches from the court of Louis XII in 1500, Machiavelli pointedly reminded the Florentine *signoria* of 'the importance of making some one here your friend, who from other motives than mere natural affection [money, of course] will watch your Lordships' interests here, and will occupy himself in your behalf, and of whose services those who may be here as your agents may avail themselves for your advantage... it is with just such weapons', the Florentine Secretary continued, 'that the Pisans defend themselves, and that the Lucchese attack you; and that the Venetians and King Frederick [of Naples], as well as all others who have any business to transact at this court, help themselves; and whoever does not do the same may be said to think of gaining a lawsuit without paying an attorney.' [37] Two years later we find Machiavelli imploring the *signoria* to persuade the merchants of Florence to pay bribes to the chancery clerks of the peripatetic court of the Duke Valentino, 'for if I do not satisfy these clerks of the Chancery, I shall never more be able to expedite anything through them, and especially confidential matters'. [38]

So the diplomat could achieve influence at foreign courts and thereby advance his government's designs because men could be bribed, intimidated or deceived as to their true interests. This was the advantage to diplomacy of the human baseness persuasively alleged by Machiavelli. But such depravity also leads to duplicity and, seeing this, Machiavelli, in a particular application of his general principle that the end justifies the means, [39] tells the prince that he cannot avoid joining the game. Since men 'would not keep their word to you,' he insists, 'you do not have to keep yours to them'. [40] In perhaps the most notorious sentence in *The Prince*, Machiavelli says that 'A prudent ruler... cannot, and should not, keep his word when keeping it is to his disadvantage, and when the reasons that made him promise no longer exist.' [41] These reasons would usually have to do with power, as he had suggested in a despatch from the court of the Duke Valentino: 'alliances between princes are maintained only by arms, inasmuch as the power of arms alone could enforce their observance.' [42] Now, diplomacy is activated not least by the desire to negotiate agreements and this would be pointless if they were not, at least as a general rule, honoured. Is Machiavelli's '*Realpolitik*' consistent with the diplomatic reflex?

If we read beyond Chapter 18 of *The Prince*, a book in which, as Butterfield reminds us, Machiavelli was concerned chiefly with emergency conditions and advising new princes how to become as safe as old ones, [43] we discover that his position was in fact more subtle. For one thing, not only did individual men vary in degrees of baseness; so did political regimes. For another, his awareness of the long-term drawbacks of faithlessness made Machiavelli's advice on this point cautious; while his urging of its advantages [44] reflected the shrewd insight that acceptance of faithlessness in some circumstances was, in a world of sovereign princes, a condition of extending faith in others. For both of these reasons, diplomacy was in serious danger neither from the real world as portrayed by Machiavelli nor from the behaviour of princes acting upon his advice.

In *The Discourses* it is notable, to begin with, how impressed is Machiavelli by the degree to which religious oaths sworn even at the point of a sword were honoured during the Roman republic, [45] which is significant for our argument since he would obviously have been aware of the diplomatic custom of his own time of reinforcing treaty signature and ratification with religious ceremonial. [46] Of course, he was also only too well aware that the modern Roman Church was corrupt and was thus no doubt in general sceptical of the current efficacy of this custom, at least in Italy, France and Spain, which he regarded as lands corrupt above all others. [47] Nevertheless, he also notes in *The Discourses* that even sophisticated city dwellers, as in his native Florence during the period of Friar Savonarola, could still be swayed by those whom they were convinced had genuine 'converse with God'. [48] Thus, since 'men are born and live and die in an order which remains ever the same', [49] the potential usefulness of religion should never be ruled out and might – it seems permissible to infer about Machiavelli's thought – even now reinforce diplomacy itself in some parts of the world. [50] In any case, it also emerges in *The Discourses* that Machiavelli did not, as it happens, believe that men were often entirely bad. [51] In short, as among individual men religious belief varied in intensity and evil was not ubiquitous, so also was variable the inclination to bad faith. [52]

Of particular importance in connection with Machiavelli's second belief in this context, that is, that faithlessness also varies between different kinds of political regime, is Chapter 59 of Book One of *The Discourses*. Here he considers 'which contracts are the more stable and on which ought more store to be set, on those made by a republic or on those made by a prince'.[53] In some situations he sees little difference between them. Both will be disinclined to honour an agreement imposed on them by force, and both will be as ready to break faith with a foreign ally if sticking to an agreement with him leads to fear 'for the safety of their estate'.[54] Nevertheless, says Machiavelli, even in the second of these circumstances a republic is likely to be more reliable, and even more so in less extreme cases, that is, when keeping an agreement with another government has ceased to suit the state's interest but is still well short of being either humiliating or fatal to its security. 'Instances might be cited of treaties broken by princes for a very small advantage,' he maintains, 'and of treaties which have not been broken by a republic for a very great advantage.'[55] For this Machiavelli appears to offer at least four explanations, to locate which we must cast our net widely in *The Discourses*. The first is that republics have more moral virtue because their governments must needs be responsive to the people, who in their naivety assume that the rules which prevail in ordinary social relationships (for example, that promises should be kept) should also prevail in the intercourse between states.[56] The second, which is closely related to the first, is that they have more respect for law in general. The third is that their officials are of better quality. And the fourth is that their constitutions require the reconciliation of divergent views, which makes their decision-making simply much slower.[57] For all of these reasons, republics are less likely than princes to break their faith with other states.[58] This being Machiavelli's argument, it is striking that one of his longest examples in *The Prince* of a promise being kept to the disadvantage of the promise-maker is of one made not by a republic but by a prince: King Louis XII of France.[59]

If Machiavelli believed that some men and some states were in their nature more inclined to honour agreements than others and thus reinforce the diplomatic impulse, he also knew that this inclination was further strengthened by the fact that princes were obliged to strive for a *reputation* for integrity in their dealings with others. Apart from the fact that a cavalier attitude to the 'law of nations', not least in regard to the immunity of diplomats themselves, could *needlessly* provoke hostility and imperil the prince's position,[60] a reputation for faithlessness made it unlikely that anyone would make an agreement with him in the first place while the opposite reputation would lead him to be courted even by recent enemies.[61] Thus, contrary to the interpretation of Meinecke,[62] even the unscrupulous prince had to keep most of his agreements since there was no other way – or at least no better way –

in which to acquire a reputation for integrity. [63] It is precisely for this reason, says Machiavelli, that 'powerful states who have a certain respect both for treaties and for one another' and desire to make war on a traditional ally will typically try to provoke him to make the first move. [64] It is also noticeable that when Machiavelli discusses the question of integrity in the context of how the ambassador, as opposed to the prince, should behave, he places even more emphasis on it, suggesting at worst that the diplomat may need to conceal a fact. [65] Had Harold Nicolson read this it is difficult to see how he could have faulted it.

A reputation for integrity was also particularly important for mercenary princes, the *condottieri* who made their living by supplying their armed retainers to other princes under a *condotta* (contract). It may be objected that, while being fairly clear, this is only implicit in Chapter 18 of *The Prince*. It is, however, explicit in the *Missions*, notably in the despatch of 11 April 1505 in which Machiavelli reported on his mission to Perugia to explore the real reasons for the announcement by Gianpaolo Baglioni of his intention to break his *condotta* to supply 135 men-at-arms to the Florentine Republic, and try to persuade him to change his mind.

Gianpaolo, Machiavelli informed the *signoria*, maintained that his own state was in imminent peril, and that for this overriding reason he must remain at home and not be bound by his contract with Florence. Machiavelli had replied to Gianpaolo, he reported, that even if this were true, he would pay a heavy price for his action for 'every one knew the obligation under which he was to your Lordships...and would regard him as a stumbling horse which nobody would ride for fear of getting his neck broken;...and that whoever attached any value to wearing armor, and desired to win honor by his arms, could lose nothing that was prized so much as the reputation for good faith'. [66]

Whether because of religious fear, moral virtue, republican inertia, or calculation of long-term advantage, good faith was still in Machiavelli's account a common reflex in interstate dealings. [67] Had it not been, he would hardly have recommended a variety of circumstances in which weak states should make terms with stronger ones (see below). Furthermore, it was also precisely because good faith remained a common reflex that, as Machiavelli noted, even those who regularly broke their own promises were quite capable of assuming that others would honour their undertakings towards them, even when circumstances should have led them to doubt it. As Machiavelli tells us, such was the case with Cesare Borgia, who mistakenly relied on the promise of Julius II (who had been badly treated by the Borgias) to make him captain-general of the papal armies in return for his support in the election which had made him pope.[68]

If on closer inspection Machiavelli is seen to believe that, unless too severely tested, good faith between states remains common and thus an incentive to negotiation, he certainly did not believe, as we have already seen, that it is universal – even when not severely tested. But where uncertainty about good faith remains, this merely makes diplomacy more important for another reason: apart from spies, only diplomats are in a position to probe the intentions of the foreign prince, as we shall see.

Machiavelli's prescription on good faith, his support for an order of morality for states quite different from that appropriate to individuals,[69] was strong meat for his times[70] but not for ours. It amounted to an acknowledgement of the reality that, since they had no other means of rectification, states would throw off treaties which no longer served their interests at the first opportunity. It was thus little more than a statement of the doctrine subsequently known to international lawyers as *rebus sic stantibus*: international obligations only endure as long as the conditions which generated them. Acceptance of this did not undermine diplomacy any more in Machiavelli's time than after it; indeed, because it acknowledged the realities of power, the flexibility which it permitted in interstate relationships was a condition of diplomacy and, for that matter, of the emerging international law itself.[71]

The Role of the Ambassador

Machiavelli's only dedicated analysis of the tasks of the ambassador[72] and the manner in which he should go about them is provided in the 'Advice to Raffaello' referred to above. What he has to say here is little more than a codification of the conventional wisdom of the age and, no doubt because of his own lack of experience as a full ambassador, somewhat one-dimensional. The analysis is typically terse and interesting nonetheless and it is possible, in any case, to add greatly to the views outlined here by working the rich veins of *The Discourses*, the *Missions*, and *The History of Florence*.

Looking at Machiavelli's writings as a whole, then, we find him suggesting that the resident diplomat has five main tasks. He must encourage the prince to whom he is accredited to pursue policies congenial to the interests of his own prince,[73] and refuse to contemplate policies hostile to them, which might well involve sabotaging the activities of diplomatic rivals. The diplomat must also submit advice on policy to his own prince, and at all costs defend his own prince's reputation. [74] He must, if his instructions require it, engage in formal negotiations, and be especially industrious in obtaining information and reporting it home; this includes the responsibility for predicting future developments, which is the most difficult of all. I shall say something more about Machiavelli's views on these last functions, and then consider what he had to say about the diplomat's general manner of proceeding.

Machiavelli gives special emphasis to information-gathering and it might be thought that this is because of his own experience as an envoy, for whom this task was customarily even more important than it was for an ambassador (see above); and, indeed, it would be surprising if this was not the greater part of the explanation. [75] Nevertheless, it is also consistent with one of the most fundamental points of Machiavelli's political theory: his optimistic belief that, to employ the paraphrase of Bernard Crick, 'virtù, if it studies necessity, can combat fortune'. [76] In other words, the audacious and skilful prince, who understands the political requirements for preserving his state and is sufficiently in tune with his times, has a good prospect of bending to his interests the swirl of contingent events and drift of underlying social tendencies. [77] But this is impossible without knowledge of the world, and this – including information concerning successful techniques of statecraft to be emulated – must be supplied in great part by the diplomat.

As for the business of negotiation, this may be undertaken with a view to securing agreement, which is the usual case, or it may not. In the last instance, states may require their ambassadors to go through the motions of negotiations with an enemy whom they have already resolved to attack in order to demonstrate that necessity forced them to war; [78] or go through the same motions in different circumstances in order to play for time. Temporizing in this manner was a role which Machiavelli the diplomat had been much resigned to playing himself [79] and was also one in the performance of which he had greatly admired the virtuosity of the Duke Valentino. [80] States might instruct their diplomats to temporize in order to make assumption of a war-footing seem less necessary to an emerging rival; to create the possibility that fortune might divert the storm elsewhere; to permit more forces to be gathered; or to enable a more propitious moment for the use of existing forces to be employed. [81]

It is, however, one thing to use diplomacy in order to temporize in the face of superior force; it is quite another to make concessions, especially if the enemy is arrogant and unsupported by confederates. This, claims Machiavelli, will merely demoralize the state's allies and cause them to desert it, while at the same time feeding the appetite of the enemy. The result will be that the war which it had been hoped to avoid by appeasement will simply have to be fought in worse circumstances. In short, if concessions are to be made at all they should be made from positions of strength, not weakness. [82] (A special case is the prince who can get away with employing peaceful methods abroad because his state still enjoys the aura of a warlike predecessor. [83]) However, when a state is confronted by overwhelming force Machiavelli does not hesitate to say that it should recognize necessity and make concessions. He envisages three such circumstances. First, when the enemy is a powerful confederation, in which case 'the wiser course is to hand over some of your possessions to one of them so as to win him to your side even after war has been declared'. [84] Secondly, when the demands made are not a threat to the state's survival and can be met as if by free will. [85] The third and final circumstance in which concession should be made to necessity is when a much stronger enemy *himself* offers peace negotiations in the course of a war already under way, 'for the terms will never be so hard but that in them some benefit will accrue to those who accept them, so that in a way they will share in the victory'. [86] Thus Machiavelli's generally convincing theory of negotiations, though it must be said that it is not clear why concessions to a more powerful enemy backed by confederates will be likely to win him over when a similar policy towards one lacking such support will merely feed an appetite for more.

In his 'Advice to Raffaello' Machiavelli maintains that the diplomat can discharge none of his functions properly unless he studies the prince and 'those who control him' – and gains their attention, if necessary by bribery. In addition, he must acquire a high reputation, especially for integrity: 'This matter is very important;' adds Machiavelli, 'I know men who, through being clever and two-faced, have so completely lost the trust of a prince that they have never afterward been able to negotiate with him.' Do not concentrate exclusively on the centre of power but also cultivate the 'different kinds of busybodies' found in all courts, advises Machiavelli. Give them 'banquets and entertainments' and pump them for information but, because 'the best means for getting information is to give it', ensure that your own government keeps you regularly informed of events elsewhere 'though they are remote from your business'.

In his 'Advice to Raffaello', Machiavelli gives close attention to the contents and tone of the reports that the diplomat must send home.

This is natural since, as the length of the *Missions* testifies, in his own hectic career as a special envoy it was quite normal for him to write one report a day, [87] though he only expected a resident ambassador such as Raffaello to write every two or three months. Machiavelli knew that diplomats were judged above all by their despatches: 'Great honor also comes to an ambassador from the reports he writes to those who send him'. They should cover three main subjects, says Machiavelli: matters decided; matters currently under discussion; and matters which are likely to arise.

In his reports home Machiavelli urges the diplomat to be cautious but not over-diffident. Much of the information which he obtains will be false and misleading, but he owes his own prince his judgement. [88] As a result, he must compare information from different sources, weigh it, and finally declare what he believes himself to be the truth. In his own despatches, however, Machiavelli customarily embellishes this method by providing the provenance of certain kinds of intelligence and cautioning the *signoria*, with its greater wisdom and more comprehensive picture of events throughout Italy, to place its own interpretation on what he has told them. When the diplomat has to use his own judgement, and especially when this involves predicting the course of events at the court to which he is attached, he must be especially careful of princely sensibilities at home, says Machiavelli, in reference to the tradition of ambassadorial reticence then prevailing. [89] Thus ' . . . because to put your judgment in your own mouth would be offensive', he tells Raffaello, you should pass, or at least share, the responsibility; 'use such words as these', he says: ' "Considering, then, everything about which I have written, prudent men here judge that the outcome will be such and such".' Machiavelli had placed unusually heavy reliance on this method in his despatches from his mission to Pope Julius II in the second half of 1506, which, in light of the fluid situation at the time and volatility of the pope, is hardly surprising. [90] A variant on this theme was Machiavelli's use of the views of a well-placed and shrewd friend who was nevertheless 'obviously fictitious'. [91]

In the 'Advice to Raffaello' Machiavelli appears to have in mind only the question of how the diplomat should present his opinions on facts and possible future developments. It is certain, however, that he was thinking of policy advice as well, which made modest and indirect presentation the more important since it was a tradition at this time that 'ambassadors were not encouraged to add personal comments or advice'. [92] Impressed with the advantages of resolute action by his close observation of the Duke Valentino [93] and constantly exasperated by the dithering of his own government, he had certainly not shirked this responsibility during his own diplomatic career. In 1510, to provide but one example, he urged upon the *signoria* the advantages of mediating a settlement between Louis XII and Julius II and the disadvantages, in the event that war should break out nevertheless, of seeking neutrality between them. [94]

This, then, was the role of the diplomat according to Machiavelli, and it is a role to which he attaches obvious importance in statecraft. But Machiavelli had no illusions about it: 'pure persuasion', even if the diplomat was sufficiently skilful to gain the attention of a prince, was rarely sufficient. For the successful pursuit of most of his functions, he needed before anything else to be backed by arms, money and resolute government, though either because he thought this self-evident, or redundant, or because he did not wish to discourage him, he did not mention this in his 'Advice to Raffaello'. It is, however, a recurring theme in the *Missions*, and is especially prominent in the first mission to France, where Machiavelli and his colleague della Casa are brought face to face with the contempt in which a diplomat is held who can boast none of the above attributes. 'Mere words' are not enough, he kept telling the *signoria*; 'they...have consideration only for those who are either well armed, or who are prepared to pay... They call you *Ser Nihilo* (Signor Nothing)' [95] – and their mission suffered accordingly. [96] In the same vein, we are told in *The Discourses* that 'Venice, having occupied a large part of Italy, most of it not by dint of arms, but of money and astute diplomacy, when its strength was put to the test, lost everything in a single battle'. [97] It is probable, therefore, that while Machiavelli would no doubt have agreed with his famous twentieth-century follower, Hans Morgenthau, that first-class diplomacy can magnify the material power of a state, [98] he would also have been quick to add some qualifications: first, that the magnification was never likely to be very great; second, that if the diplomatic means of magnification amounted to no more than promises which never issued in deeds then it would not suffice for long; and third, that even over the short term the most brilliant diplomacy would not be able to create power out of thin air. Even splitting a hostile confederation meant being able to give something worthwhile to one of its members.

Nevertheless, allowing on the one hand for Machiavelli's penchant for overstatement and, on the other, for Morgenthau's interpretation of 'diplomacy' to include the formation as well as execution of foreign policy, [99] the difference between them on this point is not great. Raymond Aron is more careful than either of them, pointing out with Machiavelli that the relations of force which require a negotiation mean that, in marked contrast to a military engagement, its general results are usually a foregone conclusion,[100] while acknowledging with Morgenthau that even among rival states negotiated agreements 'are not, in normal times, the pure and simple expression of relations of force'. Diplomatic skill thus usually has influence over the outcome, as does the authority of law.[101] Thus are reassured those modern governments, typically middle powers with long diplomatic traditions, who claim to be able to 'punch above their weight'. What none of these scholars considers, however, is the probability that the influence of diplomatic skill is likely to vary with circumstances, being the greater, perhaps, when both international issues and diplomatic procedures are more complex.

Permanent Residence and 'Express' Communications

Machiavelli clearly believed that diplomacy must be a continuous rather than episodic activity; only thus could it be a full component of the *virtù* available to the prince.[102] A prince should keep at least one resident diplomat at all courts of interest to him and at important ones have a full ambassador selected from among the most distinguished citizens of the state.[103] 'Where are the new ambassadors?' was a question which became the increasingly urgent theme of his despatches to the dilatory and parsimonious *signoria* from the court of their chief ally, Louis XII, in late August 1500.[104] 'King Frederick [of Naples] constantly keeps ambassadors near his Majesty', noted Machiavelli approvingly.[105] So that they might not be thought mendicants and their princes either impoverished or mean, such ambassadors should also be provided with sufficient money from home to meet all of their living expenses. 'I recommend myself to your Lordships,' wrote Machiavelli from the court of the Duke Valentino in December 1502, 'and beg again that you will furnish me the means of support; I have here at my charge three servants and three horses, and cannot live upon promises. I began yesterday to run into debt . . . I might have my expenses paid by the court here, and may still have it done, but I do not wish that; and have not availed myself of that privilege hitherto, for it seemed to me for your Lordships' honor and my own not to do it'.[106] Money was also needed, as we have already seen, to bribe court officials.

Machiavelli was also the first to insist that having agents abroad is not in itself enough. He is adamant that the prince must also provide them with the means to keep in constant, rapid and secure communication with home. Ideally, this meant an ample provision of messengers in the prince's own employment who were capable of travelling 'express'. By virtue of being more secure, such a system was faster still because time would not necessarily have to be spent on ciphering and deciphering messages. [107] But, not surprisingly, another theme of the *Missions* is the inadequate provision made by the *signoria* for special messengers, and we constantly read Machiavelli's complaints at having to send messages by merchants, other envoys, royal post (in France), and sometimes even 'at a venture', that is, with more or less anyone who happened to be travelling in the direction of Florence. By contrast, Machiavelli wrote to his employers from Imola in 1502, the Duke Valentino 'has spent since I have been here [two weeks] as much money for couriers and special messengers as anyone else would have spent in two years'. [108]

It is not difficult to grasp why Machiavelli believed that continuous diplomacy – permanent and at all places, with enemies as well as friends – was so vital. First, fortune was fickle and if the fleeting opportunities which it threw up were to be seized, the instruments for achieving this had to be in constant readiness; for one thing, today's apparent foe (the Duke Valentino) might be tomorrow's ally. Secondly, only permanent residence could provide the time required to gain knowledge and influence. On an objective appraisal, reported Machiavelli from Furli in 1499, its ruler, Catharine Sforza, was likely to accept a proposal which he had put to her on behalf of the Ten. 'On the other hand,' he lamented, 'I see near her Excellency the Duke of Milan's agent Messer Giovanni da Casale, who is very highly esteemed, and seems to rule everything here. This is of great importance, and may easily sway the undecided mind of the Countess to whatever side he pleases.' [109] Thirdly, the resident diplomat was also needed to consolidate any major agreement reached by special ambassadors sent by his own prince. [110] Fourthly, it is reasonable to infer that Machiavelli favoured permanent and widespread diplomatic representation since he was aware that, with some exceptions, [111] princes liked to have high-ranking ambassadors in attendance on them and that to withhold them was regarded as insulting. Only the despatch to France of new ambassadors, Machiavelli and della Casa informed the Ten in 1500, could 'remove the ill feeling and the umbrage given by the abrupt departure from here of the former ambassadors'. [112] And Machiavelli, in this regard the caricature of the professional diplomat, favoured giving offence to none. 'I hold it to be a sign of great prudence in men to refrain alike from threats and from the use of insulting language,' he wrote in *The Discourses*, 'for neither of these things deprives the enemy of his power, but the first puts him more on his guard, while the other intensifies his hatred of you and makes him more industrious in devising means to harm you.'[113]

Diplomacy: an 'Honorable Laziness'?

With the model of the Roman legions in clear view, Machiavelli believed that military service for the state fostered among citizens respect for law, authority, and religion; a love of peace and order; loyalty; a spirit of self-sacrifice; and exceptional personal courage. For these reasons military service was 'a decisive factor in the stability and grandeur of the republic'.[114] We can assume from his almost complete silence on this score, however, that it is unlikely that he was of the view that *diplomatic* service was of similar benefit to civic virtue, and probable that, if pushed, he would have admitted that it could be corrosive of it.

The nearest Machiavelli comes to saying anything at all on the subject is probably at the beginning of Book Five of *The History of Florence*, where, having rehearsed his cyclical theory of human affairs, he says: '...after good and well disciplined armies have brought forth victory, and their victories quiet, the virtue of military courage cannot be corrupted with a more honorable laziness than that of letters; nor with a greater and more dangerous deception can this laziness enter into well regulated cities'. It was for this reason, he concludes, that Cato, having seen how enamoured were the young men of Rome by the philosophers sent as ambassadors from Athens, ruled that no more philosophers should be received in the city.[115] It may, of course, be objected that it was because the ambassadors were 'philosophers' and not because they were ambassadors as such that Machiavelli alleges this corruption; and that in any case the corruption was being inflicted on a foreign city. On the other hand, his notion of 'philosopher' was clearly a broad one, and on at least one other occasion in the same volume he juxtaposes 'letters and soldiers' in such a way as clearly to suggest the distinction between diplomacy in general and force.[116] Since he was also of the view that successful embassies enhanced public reputations at home[117] it is unlikely that he would have denied the possibility that, via this route, domestic corruption would have followed in the train of foreign corruption.

It would have been obvious to Machiavelli, as someone who knew both worlds, that diplomatic service did not foster discipline in the manner of the army. Diplomats, it is true, often functioned in groups – sometimes at hostile courts – and were well advised to present a united front to the prince to whom they were accredited. Juniors (like Machiavelli himself) were obliged to follow the orders of the senior ambassador, and all were obliged to follow closely their 'instructions' from home. But the resemblance to an army ends here. Most importantly, no diplomat, as a rule, and certainly not in the Florentine service, was required to obey directives uncritically. The authority which their profession led them to respect was the authority of 'prudent' men – at home or abroad. Such, furthermore, was the impecunious plight in which diplomats were often left in foreign lands, that they were readily led into frustration with their own governments – even contempt for them if they were irresolute as well as parsimonious. Worst of all, there was the natural tendency on the part of the diplomat, noted by Machiavelli's friend Guicciardini (see Chapter 2), if not by the Florentine Secretary himself, to develop a fondness for foreign ways and even to adopt the outlook of a foreign prince. In any case, in particularly marked contrast to military service, diplomatic employment was confined to a small minority among the nobility, and perhaps it was just as well.

Conclusion

For Machiavelli, diplomacy was an important instrument of the state, especially when it was employed in a strategy of deception. For this reason it was also a valuable means whereby a citizen might enhance his public reputation. Beyond that, however, it really had no significance at all. Its agents carried in their heads no commitment to universal peace, as they were supposed to do in medieval theory; nor were they seen as the embodiment of an institution which sustained a system of states, as in the later writing of Callières (see Chapter 6). This is because Machiavelli saw foreign policy in general as little more than a struggle to increase the power of the state, which, in consequence, was in a more or less permanent condition of war. As for the elevation of the needs of the state above personal morality, subsequently known as *raison d'état*, this may have had profound implications in Machiavelli's thinking for foreign policy but not I believe for diplomacy itself. We should not be surprised, therefore, that while Machiavelli expanded on what he had to say about warfare in *The Discourses* into a full length study in *The Art of War*, it appears never to have occurred to him to write an equivalent book on the art of diplomacy. Had he done so, it would probably have resembled, in its preoccupation with technique, the long chapter on conspiracies in Book Three of *The Discourses*.

Notes

1. Friedrich Meinecke, *Machiavellism: The doctrine of raison d'état and its place in modern history*, first publ. 1924, trans. D. Scott (London, 1957), p. 41.
2. *The Evolution of Diplomatic Method* (London, 1954), pp. 31–3.
3. *The Embassador and His Functions*, first publ. 1680/1; trans. J. Digby 1716, repr. with introduction by Maurice Keens-Soper (Leicester, 1997), pp. 52–3.
4. G. Mattingly, 'Machiavelli', in J. H. Plumb (ed.), *Renaissance Profiles* (New York, 1965), p. 21.
5. Q. Skinner, *Machiavelli* (Oxford, 1981), pp. 3–6, and generally R. Ridolfi, *The Life of Niccolò Machiavelli*, trans. C. Grayson (London, 1963), ch. 2.
6. Mattingly, 'Machiavelli', p. 22; confirmed by Ridolfi, *The Life*, pp. 60, 75.
7. J. R. Hale, *Machiavelli and Renaissance Italy* (Harmondsworth, 1972), pp. 6–7.
8. Mattingly, 'Machiavelli', pp. 27–8; Ridolfi, *The Life*, pp. 96–7.
9. *The Life*, p. 25.
10. *Machiavelli and Renaissance Italy*, p. 7; see also p. 36.
11. Mattingly, 'Machiavelli', p. 29; Ridolfi, *The Life*, pp. 36, 39, 77, 100ff, 114–15, 119; Hale, *Machiavelli and Renaissance Italy*, pp. 29, 42. Federico Chabod stands between the critics and defenders of Machiavelli the diplomat, maintaining on the one hand that he 'gradually accustoms himself to the difficult art of diplomacy, which is not quickly learned, and becomes an adept at it' but on the other that 'being a diplomat by chance and not by upbringing' as well as a man of outstanding political imagination, he usually fails to conceal his feelings and is not as accurate, careful and even as acute as the Florentine and Venetian diplomats born to the art, *Machiavelli and the Renaissance*, trans. D. Moore (London, 1958), pp. 4–5, 60–2.
12. Ridolfi, *The Life*, p. 48.
13. Ridolfi, *The Life*, p. 58.
14. Following a slow political rehabilitation, Machiavelli was used on a number of more or less minor missions in the 1520s.
15. Ridolfi, *The Life*, p. 123.
16. In A. Gilbert's *Machiavelli: The Chief Works and Others* (Durham, North Carolina, 1965), vol. I, pp. 116–19.
17. Christian E. Detmold, *The Historical, Political, and Diplomatic Writings of Niccolo Machiavelli* (Boston, 1882), 4 vols. The *Missions*, together with important miscellaneous papers, are to be found in volumes III and IV, and in *Machiavelli's 'Legations'*, selected and introduced by G.R. Berridge from the trans. by Christian E. Detmold (Leicester, 2000).
18. Gilbert's *Chief Works* contains only a small selection from the *Legations/Missions*, although a very much larger selection can be found in the recent publication *Machiavelli's 'Legations'*. On the general importance of the *Missions*, see Skinner, *Machiavelli*, p. 9.
19. All references to *The Prince* are to the edition translated and introduced by Stephen J. Milner: Niccolò Machiavelli, *The Prince and Other Political Writings* (London, 1995).
20. All references to *The Discourses* are to the translation by Leslie J. Walker, edited and introduced by Bernard Crick (Harmondsworth, 1970).
21. *The Discourses*, I.6, pp. 122–3.

22. *The Discourses*, I.6, p. 123; see also J. G. A. Pocock, *The Machiavellian Moment: Florentine Political Thought and the Atlantic Republican Tradition* (Princeton and London, 1975), pp. 198–9.
23. *The Discourses*, I.4, p. 113; I.6, pp. 123–4.
24. This theme is developed to its fullest in Machiavelli's *The Art of War*; for commentary, see Neil Wood's Introduction to the revised edition of the Ellis Farneworth translation (Indianapolis, 1965), pp. xlvii–liii; and Pocock, *The Machiavellian Moment*, p. 199ff.
25. These are the terms used by Pocock to characterize the three possible methods of expansion analysed by Machiavelli in *The Discourses*, II.4, *The Machiavellian Moment*, p. 215.
26. Although Walker grouped together chapters 11–15 of Book II of *The Discourses* under the heading 'Diplomacy and War', Machiavelli himself did not use the word 'diplomacy'. This was for the good reason that it was nearly a further three hundred years before Edmund Burke invented it. Instead, and apart from simply referring to the employment of ambassadors, we find him using such phrases as 'peaceful methods', 'deceit', 'artifice' and – especially when it is contrasted with force – 'prudence'. On 'prudence' in Machiavelli's thought, see Harvey C. Mansfield, *Machiavelli's Virtue* (Chicago and London, 1996), pp. 38–41.
27. *The Prince*, pp. 77, 86.
28. *The Discourses*, II.13, p. 311; see also pp. 297, 372–4, 391, 438–40.
29. *The History of Florence*, 5/1, p. 1233.
30. *The Discourses*, II.13, pp. 310–11; see also *The History of Florence*, 7/30, pp. 1374–5.
31. *The Discourses*, II.1, pp. 271–2.
32. His second mission was to Catharine Sforza, formidable ruler of Furli; see *Missions*, vol. 3, pp. 6–26.
33. *The Discourses*, I.42, 'How easily Men may be Corrupted'.
34. Mattingly, 'Machiavelli', p. 31; also Hale, *Machiavelli and Renaissance Italy*, pp. 10–11. And, of course, *The Prince*, ch. 17, pp. 93–4.
35. T. Babington Macaulay, 'Machiavelli', prefaced to the edition of Machiavelli's *Mandragola*, trans. by Stark Young, published in New York in 1927; p. 53.
36. Nicia, whose wife is unable to bear the children he so desires, is persuaded that this can be rectified by administering to her a potion made from the herb mandragola; but, that since the first man to lie with her afterwards will assuredly die within eight days, he must also, in order to save himself, permit an unwitting stranger to assume this fatal burden.
37. *Missions*, vol. 3, pp. 100–1. It is clear from a second dispatch in which Machiavelli raises this issue that he has in mind as the Florentine's corruptible French official the well disposed General Robertet, *Missions*, vol. 3, pp. 136–7; see also vol. 4, pp. 223–4.
38. *Missions*, vol. 3, p. 251.
39. *The Discourses*, I.9, p. 132; III.41, pp. 514–15. For a discussion of this point, see the Introduction to *The Discourses of Niccolò Machiavelli*, 2 vols., trans. by L. J. Walker (London, 1950), pp. 118–28.
40. *The Prince*, p. 97.
41. Ibid; see also *The Discourses*, Third Book, ch. 42.

42. *Missions*, vol. 3, p. 202; see also *The History of Florence*, 8/22, p. 1413: 'Force and necessity... not writings and obligations, make princes keep their agreements.'
43. Herbert Butterfield, *The Statecraft of Machiavelli* (London, 1960), p. 92.
44. Though it must be admitted that, as Father Walker argues, Machiavelli assumes rather than proves that faithlessness is frequently advantageous to a prince, *The Discourses of Niccolò Machiavelli* (1950), pp. 107–8 ('Introduction').
45. *The Discourses*, I.II–15.
46. M. S. Anderson, *The Rise of Modern Diplomacy, 1450–1919* (London, 1993), pp. 15–16; Jocelyne G. Russell, *Peacemaking in the Renaissance* (London, 1986), pp. 81–2.
47. *The Discourses*, I.55, pp. 244–5.
48. *The Discourses*, I.II, p. 142.
49. Ibid.
50. Among the German states, in particular, *The Discourses*, I.55, pp. 244–5.
51. *The Discourses*, I.27, p. 177: 'Very rarely do Men know how to be either Wholly Good or Wholly Bad'; I.30, p. 185; I.55, p. 244; I.55, pp. 252–3; Preface to Book II, pp. 266–7; III.29, p. 483; see also I.3, pp. 111–12, incl. Bernard Crick's footnote.
52. As Father Walker points out, it was precisely because Machiavelli was aware of the existence of conscience among the peoples of his time that he emphasized the prudence of a prince preserving his reputation for integrity, *The Discourses of Niccolò Machiavelli* (1950), p. 106 ('Introduction').
53. p. 258; see also III.42, 'That Promises extracted by Force ought not to be kept'.
54. p. 258.
55. *The Discourses*, I.59, p. 259.
56. Strauss brings this out well, *Thoughts on Machiavelli*, pp. 263, 264–5.
57. And less secretive, adds Strauss, *Thoughts on Machiavelli*, p. 257. This is a reasonable corollary but not in fact mentioned by Machiavelli.
58. *The Discourses*, I.20, 29, 34 (p. 195), 58 and 59.
59. *The Prince*, pp. 46–7.
60. *The Discourses*, II.27, pp. 364–5; II.28, pp. 367–8. On this point, see Anthony d'Amato, 'The relevance of Machiavelli to contemporary world politics', in Anthony Parel (ed.), *The Political Calculus: Essays on Machiavelli's philosophy* (Toronto, 1972), p. 223.
61. In *The History of Florence*, Machiavelli relates with obvious approval an episode in which the Florentine republic responded with 'great promptness and zeal' to a call for help against the pope from its ally, the King of Naples, even though this seemed contrary to its interests, and how this faithfulness so impressed the pope that he subsequently favoured the republic despite its recent hostility, 8/32 and 8/33, pp. 1426–8.
62. *Machiavellism*, p. 40: 'With this [chapter 18 of *The Prince*] he helped to make any hypocritical scoundrel secure on a throne'. Meinecke seems only to arrive at this conclusion by forgetting his own advice to look at Machiavelli's work as a whole and not just rely on *The Prince*, p. 41.
63. This is the implication of *The Discourses*, III.40, p. 513, to which Bernard Crick rightly draws attention in a footnote. However, I am not sure that he is correct to suggest that what Machiavelli says here is inconsistent with what

he has to say in chapter 18 of *The Prince*, since in III.40 he merely says that faithlessness does not bring glory; he does *not* say that it should always be avoided. Again, it seems clear, Machiavelli is repeating his claim that faithlessness may sometimes be unavoidable, though it carries its own price.

64. *The Discourses*, II.9, p. 299. The omission of a comma after 'powerful states' in the Walker translation suggests that Machiavelli might here have had in mind only those powerful states which did in fact respect treaties, which would narrow its significance considerably. However, a recent translation has the following: 'This mode of setting off new wars has always been customary among the powerful, who have some respect both for faith and for each other', *Niccolò Machiavelli. Discourses on Livy*, trans. by Harvey C. Mansfield and Nathan Turcov (Chicago and London, 1996), p. 146. On the general point here, see also *The History of Florence*, 6/25, p. 1317.

65. 'Advice to Raffaello'. I am grateful to Dimitris Perdikis for drawing my attention to this important distinction. For further discussion, see the section 'The role of the ambassador', below.

66. *Missions*, vol. 3, p. 449; see also Machiavelli's observations on the anxiety of Julius II to keep his reputation for good faith and his subsequent behaviour, *Missions*, vol. 3, pp. 307, 314, 350, 352.

67. As a result, I cannot help but feel that Father Walker exaggerates when he says that 'Every breach of contract to some extent undermines that mutual confidence on which society rests, and, if breaches become the rule and not the exception, mutual confidence is destroyed. *This had happened in Machiavelli's own day and he admits that the result was deplorable...*' (emphasis added), *The Discourses of Niccolò Machiavelli* (1950), p. 108 ('Introduction').

68. '...the Duke meantime allows himself to be carried away by his sanguine confidence, believing that the word of others is more to be relied upon than his own', *Missions*, vol. 3, p. 300.

69. On the ultimate but perhaps inevitable incoherence between these two moralities, see Bernard Crick's introduction to *The Discourses*, pp. 61–7; also Meinecke, *Machiavellism*, ch. 1.

70. Though the doctrine that promises made under duress could be broken was, of course, already widely accepted, Russell, *Peacemaking in the Renaissance*, p. 82.

71. On this subject generally, see the chapter on 'The Sanctity of Treaties' in E. H. Carr's *The Twenty Years' Crisis, 1919–1939*, 2nd edn (London, 1946). For a modern introduction to the law of treaties by an international lawyer, see M. N. Shaw, *International Law*, 3rd edn (Cambridge, 1991), ch. 15.

72. In the 'Advice to Raffaello' he is, of course, thinking chiefly of the *resident* ambassador, though the distinction between resident and special ambassadors is rarely in his mind; however, for descriptions of the use of the latter by Milan and Florence when war seemed imminent, see *The History of Florence*, 4/4, p. 1190 and 6/26, p. 1318.

73. For example, the encouragement to oppose the Venetians in Romagna (where they were regarded as threatening by Florence) given by Machiavelli to Julius II in November 1503: 'No efforts are spared here', Machiavelli reported to the signoria, 'to try and stir up his Holiness against the Venetians', *Missions*, vol. 3, pp. 303, 312.

74. For example: 'Every day fresh rumours are set afloat here [at the court of Louis XII]; at one moment it is that you have sent ambassadors to the Turk, at another it is to the Emperor of Germany. We do our best to contradict these reports everywhere', *Missions*, vol. 3, p. 100.

75. Information-gathering was the most important task of all residents, M. Mallett, 'Ambassadors and their audiences in Renaissance Italy', *Renaissance Studies*, vol. 8, no. 3, Sept. 1994, p. 232.

76. *The Discourses*, p. 60.

77. *The Discourses*, pp. 53–60 [Crick's Introduction].

78. *The Discourses*, III.12, p. 442.

79. Ridolfi, *The Life*, p. 92.

80. See for example his 'Duke Valentino's Treacherous Betrayal of Vitellozzo Vitelli, Oliverotto da Fermo and Others', in *The Prince and Other Political Writings* (Milner, ed.), pp. 30–1.

81. *The Discourses*, I.33, pp. 190–3; II.25, pp. 360–1.

82. *The Discourses*, II.14, pp. 312–13.

83. *The Discourses*, I.19, p. 166.

84. *The Discourses*, II.14, p. 313; and *The History of Florence*, 8/26, p. 1419.

85. *The Discourses*, I.38, pp. 205–6.

86. *The Discourses*, II.27, p. 365; see also II.20, p. 340.

87. Such was the anxiety of the signoria for news from Machiavelli's temporary postings, that – couriers and weather permitting – he wrote even when there was no news in order to avoid keeping them in suspense; for example, *Missions*, vol. 3, p. 236.

88. In *The Discourses*, too, and though he is thinking of senior officials in general ('the advisers of a republic and the counsellors of a prince'), Machiavelli is strong on the duty of honest advice, despite its dangers – 'since all men [here meaning governments] in such matters are blind and judge advice to be good or bad according to its result', III.35, pp. 500–1.

89. Mallett, 'Ambassadors and their audiences in Renaissance Italy', p. 241.

90. *Missions*, vol. 4, 'Second Mission to the Court of Rome', pp. 10–75.

91. Gilbert, *The Chief Works*, vol. 1, p. 132, n.3.

92. Mallett, 'Ambassadors and their audiences in Renaissance Italy', p. 241.

93. Hale, *Machiavelli and Renaissance Italy*, pp. 18–20.

94. *Missions*, vol. 4, pp. 245–50. Machiavelli also attacks neutrality in general in *The Prince*, though his hostility to it is in the end heavily qualified, pp. 113–15.

95. *Missions*, vol. 3, pp. 83–4; see also pp. 117, 120, 121–2, 351.

96. See also Hale, *Machiavelli and Renaissance Italy*, pp. 28–9, 38–40.

97. *The Discourses*, I.6, p. 122.

98. Hans J. Morgenthau, *Politics Among Nations: The Struggle for Power and Peace*, 5th edn (New York, 1978), pp. 146–50; see also chs 31 and 32.

99. *Politics Among Nations*, p. 146, n.9.

100. *Peace and War: A Theory of International Relations*, trans. by R. Howard and A. Baker Fox (London, 1966), p. 61.

101. *Peace and War*, pp. 69–70.

102. Pocock, *The Machiavellian Moment*, p. 162.

103. *Missions*, vol. 3, pp. 60, 98–9, 245, 262.

104. *Missions*, vol. 3, p. 84ff.

105. *Missions*, vol. 3, p. 82.
106. *Missions*, vol. 3, pp. 250–1.
107. *Missions*, vol. 3, p. 195. It was common at this time for diplomats enjoying 'secure courier systems' to dispense with ciphers 'even for quite confidential despatches', Mallett, 'Ambassadors and their audiences in Renaissance Italy', pp. 239–40.
108. Machiavelli to the Ten, 20 October 1502, *Missions*, vol. 3, p. 171; see also Ridolfi, *The Life*, p. 57.
109. *Missions*, vol. 3, p. 21.
110. *The History of Florence*, 8/21, pp. 1411–12.
111. '...the Emperor, unlike other princes, is averse to having the envoys of other sovereigns about him, and either dismisses those that come, or confines them to some special locality which he does not permit them to leave without his orders,' *Missions*, vol. 4, p. 218.
112. *Missions*, vol. 3, p. 92.
113. *The Discourses*, II.26, pp. 361–2.
114. Neal Wood, 'Introduction', *The Art of War*, p. 50.
115. *The History of Florence*, 5/1, p. 1232.
116. *The History of Florence*, 6/36, p. 1332.
117. *The History of Florence*, 7/1, pp. 1336–7; 'Advice to Raffaello'.

Further reading

Works by Machiavelli

Machiavelli's 'Legations', selected and introduced by G. R. Berridge from the trans. by Christian E. Detmold (Leicester, 2000; available through www.allandale.co.uk). The reference to Detmold's full translation, which is long out of print and very rare, can be found at note 17 above. A few of the despatches have also been published in *Machiavelli: The Chief Works and Others*, trans. A. Gilbert, vol. 1 (Durham, NC, 1965).

The Prince and Other Political Writings, trans. and ed. Stephen J. Milner (London, 1995). There are also many other good editions of *The Prince*. Since this is short, it should be read in its entirety; nevertheless, esp. chs 8, 14–25.

The History of Florence, in Gilbert's *Chief Works*, vol. 3 (Durham, NC, and London, 1989), books 5–8 (esp. 5/1; 6/25 and 26; 7/30; 8/21, 22, 26, 32 and 33).

The Discourses, trans. L. J. Walker, ed. Bernard Crick (Harmondsworth, 1970); other good translations are to be found in Gilbert's *Chief Works*, vol. 1, and in *Niccolò Machiavelli. Discourses on Livy*, trans. by Harvey C. Mansfield and Nathan Turcov (Chicago and London, 1996). Book One, 6, 11, 12, 15, 20, 33, 34, 38, 58, 59; Book Two, 1, 4, 9, 11–15, 26, 27, 28, 30; Book Three, 11, 12, 35, 40, 41, 42.

'Advice to Raffaello Girolami when he went as Ambassador to the Emperor', in Gilbert's *Chief Works*, vol. 1, and *Machiavelli's Legations*.

Historical background

Anderson, M., *The Rise of Modern Diplomacy* (London and New York, 1993), ch. 1.
Bozeman, Adda B., *Politics and Culture in International History*, 2nd edn (New Brunswick, 1994).

Brucker, G., *Renaissance Florence* (London, 1969).

Hamilton, K. and R. Langhorne, *The Practice of Diplomacy: its evolution, theory and administration* (London and New York, 1995), ch. 2.

Hill, David Jayne, *A History of Diplomacy in the International Development of Europe* (London, 1905), vol. I, ch. 7, sec. 3; vol. II, pp. 152–8, 227–9, 233–5, 239–41, 308–17.

Mallett, M., 'Ambassadors and their audiences in Renaissance Italy', *Renaissance Studies*, vol. 8, no. 3, Sept. 1994.

Martines, Lauro, *Lawyers and Statecraft in Renaissance Florence* (Princeton, NJ, 1968), ch. 8, 'Problems of diplomacy'.

Mattingly, Garrett, *Renaissance Diplomacy* (Harmondsworth, 1965).

Potter, G. R. (ed.), *The New Cambridge Modern History*, vol. I, The Renaissance, 1493–1520 (Cambridge, 1957), ch. IX, 'International relations in the West: diplomacy and war' (J. R. Hale).

Queller, D. E., *The Office of Ambassador in the Middle Ages* (Princeton, NJ, 1967).

Russell, J. C., *Peacemaking in the Renaissance* (London, 1986), ch. 3.

Biography

Chabod, Federico, *Machiavelli and the Renaissance*, trans. David Moore (London, 1958).

Hale, J. R., *Machiavelli and Renaissance Italy* (Harmondsworth, 1972).

Ridolfi, Roberto, *The Life of Niccolò Machiavelli*, trans. C. Grayson (London, 1963).

General

Anglo, Sydney, *Machiavelli: A Dissection* (London, 1971).

Aron, Raymond, *Peace and War: A Theory of International Relations* (London, 1966), chs 2 and 3.

Berlin, Isaiah, *Against the Current* (New York, 1980).

Butterfield, Herbert, *The Statecraft of Machiavelli* (London, 1960).

Carr, E. H., *The Twenty Years' Crisis, 1919–1939*, 2nd edn (London, 1946), chs 5 ('The realist critique') and 11 ('The sanctity of treaties').

Doyle, Michael W., *Ways of War and Peace: Realism, Liberalism, and Socialism* (New York and London, 1997), ch. 2.

Gilbert, F., *Machiavelli and Guicciardini* (Princeton, NJ, 1965).

Gilmore, Myron P. (ed.), *Studies on Machiavelli* (Florence, 1972).

Gooch, G. P., *Studies in Diplomacy and Statecraft* (London, 1942), ch. IX (Politics and Morals).

Gray, Hanna, 'Machiavelli: The art of politics and the paradox of power', in I. Krieger and Fritz Stern (eds), *The Responsibility of Power* (Garden City, NY, 1967).

Hoffman, Stanley, *Duties Beyond Borders* (Syracuse, New York, 1981).

Meinecke, F., *Machiavellism: The doctrine of raison d'état and its place in modern history* (London, 1957), ch. 1.

Morgenthau, Hans J., *Politics Among Nations: The Struggle for Power and Peace*, 5th edn (New York, 1978), pp. 146–50, 529–58.

Nicolson, Harold, *The Evolution of Diplomatic Method* (London, 1954), ch. 2 ('The Italian system').

Parel, Anthony (ed.), *The Political Calculus: Essays on Machiavelli's philosophy* (Toronto, 1972), ch. by d'Amato: 'The relevance of Machiavelli to contemporary world politics'.

Pocock, J. G. A., *The Machiavellian Moment: Florentine Political Thought and the Atlantic Republican Tradition* (Princeton and London, 1975), chs. 6 and 7.

Skinner, Quentin, *Machiavelli* (Oxford, 1981), esp. ch. 1.

Sterling, Richard W., *Ethics in a World of Power: the Political Ideas of Friedrich Meinecke* (Princeton, NJ, 1958), esp. chs. 9 and 10.

Walker, L. J., trans., *The Discourses of Niccolò Machiavelli*, 2 vols (London, 1959), Introduction by Father Walker, esp. pp. 102–34.

Walzer, Michael, 'Political action: the problem of dirty hands', *Philosophy and Public Affairs*, vol. 2, no. 2, Winter 1973.

Wight, Martin, *International Theory: the Three Traditions* (London, 1991), ch. 9.

Williams, Howard, *International Relations in Political Theory* (Milton Keynes and Philadelphia, 1992), ch. 5.

Wood, Neal, Introduction to his revised edn of the Ellis Farneworth translation of Machiavelli's *The Art of War* (Indianapolis and New York, 1965).

2
Guicciardini

G. R. Berridge

Francesco Guicciardini was born into a long-established patrician family in Florence in 1483. He trained and then practised successfully as a lawyer, but in January 1512 was sent by the *signoria*, despite his youth, as ambassador to Spain.[1] His mission was conducted against a background of acute tension and at a time when the goodwill of Ferdinand the Catholic – 'that master of deceit'[2] – was of the first importance to the republic. (Ferdinand's soldiers, only recently allied to those of Pope Julius II against Florence's ally, France, were entering the nearby Romagna.) Guicciardini remained in Spain until 1514. In his absence, and despite his diplomacy, the Florentine republic was overthrown by Spanish arms, the Medici restored, and his native city subjected to the influence of Rome. This meant at least that positions in the Papal administration were open to the city's citizens, and in 1516 Leo X appointed Guicciardini governor of Modena and in the following year added Reggio to his responsibilities. This was the start of a twenty-year-long career during which he served three popes and rose ever higher in their esteem, though this did not always endear him to his fellow Florentines. He died in 1540, having served, *inter alia*, as lieutenant-general of the papal army and governor of Bologna, the most important of all the Papal lord-lieutenancies.[3]

The Relevant Writings

Guicciardini is remembered today chiefly for his writings on the constitution of Florence and above all for his great works of history, especially his *Storia d'Italia* [History of Italy],[4] in which he displayed a taste for methods well ahead of his time.[5] However, Guicciardini also committed to paper some interesting general reflections on diplomacy and on conduct relevant to diplomacy, and at somewhat greater length than his friend and fellow Florentine, Niccolò Machiavelli, though the latter enjoyed a longer and richer experience as an envoy. Guicciardini's authority to write on this subject nevertheless remained immense since, as a papal lord-lieutenant, he received envoys and dispatched his own (including Machiavelli himself);[6] he also kept a personal agent, Cesare Colombo, at Rome, in order to protect and advance his position.[7] According to Chabod, Guicciardini was a diplomat 'by nature' who viewed 'all things, at all times, through the eyes of a diplomat'.[8] A few of Guicciardini's reflections on diplomacy are to be found in his sympathetic but cautionary observations on Machiavelli's *Discourses*[9] but most are located in a volume entitled the *Ricordi*, which consists of a list of more or less elaborated maxims and observations on a miscellaneous range of topics which he began to write during his sojourn in Spain and periodically revised until 1530, when the final version, known as 'Series C', was produced.[10] This contains 221 *ricordi* in all, about fifty of which are of relevance to the student of diplomacy. It is thus chiefly on the *Ricordi*, in Hale's authoritative view 'the coolest and most cynical item in the Guicciardini canon',[11] that this chapter is based.

The *Ricordi* are important because they reveal the thinking about certain key elements of diplomacy of one of the greatest minds of the Italian Renaissance at precisely the time that diplomacy as we know it was being established. They are also a valuable antidote to the elegant caricature of the 'Italian method' of negotiation offered by Harold Nicolson, which he achieved by forgetting his own advice to keep clear the distinction between foreign policy and diplomacy.[12] It is, therefore, the more remarkable that, with few exceptions,[13] the *Ricordi* have been consistently overlooked by students of diplomacy, not least by Garrett Mattingly in his otherwise masterly *Renaissance Diplomacy*. Of course, Guicciardini does not offer us a comprehensive theory of diplomacy, any more than he offers us a systematic theory of politics.[14] He shows no interest in some of the questions which were already being raised in this area by others, and have been noted in the Introduction to this book. And when he does focus on important points he quite often fails to reveal the reasoning behind his conclusions. As Rubinstein says, 'many *ricordi* could have formed the subject of systematic discussion; however, Guicciardini chose to leave them in the lapidary form of reflections'.[15]

The partial rather then comprehensive, unsystematic and, on the whole, superficial treatment of diplomacy in the *Ricordi* was partly a

result of the fact that Guicciardini's own formal ambassadorial experience was a minor part of his career. Mainly, however, it was because,
thinking of himself as above all a man of action, his whole approach
consisted in emphasizing the importance of experience and the dangers
of abstract theory (his argument with Machiavelli).[16] In other words,
what he had to say about diplomacy was no different in character from
what he had to say about other subjects in the *Ricordi*, including the
vexed question of how best to marry off one's daughters. It should also
not be forgotten that these general reflections, in line with established
tradition, were not intended to be read beyond his family. Nevertheless,
some of Guicciardini's explicit observations on diplomacy go shrewdly
to the heart of what were to become enduring problems of the art.

The only critical edition of the *Ricordi*, by Raffaele Spongano, has not
been translated into English, which is a pity since it is much admired.[17]
Nevertheless, there is available a good translation by Mario Domandi,
introduced brilliantly by Nicolai Rubinstein, which was published in
1965 as *Maxims and Reflections of a Renaissance Statesman* (see 'Further
Reading'). All subsequent references to the *Ricordi* are to this edition.[18]

Princes and their Ambassadors

Perhaps because Guicciardini had despatched and received diplomats
as well as having been one himself, one of the major themes of his
treatment of diplomacy in the *Ricordi* is the relationship between princes
and their ambassadors. In C171 he remarks with obvious approval that
'Duke Ludovico Sforza used to say that princes and crossbows could be
tried by the same rule. Whether the crossbow is good is judged by the
arrows it shoots. So too, the value of princes is judged by the quality of
the men they send forth.' Guicciardini, of course, was no less aware than
Machiavelli of the preponderant importance of arms to the prestige of a
prince, so we can probably assume that what he had in mind here
was the direct relationship of ambassadorial quality to the prince's
reputation for sagacity, moral stature and perhaps wealth. Commonplace observation though this *ricordo* may seem, in the early sixteenth
century and for at least a further three hundred years it was nevertheless
an important one. This is because, although only eight years before
Guicciardini went as Florentine ambassador to Spain Pope Julius II had
laid down an order of precedence for the monarchs of the earth, this
was hardly uncontroversial and arguments – sometimes violent – over
diplomatic precedence were not laid to rest until the Congress of Vienna
in 1815.[19] Until this time, therefore, ambassadors had constantly to

exert themselves to obtain at foreign courts the respect to which their princes thought themselves entitled, rather than simply remain sensitive to the possibility that rights prescribed on the basis of a widely accepted principle might be overlooked. Thus Guicciardini alerts us to the fact that good ambassadors were of unusual value to the prestige of their princes during these years, and for this reason it is not surprising that he also gives attention in the *Ricordi* to the importance of their training and rewards. [20]

The directions in which the prince might shoot his diplomatic arrows, as opposed to the quality they should exhibit, is not something which is discussed by Guicciardini. Nevertheless, we can safely assume that, like Machiavelli, he favoured broad diplomatic representation. The whole thrust of the *ricordi* dealing with relations with others supports this. Thus at one point we find him saying 'harm no one and . . . help everyone as much as you can', [21] which is hardly possible in interstate relations without envoys everywhere. Since everyone has faults, at another point he stresses the importance of tolerance. [22] Elsewhere he says this: 'Though few men can do it, it is very wise to hide your displeasure with others, so long as it does you no shame or harm. For it often happens that later you will need the help of these people, and you can hardly get it if they already know you dislike them. It has happened to me very often that I have had to seek help from someone towards whom I was very ill disposed. And he, believing the contrary, or at least not knowing the truth, served me without hesitation.' In short, maintain diplomatic relations as widely as possible.

Also of interest under this head (as well as under the head of 'negotiations', where it would be equally appropriate to discuss it) is Guicciardini's relatively lengthy consideration of the question of whether or not princes should take their own ambassadors fully into their confidence and, if so, in what circumstances. 'Some princes confide to their ambassadors all their secret intentions, and tell them the goals they intend to achieve in their negotiations with the other princes', says Guicciardini in C2. 'Others deem it better to tell their ambassadors only as much as they want the other prince to believe.' Each of these courses has its advantages and disadvantages, he remarks. In favour of the latter course, an ambassador might be expected to deliver his case with more conviction if he believed himself to be truly presenting his prince's mind. Furthermore, if he did not know of any secret intentions harboured by his prince he would be unable, either out of 'levity or ill will', to reveal them. 'On the other hand,' observes Guicciardini, 'it often happens that an ambassador who believes his false instructions to be genuine will be more insistent than the matter requires. For if he believes his prince really wishes to achieve a specific end, he will not be as moderate and circumspect in his negotiations as he would have been had he known the truth. It is impossible', continues Guicciardini, 'to give ambassadors instructions so detailed as to cover every circumstance; rather discretion must teach them to accommodate themselves to the end generally being pursued. But if the ambassador does not fully know that end, he cannot pursue it, and therefore he may err in a thousand ways.'

It thus emerges that Guicciardini's own view is that the prince should take his ambassadors fully into his confidence. [23] Only when they enjoy this position can they be subtle and flexible instruments of his will. He might have added that ambassadors who are kept in the dark are bound to find out sooner or later, as is the prince to whom they are accredited. This harms the morale of the ambassador, increases his distrust of his own prince, and weakens his authority in the eyes of his host, though it is true that these strictures apply less to the special envoy than to the resident ambassador, and it may be that it was the former which Guicciardini had chiefly in mind.

Guicciardini concludes his discussion of this point by adding an important condition: the prince should only take his ambassadors fully into his confidence if they are 'prudent and honest . . . , well-disposed toward him, and well-provided for, so that they have no reason to depend on others.' [24] Among the reasons why an ambassador may not be trusted by his government and therefore should not be given its full confidence is the suspicion that he may have 'gone native' or, in the current American expression, fallen victim to 'localitis'. However, consistently with his preference for trusting the ambassador, in another *ricordo* (C153), Guicciardini, one of the earliest writers to note this phenomenon, provides an account which displays understanding and sympathy for the diplomat. 'It seems that ambassadors often take the side of the prince at whose court they are', he notes. 'That makes them suspected either of corruption or of seeking rewards or at least', he continues, 'of having been bedazzled by the endearments and kindnesses shown them. But the reason', he rightly points out, 'may also be that the ambassador has the affairs of that prince constantly before his eyes, and since he sees no others in as much detail, they assume greater importance than they really have. But the same is not true of the ambassador's own prince, whose distance allows him to see everything equally well. He quickly detects the mistakes of his minister and will often attribute to evil design what is more probably caused by bad judgement. If you are to become an ambassador,' he concludes, 'heed this well, for it is a matter of great importance.'

The unusually long *ricordo* (C2) on whether or not a prince should take his ambassadors fully into his confidence is particularly interesting, since in present-day textbook discussions of this relationship the question rarely arises: that ambassadors will have nothing of relevance to their posting concealed from them tends to be taken for granted. In suggesting that this was certainly not always the case, a reading of Guicciardini reminds us that, the textbooks notwithstanding, it may still not always be the case. In fact, it seems probable that ambassadors as a class are actually kept in the dark by their governments more today than in the time of Guicciardini. This is partly because the reasons why governments might want to do this remain at least as strong while their opportunities for doing so have increased. Disloyalty on the part of ambassadors prompted by party or ethnic considerations is still a common fear, while prejudices embedded within foreign ministries and diplomatic services which are from time to time inconsistent with prevailing policy have come in the train of the bureaucratization of diplomacy, a post-Renaissance phenomenon. Besides, developments in transport and communications since the middle of the nineteenth century have made it possible for political leaders to conduct, or believe that they can conduct, their own diplomacy, thereby reducing their dependence on their ambassadors. The British prime minister Anthony Eden deceived his 'pro-Arab' Foreign Office about the real intentions behind his policy towards Egypt in 1956, and in the early 1970s Henry Kissinger, National Security Adviser to United States president, Richard Nixon, was famous for his habit of employing 'back-channels' in order to bypass a State Department which he regarded as ponderous, prone to leaks and, above all, incapable of responding enthusiastically to a diplomacy inspired by *Realpolitik*. [25] Many other cases could no doubt be cited.

Negotiations and *Ragione di Stato*

As with Machiavelli, so with Guicciardini the value of procrastinating never seems far below the horizon when negotiation is being considered. This is not surprising since, prompted by a sense of relative military weakness, dependence on trade, and a firm belief in the potency of reason (for which diplomacy was, of course, the vehicle), it was a general Florentine reflex. [26] Procrastination is certainly not to be used in all circumstances, since 'opportunity knocks at your door just once, and in many cases you have to decide and to act quickly'. [27] Nevertheless, says Guicciardini, 'when you are in difficult straits or involved in troublesome affairs, procrastinate, and wait as long as you can. For often time will enlighten or free you' (C79). [28]

The tactics to be employed in genuine negotiations and the most favourable circumstances for them are perhaps the major theme of Guicciardini's reflections on diplomacy in the *Ricordi*. Like Machiavelli, he believed that diplomacy issued from the balance of power but unlike his friend he gave more attention to the reverse side of this equation, namely, to the exceptional significance of diplomacy in the *maintenance* of the balance of power by providing constant vigilance and creating 'counterpoise' by the negotiation of alliances. Indeed, students of equilibrium such as Moorhead Wright have emphasized the greater importance of Guicciardini among the earliest writers to identify and analyse the working of this principle in Europe. [29] Man of action as he saw himself, however, in the *Ricordi* there is little hint of theorizing at this level and we find instead Guicciardini at once immersed in consideration of the tactics of negotiations. The first of these tactics is concerned with timing.

'In my various administrative posts', Guicciardini notes in C43, 'I have observed that when I wanted to bring about peace, civil accord, and the like, it was better, before stepping in, to let matters be debated thoroughly and for a long time. [30] In the end,' he records, 'out of weariness, both sides would beg me to reconcile them.' And in C78, where it is reasonable to suppose that he also had negotiating in mind, he develops the same theme in a more sophisticated manner and in almost twentieth-century language. 'If you attempt certain things at the right time,' says Guicciardini, 'they are easy to accomplish – in fact, they almost get done by themselves. If you undertake them before the time is right, not only will they fail, but they will often become impossible to accomplish even when the time would have been right. Therefore, do not rush things madly, do not precipitate them; wait for them to mature, wait for the right season.' Thus Guicciardini's version, offered a century prior to one view of its origins, [31] of what in a later idiom came to be known as the doctrine of the 'ripe moment'. [32]

What is particularly interesting about Guicciardini's theory of negotiation here is his claim that any attempt to launch a negotiation before 'the right season' will not only fail but make success less likely if and when this juncture is reached. Failure in such circumstances is not difficult to comprehend; by definition, at least one of the parties in conflict will believe that it can get what it wants by other means, such as force, or that the passage of time will deal it a better hand in resumed talks. By contrast, why premature negotiations should actually make matters worse is not self-evident, and is positively disputed by many modern scholars. [33] On the explanation of his claim, Guicciardini himself is silent. [34] In fact, 'premature' negotiation need not always exacerbate a conflict; it depends on the form which it takes and the goals which those bent on this course set themselves. If the latter are modest and the former is low-key, it is unlikely that the situation will deteriorate when the negotiations stall and it would be very surprising indeed if, as Guicciardini seems to suggest, the problem were to become altogether impossible of resolution. On the contrary, useful advances on procedure, the building of trust and even on broad principle may be made which will make seizing the opportunity that much easier when the time really is ripe for substantive negotiations. [35] Besides, diagnosing 'ripe moments' is not exactly a scientific exercise and it is not always possible to tell if these circumstances exist until they are put to the test, that is, by negotiation. [36] The very fact that such a move is made can itself also affect the degree of 'ripeness' for settlement.

It remains true, however, that if negotiations launched in unpropitious circumstances are ambitious and conducted with much fanfare, and if in consequence they fail, then they can indeed be counterproductive. There are at least three reasons for this. In the first place, the leaders and domestic groups on which political support for negotiations rests will be at least temporarily discredited. [37] In the second, pessimism about reaching an agreement will be deepened where optimism is so important if the risks of restarting negotiations (exploitation by the other side and charges of weakness, or even treason, by radical elements at home) are to be taken; in other words, the view that the conflict is intractable will be strengthened. [38] And in the third place, one or both of the parties to the conflict may take provocative measures in reaction to the failure of the negotiations. [39] Guicciardini would probably have condemned the abandonment by Jimmy Carter in the years 1977 and 1978 of Henry Kissinger's 'step-by-step' approach to the Arab–Israeli conflict in favour of an attempt to seek a 'comprehensive' settlement, that is, one encompassing the political fate of the Palestinian people as well as the Arab territories seized by Israel in the 1967 war. This is because the time was *clearly* still not ripe to tackle the first of these questions, and the attempt merely led, among other things, to the ostracism of Egypt's moderate leader within the Arab world and ultimately to his assassination.

When negotiation is joined, says Guicciardini, in a *ricordo* which is now a commonplace, always conceal the least for which you will settle. 'I have learned', he says, 'the most advantageous way to negotiate in all matters: namely, do not reveal immediately the ultimate point to which you would be willing to go. Rather remain distant from it, let yourself be pulled toward it step by step, reluctantly. If you do this, you will often get more than you had expected (C132).' In four separate *ricordi*, though never with explicit reference to negotiation, he also emphasizes the general importance of secrecy,[40] while conceding in C186 that some information must be imparted if other information is to be obtained. Voicing elsewhere a sentiment with which five centuries later Henry Kissinger would have expressed heartfelt agreement, he also notes that secrecy in negotiation is much easier to obtain in princely states than in those where the people have more influence.[41]

Most agreements produced by negotiation are compromises, which is another way of saying that, from the point of view of each party, their provisions are less than perfect. What Guicciardini points out in two separate *ricordi*, however, is that in this regard the decisions contained in negotiated agreements are no different from any other decisions: 'the nature of things in this world', he says, 'is such that nearly everything contains some imperfections in all its parts'.[42] This is a useful point to marshal against critics of diplomacy but Guicciardini's observations on universal imperfection have a further significance. Perfectionism is not only futile but, because opportunities may be lost in its pursuit, dangerous as well.[43] Here again speaks the man of action.

By not overlooking the importance of following up a deal which has been formally concluded, Guicciardini reveals with exceptional clarity his practical experience as a negotiator and generally as a man of public affairs. In light of what he describes here as 'the negligence, the ineptitude, and the wickedness of men', he says that 'it is not enough to begin things, give them their direction, and get them moving; you must also follow them up and stay with them until the end. . . . Anyone who does business otherwise often assumes that a deal is concluded when in fact it is hardly begun, or has many obstacles before it (C192).' Difficult in Guicciardini's own day chiefly because diplomacy was not bureaucratized, this is difficult in our own principally because of the number of international issues with which governments have to deal. It is for this reason that good practice now sees the creation in important agreements of standing committees of diplomats and technical experts designed precisely to oversee the implementation of these agreements. No theory of negotiation is adequate which overlooks the need for, and most appropriate mechanisms of, implementation, and in this regard Guicciardini does not entirely disappoint us.

Should the agreements which issue from negotiations be kept? It has been pointed out that in his 'Considerations' Guicciardini is critical of Machiavelli's doctrine of 'fraud'. Arguing correctly that Machiavelli's use of this term is permissive, covering 'every astute trick or dissimulation' as well as criminal dishonesty, Guicciardini goes on to say that while acceptance of the former is one thing, acceptance of the latter, especially where breach of faith is concerned, is quite another. Contradicting Machiavelli, he adds that in any case the historical evidence does not support the view that breaking promises is important to political success, concluding that 'while by deception one may bring off some fine things, [44] too often a reputation for deceit spoils one's chances of attaining one's ends'. [45] Nevertheless, it does not do to lay too much stress on the difference between Guicciardini and Machiavelli which seems apparent here. This is partly because, as argued in the previous chapter, Machiavelli's view on good faith was in fact less extreme than suggested in the discourse drawn on here by Guicciardini, while the latter's general moral stance was identical to that of Machiavelli.

Like Machiavelli, Guicciardini noted examples of the 'faithlessness of princes' [46] and believed that the norms of private morality could not always be respected in public affairs; he believed, in other words, that the requirements of the state's security (internal or external) could justify *any* course of action. [47] Guicciardini himself has even been credited with employing, if not necessarily with coining, the phrase which encapsulated this new doctrine, *'ragione di stato'*, [48] which later became better known in its French usage, *raison d'état*, [49] even though Meinecke himself was doubtful on this point [50] and there is less explicit evidence for Guicciardini's belief in the theory of the reason of state in the *Ricordi* themselves than Hale suggests. [51] Be this as it may, Guicciardini is emphatic that deceit was sometimes necessary (C104) and the more valuable since men were gullible and stupid. [52] The less plausible a lie the more fervently it should be employed. 'For, though there be much – even conclusive – evidence to the contrary, a fervent affirmation or denial will often create at least some doubt in the mind of your listener' (C37). Elsewhere he says further that 'Even though a man be a known dissimulator and deceiver, his deceptions will nevertheless, on occasion, find believers. It seems strange, but it is very true. I remember', he continues, 'that His Catholic Majesty [the King of Spain], more than any other man, had such a reputation; and yet there was never any lack of people who believed him more than they should. This stems necessarily either from the simplicity or from the greed of men. The latter believe too easily what they wish were true; the former simply do not know what is happening' (C105). Nevertheless, he notes that deception should only be used in 'very rare, important matters'. This is partly because it is 'odious' (C104); [53] and partly because excessive use will jeopardize one's reputation for integrity, which is so valuable. [54] Besides, he adds, with a perfect example of the cynicism which subsequently gained him a name as bad if not worse than that of Machiavelli, a reputation for being 'open and genuine' will be invaluable since 'in those very important matters, you will reap even greater advantage from deception, because your reputation for not being a deceiver will make your words be easily believed (C104).' [55]

Conclusion

It might be imagined that in its emphasis on the importance of seizing opportunities and admitting reason of state, Guicciardini's thought provides support for the picture of fevered opportunism and indifference to the 'gradual creation of confidence' conjured up by Harold Nicolson to describe the 'Italian method' of diplomacy during the Renaissance. Nothing could be further from the truth.

Guicciardini shows how important it is for the prince to choose his ambassadors carefully, train and reward them well, and take them into his confidence when this is justified by their performance. These ambassadors should be sent into all states of consequence and not be placed under immediate suspicion if they should appear to have taken 'the side of the prince at whose court they are'. In contemplating negotiation, he emphasizes the importance of waiting for the 'right season' and being sure to follow up any agreement which is reached. As to *ragione di stato*, it is true that this is accepted by Guicciardini. However, his reservations are emphatic: good reputation is so valuable in diplomacy that only in exceptional circumstances should it be put at jeopardy by breaking an agreement. Calculating, bitter and often cynical though Guicciardini is, there is a cautiousness and moderation in this account of diplomacy which is not recognizable in Nicolson's account of the 'Italian method'. It is in fact in broad outline as consistent with the requirements of the balance of power, which he also identified, as any diplomatic system could be, and there are many echoes of it in modern diplomatic theory. Of course, in Guicciardini's time diplomacy was a horse which needed to be ridden swiftly, and perhaps was ridden too swiftly; however, if this was the case it was the fault of the rider and not the horse; nor did it in the process make the horse a significantly worse horse. In the circumstances, Guicciardini's very modern thoughts on diplomacy are the more remarkable.

Notes

1. He was handed his instructions by Niccolò Machiavelli, then secretary to the Ten of War. For a lively account of this formative mission, see Roberto Ridolfi, *The Life of Francesco Guicciardini*, trans. C. Grayson (London and New York, 1968), pp. 23–46. A brief and somewhat self-satisfied account is given by Guicciardini himself in his *Ricordanze*, a combination of personal financial accounts and elaborated *curriculum vitae*; see *Francesco Guicciardini: Selected Writings*, edited and introduced by Cecil Grayson, translated by Margaret Grayson (London, 1965), pp. 145–7, 149–50.
2. Ridolfi, *The Life of Francesco Guicciardini*, p. 35.
3. For Guicciardini's life, see Ridolfi, *The Life of Francesco Guicciardini*; Nicolai Rubinstein's introduction to *Maxims and Reflections of a Renaissance Statesman (Ricordi)* (New York, Evanston and London, 1965); John Hale's Introduction to *Guicciardini: History of Italy and History of Florence*, trans. by Cecil Grayson (London, 1966). For a highly coloured nineteenth century version, see the entry on 'Guicciardini' by J. A. Symonds in the *Encyclopaedia Britannica* (1885). Despite his contempt for Guicciardini's morality, elsewhere Symonds says of the *Ricordi* that they 'have all the charm which belongs to occasional utterances, and are fit, like proverbs, to be worn for jewels on the finger of time', *Renaissance in Italy: Age of the Despots*, 2nd edn (London, 1880), p. 243.
4. First publ. 1561. All subsequent references are to the Princeton University Press edition of the Alexander translation, 1984; see 'Further reading' for full citation.
5. His insistence on the importance of documentary sources in historical writing is generally held to make him the first truly modern historian. On his historical method, see, for example, Ridolfi, *The Life of Francesco Guicciardini*, pp. 190–1.
6. Ridolfi, *The Life of Francesco Guicciardini*, p. 160; J. R. Hale, *Machiavelli and Renaissance Italy* (London, 1961), pp. 227, 233.
7. Ridolfi, *The Life of Francesco Guicciardini*, p. 106 (and esp. fn. 12). In C94 Guicciardini says: 'If you frequent the court of a prince, hoping to be employed by him, keep yourself constantly in view. For often, matters will arise suddenly; and if you are in sight, he will remember you and commit them to your trust, whereas if you are not, he might entrust them to another.' The subtext to this is probably that if you cannot be there yourself make sure you have a representative acting on your behalf. The importance of this during the papacy of Clement VII was especially great since he was notorious for delaying decisions and consulting as widely as possible among the many pressure groups surrounding him, Judith Hook, *The Sack of Rome, 1527* (London, 1972), pp. 39–41.
8. Federico Chabod, *Machiavelli and the Renaissance*, trans. by D. Moore (London, 1958), pp. 4, 61–2, 110.

9. 'Considerations on the "Discourses" of Machiavelli', in the Graysons' *Francesco Guicciardini: Selected Writings* (hereafter 'Considerations'); also F. Gilbert, *Machiavelli and Guicciardini* (Princeton, NJ, 1965).

10. On the origins of the *Ricordi* and disputes over the various texts, see Ridolfi, *The Life of Francesco Guicciardini*, chs 18 and 19.

11. Introduction to *Guicciardini: History of Italy and History of Florence*, p. viii.

12. *The Evolution of Diplomatic Method* (London, 1954), pp. 31–2, 33, 46; cf. G. R. Potter (ed.), *The New Cambridge Modern History*, vol. I, *The Renaissance 1493–1520* (Cambridge, 1957), ch. 9 (J. R. Hale) and Garrett Mattingly, *Renaissance Diplomacy* (Harmondsworth, 1965), p. 109.

13. Among these are Hale, in *The New Cambridge Modern History*.

14. Though there is a clear Aristotelian (mixed government) thrust to his thinking, as Rubinstein points out, *Maxims and Reflections of a Renaissance Statesman*, pp. 12–16.

15. *Maxims and Reflections of a Renaissance Statesman*, p. 20.

16. Rubinstein, *Maxims and Reflections of a Renaissance Statesman*, p. 20.

17. *Francesco Guicciardini: Ricordi Edizione Critica* (Firenze, 1951).

18. After completing this chapter, I decided to reprint in full another excellent translation of the Ricordi (by Ninian Hill Thomson), with the maxims grouped together by subject, including diplomacy. See 'Further reading'.

19. Harold Nicolson, *Diplomacy*, 2nd edn (London, 1950), p. 179.

20. C3. Though it is clear that in this *ricordo* Guicciardini is referring to senior government officials in general (*ministri*) and not to diplomatic 'ministers', there is no reason to suppose that he did not intend *ministri* to include diplomats, especially since this *ricordo* follows immediately after the one dealing explicitly with ambassadors. Of course, in C2 he uses '*imbasciadore*', Spongano, *Francesco Guicciardini: Ricordi Edizione Critica*, pp. 4–7.

21. C159.

22. C214.

23. In adopting this view in the final redaction, Guicciardini may well have changed his mind. In any event, in Series B of 1528 he had given the general issue much briefer consideration and quite ignored the disadvantages of deceiving the ambassador: 'Any one, whether prince or private citizen, who wants to use an ambassador or some other representative to have others believe a lie, must first deceive the ambassador. For if he thinks he is representing the thoughts of his prince, an ambassador will act and speak more effectively than he would if he knew he were lying' (B24).

24. Guicciardini's own agent at Rome, Cesare Colombo of Modena, was very much in his master's debt. While Governor of Modena, Guicciardini had successfully obstructed an attempt by Pope Leo X to dispossess Colombo of his castle, and he subsequently made him a citizen of Parma (of which at the time Guicciardini was also governor) for bravery in defence of the city against the French at the end of 1521. Ridolfi believes that Guicciardini paid him a salary of 50 ducats a month to serve as his agent in Rome, *The Life of Francesco Guicciardini*, n. 12, p. 298.

25. A particularly well documented case, albeit involving chiefly a different agency in Washington (the Arms Control and Disarmament Agency), is provided by the relationship between Henry Kissinger and Gerard Smith, the chief American negotiator in SALT I. See Gerard Smith, *Doubletalk:*

The story of the first Strategic Arms Limitations Talks (Garden City, New York, 1980).

26. Hook, *The Sack of Rome*, p. 27, and especially F. Gilbert, *Machiavelli and Guicciardini: Politics and History in Sixteenth Century Florence* (Princeton, 1965), pp. 30–4.

27. C79.

28. See also C1, C23, C30, C58, C59, C81, C85, C96, C114, C116, C127, C163 and C182.

29. Guicciardini's analysis of the working of the balance of power in Italy prior to the death of Lorenzo the Magnificent and the first French invasion in 1494, is found in the opening pages of his *Storia d'Italia*; see also Moorhead Wright (ed.), *Theory and Practice of the Balance of the Power, 1486–1914* (London, 1975), p. xi. See also Chabod, *Machiavelli and the Renaissance*, pp. 14–15.

30. In Series B, Guicciardini had said at this point that 'by proposing various postponements and delays, I caused the parties to seek a settlement themselves' (B118).

31. 'Diplomatic writers from the seventeenth century were always telling their readers to learn to seize upon the right moment...', I. William Zartman and Maureen R. Berman, *The Practical Negotiator* (New Haven and London, 1982), p. 50.

32. There is a considerable debate on the notion of 'ripeness' in the modern literature on negotiation, especially mediation; for example, Richard N. Haass, 'Ripeness and the settlement of international disputes', *Survival*, May/June 1988, and his *Conflicts Unending: the United States and Regional Disputes* (New Haven, CT, 1990); L. Kriesberg and S. T. Thorson (eds), *Timing the De-escalation of International Conflicts* (Syracuse, New York, 1991); I. William Zartman, *Ripe for Resolution: Conflict and Intervention in Africa* (New York, 1985); and I. William Zartman (ed.), *Elusive Peace: Negotiating an End to Civil Wars* (Washington, 1995). However, one of the most elegant, succinct and suggestive accounts is to be found in Dean G. Pruitt, 'Ripeness theory and the Oslo talks', *International Negotiation*, vol. 2(2), 1997.

33. For example, by Jeffrey Z. Rubin: '... there is no such thing as a "wrong time" to attempt de-escalation. The worst that can happen is that no agreement results and, perhaps, the disputants take a bit longer than they might have otherwise to achieve the hurting stalemate that predisposes them to negotiate', 'The timing of ripeness and the ripeness of timing', in Louis Kriesberg and Stuart J. Thorson (eds), *Timing the De-escalation of International Conflicts* (Syracuse, New York, 1991), p. 238.

34. The Series B version gives us no more evidence of his thought on this point: 'If you undertake things at the wrong time, you will find not only that they do not succeed but also that you risk spoiling them even for the time at which they might easily have succeeded' (B117).

35. Chester A. Crocker, *High Noon in Southern Africa: Making Peace in a Rough Neighbourhood* (New York and London, 1992), p. 471.

36. This argument is not, as sometimes suggested, tautological since ripe moments can be botched as well as missed altogether.

37. In Pruitt's language (although unfortunately he does not consider the question of premature negotiation), these would be 'perceived valid spokesmen' and the ' "bridge" people on both sides who have sufficient contact with and

understanding of each other to spring into action when a period of motivational ripeness arrives', 'Ripeness theory and the Oslo talks', p. 247. See also the Introduction by Kriesberg in Kriesberg and Thorson (eds), *Timing the De-escalation of International Conflicts*, p. 19.

38. The importance of optimism as a component of ripeness (or 'readiness') is persuasively emphasized by Pruitt, 'Ripeness theory and the Oslo talks'; and Kriesberg in *Timing the De-escalation of International Conflicts*, p. 20.

39. Haass, *Conflicts Unending*, p. 139.

40. C49, C88, C103 and C184. Note, though, that the Series B version of C88, B48, is more illuminating: 'It is incredible how useful secrecy is to a ruler. Not only can his plans be blocked or upset if they are known, but what is more, ignorance of them keeps men awed and eager to observe his every move . . .'.

41. *The History of Florence*, NEL edition (see 'Further reading'), p. 53. See also 'Considerations' II, p. 63.

42. C126. See also C213: 'In all human decisions and actions there is always a reason for doing the opposite of what we do, for nothing is so perfect that it does not contain a defect.'

43. C126.

44. Walker translates this as 'neat strokes', *The Discourses* (Harmondsworth, 1970) vol. 1, p. 105.

45. 'Considerations', no. XIII, p. 113.

46. For example, in *The History of Florence*, NEL edition, p. 20; see also *ricordi* B33 and its even more sceptical version, C27.

47. 'Considerations', no. IX, p. 76: 'There is no doubt that . . . in a disordered city anyone deserves praise, who, being unable to re-order it otherwise, resorts to violence, fraud, or other extraordinary means'. See also no. XXVI.

48. Hale, Introduction to *Guicciardini: History of Italy and History of Florence*, p. xx. (Unfortunately, Hale does not indicate the source of the quotation in which Guicciardini employs the phrase *'ragione di stato'*.) See also Gilbert, *Machiavelli and Guicciardini*, pp. 120–1.

49. Hale, Introduction to *Guicciardini: History of Italy and History of Florence*, p. xx.

50. Friedrich Meinecke, *Machiavellism: The doctrine of raison d'état and its place in modern history*, first publ. 1924, trans. from the German by D. Scott (London, 1957), pp. 46–7.

51. In the first place, the *ricordo* cited by Hale is somewhat ambiguous on this point: 'He who has to exercise authority over others must not be too nice or scrupulous in issuing his commands. I do not say that he is to lay aside all scruples, but that in excess they are harmful.' (This is found in Series B, no. 12, and in Notebook 2, no. 15; the Domandi translation is essentially the same.) In the second place, this *ricordo* is virtually unrecognizable in the form that it assumes, according to Domandi's 'Table of Correspondence', in the final version, Series C, namely, in C41: 'If men were wise and good, those in authority should certainly be gentle rather than severe with them. But since the majority of men are either not very good or not very wise, one must rely more on severity than on kindness. Whoever thinks otherwise is mistaken. Surely, anyone who can skilfully mix and blend the one with the other would produce the sweetest possible accord and harmony. But heaven endows few with such talents; perhaps no one.' Though it is compatible with it, a doctrine of severity is not in itself a doctrine of *ragione di stato*.

52. See also C26, C36, C49, C157, C192 and C200.
53. See also B87.
54. Guicciardini's stress on the point that only a small distance between appearance and reality is tolerable is to be found expressed best in *ricordo* B2, which corresponds to C44.
55. In his *History of Italy*, Guicciardini observed that it was for this reason that Pope Julius II guarded his reputation for keeping his promises, though he admits later that this did him no good in his negotiations with the Venetians in the interval between the signing and the ratification of the League of Cambrai in 1509, pp. 173–4, 199.

Further reading

Works by Guicciardini in English translation (excepting Spongano)

Francesco Guicciardini, *Maxims and Reflections of a Renaissance Statesman (Ricordi)*, translated by Mario Domandi, introduced by Nicolai Rubinstein (New York, Evanston and London, 1965). Contains Series B and Notebook 2, as well as the final version of the *Ricordi*, Series C, together with a very useful 'Table of Correspondence'.

Raffaele Spongano, *Francesco Guicciardini: Ricordi Edizione Critica* (Firenze, 1951).

Francesco Guicciardini, *Selected Writings*, edited and introduced by C. Grayson, trans. M. Grayson (London, 1965). This contains the *Ricordi* (Series C only), 'Considerations on the "Discourses" of Machiavelli on the First Decade of T. Livy', and the *Ricordanze*.

Guicciardini's Ricordi: Counsels and Reflections of Francesco Guicciardini, trans. by Ninian Hill Thomson [first publ. 1890], edited by G. R. Berridge (Leicester, 2000; available through www.allandale.co.uk).

Francesco Guicciardini, *The History of Italy* [1561], translated, edited, with notes and introduction by Sydney Alexander (New York and London, 1969; Princeton, NJ, 1984) – esp. Book One, pp. 3–9, on the balance of power. These famous pages are also reproduced in Moorhead Wright's excellent collection: *Theory and Practice of the Balance of Power, 1486–1914: Selected European writings* (London, 1975), pp. 7–12.

Guicciardini: History of Italy and History of Florence, trsl. by C. Grayson, edited and abridged with an Introduction by John Hale (London, 1966). This heavily abridged work only covers the parts of Guicciardini's two histories dealing with the years from 1492 to 1498, though the parts which are reproduced are themselves uncut. Hale's introduction is very useful, though it is poorly sourced.

Historical background

As for Machiavelli; see previous chapter.

Biography

Ridolfi, R., *The Life of Francesco Guicciardini*, trsl. C. Grayson (London, 1967; New York, 1968), chs 4, 5, pp. 146–7; chs 18 and 19.

Whitfield, J. H., *Discourses on Machiavelli* (Cambridge, 1969), ch. 5 ('The case of Guicciardini'). This is a long, favourable review of Ridolfi's biography, in which Whitfield makes comparisons between Guicciardini and Machiavelli.

General

Butterfield, H. and M. Wight (eds), *Diplomatic Investigations: Essays in the Theory of International Politics* (London, 1966), ch. 6 (Butterfield, 'The balance of power').

Chabod, Federico, *Machiavelli and the Renaissance*, trans. from the Italian by D. Moore (London, 1958), index refs. to 'Guicciardini'.

Gilbert, F., *Machiavelli and Guicciardini* (Princeton, NJ, 1965), ch. 7.

Hale, J. R., 'Introduction' to *Guicciardini: History of Italy and History of Florence* (see above).

Luciani, V., *Fr. Guicciardini and his European Reputation* (New York, 1936).

Symonds, J. A., 'Guicciardini', *Encyclopaedia Britannica* (1885).

Wright, Moorhead (ed.), *Theory and Practice of the Balance of Power, 1486–1914: Selected European Writings* (London, 1975), pp. ix–xii.

3
Grotius

G. R. Berridge

Hugo Grotius (Huig de Groot) was born into a well-connected patrician family in Delft in Holland in 1583 and died in 1645, three years before the Thirty Years' War was brought to an end in the Peace of Westphalia. [1] A moderate Protestant, from the beginning it seems likely that Grotius had political ambitions and throughout his life appears to have regarded his writing as a second-order activity. [2] In 1599 he set himself up as an advocate in The Hague, where his growing reputation caused his opinion to be sought both by the Stadtholder, Prince Maurice, and the Dutch East India Company. Only eight years later he was elevated to the position of Advocate-Fiscal of the States of Holland. It was serving the interest of the Dutch East India Company in its struggles with the Portuguese and the Spanish that he directed his thoughts to maritime law and in 1609 he published *Mare Liberum*, his famous pamphlet in defence of the freedom of the seas. By now the protégé of the powerful Advocate of Holland, Oldenbarnevelt, in 1613 Grotius accepted his offer of the position of pensionary of Rotterdam. This made him the Advocate's first lieutenant in the States of Holland and thus carried real political power. Unfortunately for Grotius, Oldenbarnevelt did not survive the acute internal theological controversy which had been affecting the Dutch Reformed State Church since 1610 and when he fell in 1618 Grotius, who had opposed the strict Calvinists with some gusto, fell with him. The Advocate was executed and his lieutenant condemned to life imprisonment. Nevertheless, Grotius spent only two years in prison, escaping from the Castle of Loevestein in March 1621 and fleeing into exile in France, where he was given a pension and encouraged to make his home.

Grotius was welcomed in France not only because of his reputation as a great scholar, lawyer and publicist but also because of his close association with Oldenbarnevelt, who had put *raison d'état* before solidarity with his Huguenot coreligionists and supported France as a counterweight to his Habsburg enemies. It was during his French exile that Grotius produced his account of diplomatic law in the great work *De Jure Belli ac Pacis Libri Tres* while hoping – like Machiavelli in similar circumstances – for a resumption of his political career. In October 1631 he took the risk of returning to the Dutch Republic but in the following April was threatened with rearrest if he did not depart; once more, therefore, the miracle of Holland was obliged to retreat, this time to Hamburg. This, however, was merely a staging post for a return to his French exile, for in May 1634, following negotiations with the Swedish Chancellor, Axel Oxenstierna, he agreed to become Sweden's ambassador in Paris. This position – 'the top post in the Swedish diplomatic service' [3] – was occupied by Grotius until 1644, the year before his death.

Though Grotius was thus a resident ambassador for a full decade, it will be clear from this brief curriculum vitae that the experience post-dated his writing on diplomatic law. Nevertheless, he was far from a diplomatic innocent by this time. Already in 1607, when he was appointed official legal adviser to the States of Holland, he was collaborating with Oldenbarnevelt in negotiations with Spain. These were mediated by England and France and were the occasion for encounters between Grotius and the plenipotentiaries of these countries in The Hague. In the spring of 1613, following his elevation to the position of pensionary of Rotterdam, he was the *de facto* leader of a diplomatic mission to the court of James I of England. Concerned chiefly with Asian affairs but given a religious twist by the shared interest of James and Grotius in theological controversy, [4] this conference was succeeded by another one in 1615 in which Grotius also played a key role. [5] While Oldenbarnevelt's lieutenant until his arrest in 1618, Grotius preserved his connections with the world of diplomacy by maintaining intimate contact with foreign ambassadors in The Hague.

The Relevant Writings

Grotius was a prolific writer, and among his works generally reckoned to be of most importance by students of International Relations are *De Jure Praedae*, which was written in the first decade of the seventeenth century but not published until 1868; *Mare Liberum*, his famous defence of the freedom of the seas, which was first published in 1609; [6] and above all his magisterial *De Jure Belli ac Pacis Libri Tres* [*Three Books On the Law of War and Peace*]. For students of diplomacy it is the last which commands attention. This work first appeared in 1625 and was, as already noted, the fruit of his first years of exile in France. It was subsequently republished many times, the English edition, which is most accessible today, being the translation published by Francis W. Kelsey in 1925 (see 'Further reading'). Though students of jurisprudence argue over the scope and general significance of *De Jure Belli ac Pacis*, there is now wide agreement that it was of great importance in the general development of international law, the theory of the just war, and the notion of an international society.[7]

The central theme of *De Jure Belli ac Pacis* is the law of war,[8] and diplomatic law itself is not much more than a long footnote: Chapter 18 of Book 2, which Grotius entitled 'The Right of Legation'. Partly because of the brevity of this treatment[9] and partly because of its influence on Grotius, it will also be instructive to make frequent reference to a much longer account of diplomatic law written only forty years earlier. This is *De Legationibus Libri Tres*, published by Alberico Gentili, a Protestant from the March of Ancona who had sought refuge from the Italian inquisition in the England of Queen Elizabeth I and been appointed to teach Roman Law at Oxford. Gentili came to attention when in 1584 he invoked the doctrine of the right of embassy to argue against the legality of punishing the Spanish ambassador, Bernadino de Mendoza, for complicity in the Throckmorton plot against Elizabeth. His own book was the product of his involvement in this case and, like that of Grotius, has been reprinted in the 'Classics in International Law' series (see 'Further reading'). It has been authoritatively described as 'the earliest major work on diplomatic law'.[10]

Diplomacy in the System of Grotius

Despite the customary description as 'Grotian' of that view of international relations in which centre stage is commanded by an international society embodied in rules and institutions such as diplomacy, it is true that only a pale version of this perspective is to be found in Grotius himself.[11] Excepting war and international law, he pays relatively little attention to the remaining institutions of international society, among them – as already noted – diplomacy itself.[12] But it is clear from the 'Prolegomena' that this is because he regards subjects such as diplomacy as beyond his remit and not because he considers them unimportant.[13] In any case, there remains explicit testimony in parts of *De Jure Belli ac Pacis* – as well as implicit testimony throughout – that diplomacy plays a vital role in his general system.

The implicit testimony is found in his belief that all aspects of the relations (including belligerent ones) between states (including non-Christian ones) are subject to law, for what is one of the greatest contributors to this law but diplomacy? [14] A corollary of this is that Grotius expects diplomacy to be successful and this is because he has great faith in the goodness, rationality and above all sociability of human beings. [15] In particular, he expects states (which are merely associations of individuals) to be able to take the long view of their interests and thus, among other things, always to keep their promises. In any event, they certainly *should*, whether these promises are given to pirates, tyrants, or enemies, and irrespective of whether or not they are infidels, since, as Lauterpacht stresses, for Grotius this is 'the principal tenet of the law of nature'. [16] In this as in other ways rejecting *raison d'état* out of hand (as much by a refusal to notice its leading proponents as by his repeated insistence on the fundamental rule that good states should behave as good individuals) [17] he even has a 'very restrictive approach' to the doctrine of *rebus sic stantibus*. [18]

The explicit testimony to the vital role played by diplomacy in the system of Grotius emerges because of his great hostility to war. Resort to war may only be had when it is just; furthermore, its calamitous consequences dictate that when there is doubt on this score it must be renounced, as for the same reason when the evidence produced in a trial dealing with a capital crime is inconclusive it is better to acquit a guilty person than to condemn an innocent one. [19] In any case, adds Grotius, there are 'three methods by which disputes may be prevented from breaking out into war', and it is no surprise to find that the first of these listed is negotiation, or what Grotius calls the 'conference' method. [20] The second is arbitration, to which Christian kings have a particular duty to resort. While Grotius clearly sees this as a judicial process rather than mediation, it is equally evident that he regards diplomacy as necessary in order to establish and hold together arbitral conferences. He would probably also have agreed that it is essential to secure acceptance of their judgements. What he actually says is that 'it would be advantageous, indeed in a degree necessary, to hold certain conferences of Christian powers, where those who have no interest at stake may settle the disputes of others, and where, in fact, steps may be taken to compel parties to accept peace on fair terms.' [21] The third method noted by Grotius for settling disputes without war is determination by lot or a variant on it, single combat. [22] Though he does not say so, it is also difficult to see how either of these methods could be determined and activated except by means of diplomacy.

Finally, if war breaks out nevertheless, Grotius observes that 'not only do very many matters come up in war which cannot be handled except through ambassadors, but also peace itself is hardly to be made by any other means'. [23]

Ambassadors and Sovereignty

In chapter 18 of *De Jure Belli ac Pacis*, however, we find Grotius dealing explicitly with diplomacy, though he restricts himself to providing an account of the law surrounding the work of diplomatic agents. Mercifully enough, he spares us the extended preliminaries provided by Gentili in his own account of diplomatic law [24] but provides a few anyway and they are not without interest. He begins by stating, in this connection with uncharacteristic baldness, [25] that the right of legation does not derive from natural law but from the 'law of nations', that is, the customary practice of states. [26] However, the cases he subsequently cites in order to demonstrate customary practice come largely from ancient Greece and Rome. [27] In any event, Grotius insists next that the right of legation is, with one exception, an exclusive attribute of sovereignty. In other words, while provincial governors for example may employ representatives at other places (one thinks of the agent maintained by Guicciardini at Rome to protect his personal interests, see page 34 above), only those sent by 'rulers with sovereign powers' to similar bodies enjoy the right of legation. This was uncontroversial. Gentili had made the same point before him and Wicquefort was to develop it at greater length not long afterwards. [28] However, Grotius maintains that an exception is provided by the circumstance of civil war, and on this he goes beyond Gentili and is taken to task for it by Wicquefort.

'In civil wars, however,' says Grotius, 'necessity sometimes opens the way for the exercise of this right [of legation], though in an irregular fashion. Such a case will arise', he continues, 'when a people has been divided into parts so nearly equal that it is doubtful which of the two sides possesses sovereignty; and again, when two persons with practically equal rights are contending for the succession to the throne. Under such circumstances', concludes Grotius, 'a single people is considered for the time being as two peoples'. In fact, says Wicquefort, this claim is not supported by seventeenth-century state practice, though he admits that it would be sensible if each party in a civil war were to concede the right of legation to the other, [29] which, as it happens, was Gentili's interpretation of the law. [30]

The position of Grotius on this question is clearly the more radical, and remarkably realistic: it suggests the inescapability of recognizing power. Nevertheless, it presents major difficulties. The first of these is the problem of deciding on what basis to determine the weight of the respective parties in the civil war and then applying it in light of the facts, which will no doubt themselves be disputed. Is the deciding factor to be the nominal relative strength of their armed forces, or the proportion of the territory, population and economic and strategic assets in their possession? The second problem derives from Wicquefort's widely admitted observation that 'there is not a more illustrious mark of sovereignty than the right of sending and receiving embassadors'. [31] This being the case, outside acceptance of 'ambassadors' from the warring parties would confer sovereignty on separate 'peoples', as Grotius acknowledges. However, this would presumably be unacceptable to the parties because if they agree on anything at all it is that they form parts of *one* people or state. This, of course, is why in the period since the revolution in China in 1949 the 'Republic of China' (ROC) on Taiwan could never contemplate diplomatic relations with a state which had similar relations with the 'People's Republic of China' (PRC): like the PRC, it claimed to be the government of the whole of China.

It is significant nevertheless that in recent years a pragmatic solution has been found to the problem confronted but not satisfactorily resolved by Grotius. This has been simply for outside states to have formal diplomatic relations with one party to a civil conflict and informal ones with the other, the differences in practice not usually being of great moment. Thus in the 1970s the United States welcomed a 'liaison office' from the PRC in addition to the existing 'embassy' of the ROC, while a sizeable number of states admit a similar kind of representation from the almost universally unrecognized 'Turkish Republic of Northern Cyprus' in addition to an embassy or high commission from the Republic of Cyprus. [32]

Should Ambassadors Always be Received?

Having established that ambassadors may only be employed by 'rulers with sovereign powers' in their relations with similar rulers, Grotius next considers whether or not they must always be 'admitted', noting the claim of certain authors that this is indeed one of the 'rights' of ambassadors. In fact it was not at that time, as Grotius was fully aware, and is not today, for the Vienna Convention on Diplomatic Relations 1961, which codified the customary law of diplomacy, [33] states early and unambiguously that 'The establishment of diplomatic relations between States, and of permanent diplomatic missions, takes place by *mutual* consent.'[34] As Gentili had earlier pointed out, 'unless one had the privilege of forbidding the coming of embassies, considerable confusion would be introduced by this alone into international law, which insists and orders that control over one's own affairs shall be final and inviolable'.[35] It is true, Grotius states, that the law of nations forbids the rejection of ambassadors 'without cause' but he at once offers a succinct list of the reasons which amply justify a ruler in barring his door: 'The cause ... may arise in the case of the one who sends the ambassador, or in the case of the one who is sent, or in the reason for the sending.'

In the first place, then, Grotius maintains that a state may refuse to admit ambassadors if objection is taken to the country from which they originate, typically because it is either 'wicked' or an enemy. There is no doubt that he was on firm ground here though he might have added *a propos* 'wicked' states that the right of denial in such circumstances was one thing but its exercise another. As Gentili had previously pointed out, it was already common for ambassadors to be admitted from states held to be in the grip of infidels or even heretics.[36] Indeed, his own book was inspired by a case concerning an ambassador from a Catholic state (Spain) to a Protestant one (England). It was also published just two years after England's first permanent embassy to the Muslim empire of the Ottoman sultan was created in Istanbul, where it joined two other Christian embassies already long established, those of Venice and France.

In the second place, Grotius notes that ambassadors may also be rejected if they are regarded as personally objectionable by reason of their beliefs or character, even if they come from states to which there is no objection in principle to the establishment or continuation of diplomatic relations. The Vienna Convention notes essentially the same right of the receiving state, making clear that a sending state must secure the latter's agreement to the named head of mission it is proposing to dispatch.[37] However, the law has been, as the lawyers say, 'developed' more than a little on this point since the time of Grotius. In particular, the Vienna Convention limits the right of rejection by the receiving state to heads of mission and service attachés,[38] whereas by implication Grotius permits it to reject any member of a diplomatic mission. The 1961 Convention also says that no reason need be given by a receiving state for a refusal of *agrément*,[39] while Grotius is silent on this point.

Finally, Grotius says that ambassadors may be denied entry if there are grounds for suspecting that they have been dispatched for some purpose damaging to the interests of the prospective receiving state. In this connection he mentions 'stirring up the people', which was, of course, a great fear at that time and has remained a source of concern ever since. Not surprisingly, therefore, this rule has echoed down the centuries and appears at more than one point in the Vienna Convention. Grotius adds as afterthoughts under this head that an 'embassy' may also be rejected when it is 'not of proper rank, or when it comes at an inopportune time'. And his much remarked parting shot is that 'permanent legations, such as are now customary, can be rejected with the best of right; for ancient custom, to which they were unknown, teaches how unnecessary they are'. [40]

These afterthoughts suggest that Grotius believed that a state could refuse to admit an ambassador into its territory for more or less any reason at all, although what is not clear from his sparse account is whether he thought that the law of nations imposed an obligation to make known this reason, either publicly or confidentially. Gentili is not much less ambiguous, observing only that 'prohibition should be based on some reason, for without reason the eternal laws of nations can not be changed or abolished by anyone'. [41] The ambiguity of both on this point was probably a reflection of the uncertainty of practice, while also being symptomatic of the tension in their thought between recognition of the fundamental importance of sovereignty on the one hand and the great value of diplomacy on the other, the former arguing against any need for the provision of reasons and the latter arguing for it so that frivolous or trivial rejections of ambassadors might be discouraged. Be that as it may, there is no requirement for justification of any kind in modern diplomatic law and it is perhaps as well. The reason for the refusal of diplomatic relations or for rejection of a particular ambassador will usually be self-evident and any explicit statement of it may simply make matters worse.

An additional weakness of Grotius's account of this question should be noted. This is his failure to distinguish between any obligation to *admit* a foreign ambassador within the state's borders and any obligation to *hear* him. This is an important oversight because even in the early seventeenth century an ambassador could be 'heard' without being 'admitted', as Emmerich de Vattel, another great international lawyer who had also served as a diplomat, [42] later pointed out. Agreeing with Grotius that ambassadors could be denied entry 'into the interior of the country' provided there were good grounds, Vattel nevertheless stresses that the obligation of mutual intercourse is such that in these circumstances they should be met at the frontier: the sovereign, he says, 'may appoint a place upon the frontier where the minister will be met and his proposals heard. The minister must stop at the appointed place; it is sufficient that he be given a hearing, and that is the extent of his right'. [43] Of course, today telecommunications make it relatively simple for foreign ministries to gain a hearing without any need for their agents to be physically admitted into a foreign territory. [44] Contact can also be made at third places of the kind which just did not exist at the time when Grotius was writing, the most obvious example being the United Nations.

The Inviolability of Ambassadors

It is in section 4 of chapter 18 of the second book of *De Jure Belli ac Pacis* that Grotius comes to the larger and more important part of diplomatic law, perhaps the most important of all questions of international law in his own day. [45] This is that providing for the special treatment of ambassadors, especially when they are accused of grave offences – what today we call loosely 'diplomatic immunity'. He remarks immediately that this question is 'more difficult' and indicates the need to approach it via a key distinction: 'We need to speak of the persons of ambassadors, then of their suite and property.' As to the ambassador himself, Grotius indicates that the issue is the extent to which the law of nations offers him special protection and on what grounds. Unfortunately, he says, state practice provides no consistent guide and 'the opinions of wise men' vary. He concludes therefore that it is necessary not only to consider their views but also 'the implications'; in other words, to stick one's neck out and suggest what the law *ought* to be.

Why, to begin with, should ambassadors receive special privileges of civil and criminal immunity at all? Grotius answers in unmistakably modern language. Embassies, he insists, are at all times useful [46] and – as already noted earlier in this chapter – in war indispensable. Unfortunately, he continues, their safety 'is placed on an extremely precarious footing' if they can be tried under the laws of the receiving state. 'For since the views of those who send the ambassadors are generally different from the views of those who receive them, and often directly opposed', it is not difficult for their actions to be made to seem criminal. [47] In circumstances such as these, then, where it is so easy to intimidate ambassadors, embassies are less likely to be sent in the first place and if sent – we can safely infer from his thought – not likely to function effectively. What Grotius himself says is that 'the ease in sending embassies is best promoted by making their safety as secure as possible'. [48]

This is a fairly unambiguous statement of what is today called the functional theory of diplomatic privileges and immunities: special privileges are needed by diplomats because without them they cannot carry out their important work efficiently. That this was the position of Grotius is further supported by his use of the word 'fiction' in his passing treatment of both of the more popular theories of his own time which were employed to justify the exceptional treatment of ambassadors – the theories of sovereign representation and exterritoriality – even though it is also clear that he regarded these as convenient. What is remarkable about Grotius's account is the extent to which he was ahead of his time. The functional theory to which he so clearly gives pre-eminence [49] did not, despite the further push provided to it by Vattel in the middle of the eighteenth century, [50] unambiguously achieve centre-stage in diplomatic law for almost another three and a half centuries, in its codification in the Preamble to the Vienna Convention on Diplomatic Relations in 1961. As Lyons wrote in 1953, 'the modern view... is a reversion to that of Grotius'. [51]

Grotius believes, then, that ambassadors accused of lawbreaking should be given special immunities from prosecution in local courts. In addition, he offers the essentially political judgement that 'the security of ambassadors outweighs any advantage which accrues from a punishment'. [52] Nevertheless, he is naturally aware that the receiving state pays some price for withholding punishment from an errant ambassador, since natural law demands the punishment of offenders whoever they may be. [53] While Grotius gives almost total immunity to deviant ambassadors, therefore, he by no means suggests that they be spared all embarrassment, or even punishment; it all depends on the nature of their illegal activity and, in practice, on the attitude of their own masters. A minor infraction should be overlooked, while a more serious one should result in the expulsion of the ambassador. [54] 'If the crime should be particularly atrocious and bid fair to bring harm to the state,' says Grotius, 'the ambassador should be sent back to the one who sent him, with the demand that he be punished or surrendered [for punishment in the receiving state].' [55] Should these demands be refused, as Gentili had earlier argued was invariably the case (even by the virtuous Romans), [56] 'punishment by means of war can be exacted from him as having approved the crime'. [57] In 'dire necessity', when the action of an ambassador produces 'an immediately threatening peril' to the state (for example by inciting rebellion) and when 'there is no other proper recourse', an ambassador may be 'detained and questioned'. [58] An ambassador may only be killed if he should 'attempt armed force' and even then 'not by way of penalty, but in natural defence'. [59]

On the question of the ambassador's criminal liability there is little doubt that Grotius had in general got it right and diplomatic law has in consequence changed little in this regard since his time. His political touch was surer than that of Gentili, who had argued among other things that an ambassador who had successfully harmed the sovereign to whom he was accredited (as opposed merely to planning to harm him) should be subject to local criminal jurisdiction and be liable to suffer death as the penalty for his crime. [60] On the face of it, it is true that Grotius may have seemed naive in suggesting that 'punishment can be inflicted through the one who sent the ambassador' but his position hardly depended on this possibility and, as it has turned out, it is by no means unknown for sending states to waive the immunity of diplomats accused of offences, albeit this is normally a practice confined to the relations between friendly states.

Can the right of retaliation be claimed against ambassadors?

An interesting footnote to the issue of ambassadorial inviolability, which Grotius touches on only briefly, is whether or not it is right that ambassadors might be punished in retaliation for an objectionable act on the part of the state which has sent them. In the Ottoman Empire it was in fact a long-established tradition that ambassadors were hostages for the good behaviour of their governments. In the event of war breaking out between the Turks and a state with an ambassador in Constantinople the latter was at once despatched to the prison of the Seven Towers, where he could languish for some years. This practice was not discontinued for almost two hundred years after Grotius presented his thoughts on diplomatic law. [61]

Grotius is unambiguously hostile to the notion that receiving states have a right of retaliation against ambassadors who are personally innocent, though he acknowledges that this right has been asserted and exercised often enough in the past. Once ambassadors have been received, he repeats, a 'tacit agreement' is made between them and their host government which establishes their inviolability: they are not simply a limb of the sending state but persons with their own rights, the rights of embassy. In any case, he says, it makes no sense to kill or mistreat ambassadors in the event of war since they will almost certainly be needed for one important task or another. Gentili had made explicit what was only implicit in Grotius's account here by stating that following the outbreak of war the most that a prince might do was to order the departure of ambassadors but whether he did or not he remained under a special obligation to secure their safety.[62] This of course remains the position under the Vienna Convention.

Grotius however does not provide an altogether satisfactory discussion of this question, overlooking in particular what subsequently came to be acknowledged as the most vital principle in defence of the rights of embassy. This is the principle of reciprocity, that is, the prudential rule that states, being invariably senders as well as receivers of ambassadors, should treat foreign ambassadors with lawful respect in order to encourage similar treatment of their own, a rule which would hardly carry weight if disrespect on one side was not matched with disrespect on the other.[63] In this connection it is instructive to turn once more to Gentili, who it transpires does not altogether agree with Grotius here and in general provides a more sophisticated analysis. Gentili begins by maintaining that the argument subsequently advanced by Grotius that the innocent should not be made to suffer for the guilty is quite wrongheaded. 'But how', asks Gentili, 'can he be called innocent who is the personal representative of one who is notoriously guilty?' If this were possible, he continues, even war would be ruled out since it would be illegal to attack the innocent soldiers of their guilty sovereign! Like Grotius, as we have seen, he certainly does not believe that ambassadors should be punished following the outbreak of war, since they are useful and since war is in any case permitted under the law of nations. Indeed, he does not even believe that they should be punished in retaliation for breaches of the law of nations by their own prince – except in one all-important case. Thus Gentili believes that a prince is entitled to punish ambassadors accredited to him only in retaliation for the mistreatment of his own ambassadors by the sending prince. This is because no other law of nations compares to that prescribing the inviolability of ambassadors 'in majesty and prestige' and because 'to withhold rights from one who has violated them is believed to be not a violation but a rendering of justice'.[64] Gentili is right and Grotius wrong. Gentili is speaking of the reciprocity which, reflecting the balance of power, is the cement of the institution of diplomacy. So when the Ottomans threw ambassadors into the Seven Towers in retaliation for an act of war against them there was nothing in principle wrong with what they did. By the norm of state practice it was in general simply crude and inappropriate; that is, they should have reserved it as a deterrent against similar abuse of their own diplomats. All diplomats are 'hostages' for the good behaviour of their own states towards their fellow professionals.[65]

Is the ambassador inviolable in a third country?

Those who had maintained that an ambassador derived his inviolability from the sacred quality of his mission naturally believed that his privileged position held good wherever he happened to be. This was a more important question in the days before air travel since it was often unavoidable that an ambassador would have to travel over the territory of third states, some of which may have been unfriendly, in order to reach the court for which alone he possessed letters of credence. One of the important new principles established by Gentili, however, was that the special privileges and immunities of ambassadors began only with their official acceptance by the receiving state, the obvious corollary of which was that such privileges had no legal basis in third states. [66] However, he diluted its impact with the rather unconvincing qualification that this represented a 'rigid interpretation of the law' and that since 'the mission of ambassadors is one of peace' and their role 'sacred', while in transit they should remain 'sacrosanct and inviolable, even in the sight of an enemy'. [67] Grotius is less sentimental, adopting Gentili's principle without even a passing reference to his qualification. [68] According to Grotius – who is under no illusion that the missions of ambassadors are always pacific – those apprehended travelling across a state to or from its enemies, or 'planning any hostile measure', can quite properly be imprisoned and even killed. But this did not threaten diplomacy as much as might at first appear, since a safe-conduct might be obtained from the government of any third state intervening between the sender and the receiver. This custom is of course noted by Grotius, though he is silent on the issue of whether or not a safe-conduct granted any special immunities in the third country. In fact it rarely did in this period, whereas the Vienna Convention now provides limited immunities to the transit diplomat with a passport visa, if this is necessary, although in order to obtain them he must be accredited to a specific receiving state and serve a government recognised by the third country; he must also be on official and not private business. [69]

The suite and property of the ambassador

By the early seventeenth century it was well established that the suite and property of the ambassador should also enjoy special privileges, since he could hardly function without them. 'What does the power of privilege attached to the person of ambassadors amount to,' Gentili had asked, 'if it does not apply to their effects also?' [70] There is therefore nothing extraordinary in the bald statement of Grotius that 'the suite also, and the effects of ambassadors, in their own way are inviolate'. If a member of his suite commits a serious offence, the ambassador can surrender him to local jurisdiction if he so chooses, and in this respect he stands in relation to his diplomatic staff in the same way that his sovereign stands to him. If he refuses to waive immunity, therefore, the receiving state must proceed towards the errant member of his suite as it would towards the ambassador in identical circumstances, which would normally be to expel him. [71] The movable goods of an ambassador fallen into debt cannot be seized by or on behalf of creditors. [72] Under the law of nations, adds Grotius, the ambassador himself has no right of jurisdiction over his suite; nor does he have the right to grant asylum to any seeking refuge in his residence. [73] Any such rights depend on their grant by the receiving government.

What became a sensitive issue (not for the first time) in connection with the ambassador's suite when diplomatic law was being codified in the late 1950s is passed over in silence by Grotius, though the fearless and argumentative Gentili had grappled with it in lively fashion. This was the issue of who precisely was to be *included* in 'the suite', [74] especially since it invariably embraced a 'rabble' of 'attendants, followers, menials, and hostlers'. It is true, conceded Gentili, that the normal definition of the suite restricted it to those who were of direct assistance to the ambassador in his diplomatic work but the ancient tradition of entering their names in public records (the 'diplomatic list' of a later era) had unfortunately lapsed. Besides, he continued, warming to his theme, since no distinction was attempted between those effects of the ambassador enjoying immunities and those not, it would be inconsistent to discriminate between different persons in his employ-ment. 'The term "suite"', he concluded, 'should be taken in a broader sense.' [75]

Grotius gives us no clues as to whether he shares the broad or the narrow view of the ambassador's suite, and perhaps he was wise to duck this tricky question at this juncture, when in fact as well as in theory it was often impossible to distinguish between 'diplomatic staff' and 'private servants' of the ambassador. [76] There is force in Gentili's logic, although enlarging the number of those enjoying immunities (not least from local taxation) increases popular resentment against diplomats, especially if ambassadors are permitted to insist that their suites include nationals of the receiving state. [77] As a result, when the Vienna Conven-tion codified diplomatic law in 1961 Gentili's broad view of the ambas-sador's suite was still clearly discernible, though it is qualified by distinctions which permit concentration of most privileges where they are most needed and most tolerable; it also generally excludes from enjoyment of immunities altogether those who are nationals of or permanently resident in the receiving state. [78] The staff of the mission, as they are now known, is divided into three categories, hierarchical by extent of immunities possessed: the diplomatic, administrative and technical, and service staff. Servants employed privately by members of the mission were also added. Members of the families of diplomats were included in the 'diplomatic staff'. This is probably as good a compromise as one could hope to achieve between the desirable and the politically tolerable.

Finally, it is perhaps appropriate to notice here that there is no mention at all in Grotius of the inviolability of the embassy premises themselves or, if separate, the ambassador's private residence. [79] Indeed, as already noted, he states that asylum cannot be granted in the embassy unless this is permitted by the receiving government. The whole emphasis in his writing is upon the inviolability of the *person* of the ambassador. This was not an oversight but how the law stood at that time, no doubt because the permanent embassy was a relatively recent invention and one of which Grotius himself disapproved. However, he stood at a watershed in this respect for only shortly afterwards state practice began to settle very firmly on the 'exterritoriality' of the embassy's premises, [80] and by the time of the Vienna Convention we find that its inviolability is significantly stronger than that of the person of the ambassador. This is because diplomacy can tolerate some constraints on its agents but might be fatally wounded if its buildings and papers could be compromised. [81]

Conclusion

Grotius believes that all aspects of the relations between states are subject to law, and that resort to war is permissible only when its justice is beyond reasonable doubt. Both of these views place diplomacy at a premium in his system, though his acknowledgement of the supreme importance of sovereignty leads him to reject the idea that diplomacy should be imposed on unwilling states and he is certainly not in advance of his times in his coolness to the permanent embassy.

It is, however, precisely because diplomacy in general is so important that Grotius believes that ambassadors, together with their effects and their suite, should have special immunities from criminal and civil jurisdiction in the countries of their accreditation. Unable to function effectively in the absence of such immunities, since it would be so easy for charges against them to be fabricated in unfriendly quarters, these immunities should also be virtually complete, extending even to immunity from retaliation equivalent to any action by their own government against the ambassadors despatched from the state of their accreditation. In both of these respects – the functional theory of diplomatic immunity and the comprehensiveness of the immunities he claimed – Grotius goes well beyond his predecessors, including Gentili. [82] It is in *De Jure Belli ac Pacis* – despite the sparseness of its account of diplomatic law, and the omissions and the gloss over some important distinctions in this treatment – that 'the outlines of the modern law [on diplomacy] are for the first time clearly recognizable'. [83] This is the real importance of Grotius for the development of diplomatic thought, and it must be admitted that it is not developed diplomatic theory. For Grotius the vast importance of diplomacy in international relations was something which he tended to take for granted, and its political elaboration something which his conception of the division of professional and intellectual labour allotted to others.

Notes

1. This biographical introduction leans heavily on 'Grotius and the international politics of the seventeenth century', the outstanding chapter by C. G. Roelofsen in H. Bull, B. Kingsbury and A. Roberts (eds), *Hugo Grotius and International Relations* (Oxford, 1992) [hereafter *HGIR*].
2. Though compare this claim with Hersch Lauterpacht, 'The Grotian tradition in international law', *International Law: Collected Papers*, ed. E. Lauterpacht, vol. 2, The Law of Peace, Part I, International Law in General (Cambridge, 1975), p. 309.
3. Roelofsen, *HGIR*, p. 127.
4. Grotius was granted a private audience with the king.
5. Peter Haggenmacher, 'Grotius and Gentili: A reassessment of Thomas E. Holland's inaugural lecture', *HGIR*, p. 144.
6. It was chapter 12 of the draft of *De Jure Praedae*.
7. *HGIR*, pp. 2–6; on the external reasons for the success of *De Jure Belli ac Pacis* [hereafter *JBP*], see Lauterpacht, 'The Grotian tradition in international law', pp. 324–6.
8. *HGIR*, p. 3.
9. For his own purposes Grotius regarded this as a virtue of his style, remarking that he had adopted 'a mode of speaking at the same time concise and suitable for exposition, in order that those who deal with public affairs may have, as it were, in a single view both the kinds of controversies which are wont to arise and the principles by reference to which they may be decided', *JBP*, Book I, p. 30. In short, his style is what would today no doubt be called that of the 'executive summary'.
10. E. Young, 'The development of the law of diplomatic relations', *British Yearbook of International Law*, vol. 40, 1964, p. 149.

11. *HGIR*, pp. 6–15. However, the introduction ('Prolegomena') to the *JBP* remains a powerful and eloquent statement.
12. *HGIR*, pp. 26–7, 89–90.
13. 'I have refrained from discussing topics which belong to another subject, such as those that teach what may be advantageous in practice. For such topics have their own special field, that of politics, which Aristotle rightly treats by itself, without introducing extraneous matter into it,' *JBP*, Book I, p. 29.
14. 'Greatest' rather than sole contributor, of course, because of the major role given by Grotius to natural law; see Lauterpacht, 'The Grotian tradition in international law', pp. 327–31.
15. *JBP*, Book I, Prolegomena, pp. 9–13; Lauterpacht, 'The Grotian tradition in international law', pp. 333–6.
16. 'The Grotian tradition in international law', p. 353.
17. *JBP*, Book I, Prolegomena, esp. pp. 9–20; Lauterpacht, 'The Grotian tradition in international law', pp. 336–46; Draper, *HGIR*, pp. 199–201.
18. O. Yasuaki, 'Agreement', ch. 6 in Yasuaki (ed.), *A Normative Approach to War: Peace, War, and Justice in Hugo Grotius* (Oxford, 1993), p. 204.
19. *JBP*, Book II, pp. 559–60.
20. *JBP*, Book II, pp. 560–1.
21. *JBP*, Book II, pp. 561–3.
22. *JBP*, Book II, pp. 563–4.
23. *JBP*, Book II, p. 446.
24. Though they are short, the twenty chapters of Gentili's Book I are concerned entirely with the definition of terms, chiefly by reference to Roman practice. Since Book I has no introduction it is actually best to begin by reading chapter 1 of Book II, where Gentili justifies his approach in Book I.
25. Lauterpacht, 'The Grotian tradition in international law', p. 311.
26. Grotius also called this 'volitional' law. Today we would be inclined to call it 'positive law', that is, law which – unlike natural law – is entirely the product of human agency.
27. In this regard he was more like Gentili, for at that time it was necessary for any work of this sort wishing to be taken seriously to be adorned with such examples. See Lauterpacht, 'The Grotian tradition in international law', p. 310; and E. R. Adair, *The Exterritoriality of Ambassadors in the Sixteenth and Seventeenth Centuries* (London, 1929), p. 27.
28. Abraham de Wicquefort, *The Embassador and His Functions* [first publ. 1680/1], trans. by J. Digby (London, 1716), repr. with an Introduction by H. M. A. Keens-Soper (Leicester, 1997), chs. 2–6.
29. Wicquefort, *The Embassador and His Functions*, p. 7.
30. *De Legationibus*, Book 2, Ch. 9: 'Does the right of embassy hold in civil strife?'
31. Wicquefort, *The Embassador and His Functions*, p. 6.
32. On this subject, see my *Talking to the Enemy* (London, 1994), ch. 3; and M. J. Peterson, *Recognition of Governments: Legal Doctrine and State Practice, 1815–1995* (London, 1997).
33. The definitive account of this is to be found in Eileen Denza's *Diplomatic Law: Commentary on the Vienna Convention on Diplomatic Relations*, 2nd edn (Oxford, 1998). The text of the Convention is also reproduced as an appendix to my *Diplomacy: Theory and Practice*, 2nd edn (Leicester, 1999).

34. Article 2, emphasis added. See also Denza, *Diplomatic Law*, p. 20.
35. *De Legationibus*, p. 69.
36. *De Legationibus*, pp. 90–1. Gentili's own phrase here was 'the universal practice', which was probably going too far.
37. Article 4(1).
38. Articles 4(1) and 7.
39. Article 4(2).
40. Less often remarked is that Gentili's view of the utility of what he sometimes calls 'time embassies' is essentially the same: 'appointed for the purpose of showing a courtesy more than anything else' (*De Legationibus*, p. 99), he regards them as useful but hardly essential; see also *De Legationibus*, pp. 14, 52–3, 94–9, 169–70.
41. *De Legationibus*, p. 69.
42. Vattel was employed in the diplomatic service of the Elector of Saxony from 1746 until 1758. On the importance of Vattel, see P. F. Butler, 'Legitimacy in a states-system: Vattel's *Law of Nations*', in M. Donelan (ed.), *The Reason of States: A Study in International Political Theory* (London, 1978), pp. 45–63.
43. Emmerich de Vattel, *The Law of Nations [Le Droits des Gens] or the Principles of Natural Law Applied to the Conduct and to the Affairs of Nations and of Sovereigns*, trans. of the edition of 1758 by C. G. Fenwick, repr. 1964, New York and London, p. 364.
44. See also Denza, *Diplomatic Law*, p. 22.
45. Adair, *Exterritoriality*, pp. 12–13.
46. *JBP*, Book II, p. 442.
47. *JBP*, Book II, p. 443.
48. *JBP*, Book II, p. 442.
49. The Frenchman Pierre Ayrault had advanced the functional argument in 1576 but had not given it ascendancy over the sovereign representative character and exterritoriality of the ambassador; see Young, 'The development of the law of diplomatic relations', p. 147.
50. *Le Droit des Gens*, vol. 3, esp. p. 376.
51. A. B. Lyons, 'Immunities other than jurisdictional of the property of diplomatic envoys', *British Yearbook of International Law 1953*, vol. 30, p. 148; see also Adair, *Exterritoriality*, p. 76.
52. *JBP*, Book II, p. 443.
53. Against the need to ease the sending of embassies, he says, 'lies the advantageousness of punishment of grave offenders', *JBP*, Book II, p. 442.
54. *JBP*, Book II, p. 443.
55. *JBP*, Book II, p. 444.
56. *De Legationibus*, pp. 115–16.
57. *JBP*, Book II, p. 443.
58. *JBP*, Book II, p. 444.
59. *JBP*, Book II, p. 444.
60. *De Legationibus*, pp. 113–14. For more general comment on Gentili's view of the criminal liability of the ambassador, see Young, 'The development of the law of diplomatic relations', p. 149.
61. In 1798 the French chargé d'affaires was sent to the Seven Towers in retaliation for Napoleon's invasion of Egypt. This was the last occasion on which the Sultan resorted to this extremity.

62. *De Legationibus*, p. 96; see also p. 73.
63. This principle is, of course, a powerful support to international law in general, see Malcolm Shaw, *International Law*, 3rd edn, p. 8.
64. *De Legationibus*, p. 73.
65. Cornelius van Bynkershoek, *De Foro Legatorum* [1721], trans. of the edition of 1744 by G. J. Laing, repr. 1964, New York and London, p. 119; Vattel, *Le Droit des Gens*, vol. 3, p. 383; Young, 'The development of the law of diplomatic relations', p. 181; and P. Cradock, *Experiences of China* (London, 1994), pp. 65, 66, 73–4.
66. *De Legationibus*, Book 2, ch. 3; Young, 'The development of the law of diplomatic relations', p. 149.
67. *De Legationibus*, p. 63.
68. Adair notes that this was the more common view, *Exterritoriality*, p. 110.
69. Article 40. See also *Satow's Guide to Diplomatic Practice*, ed. Lord Gore-Booth, 5th edn (London and New York, 1979), ch. 18.
70. *De Legationibus*, p. 104.
71. However, Adair interprets Grotius to state that if the ambassador refuses to surrender an errant member of his suite 'the only thing to be done is to appeal to the king his master or even, in extreme cases, to demand the *ambassador's* immediate withdrawal' [emphasis added], *Exterritoriality*, p. 120. What Grotius actually says is: 'If, however, the ambassador is unwilling to surrender such members of his suite, the same course will need to be pursued as we just now mentioned in the case of an ambassador'. Make up your own mind, gentle reader.
72. Adair notes that on immunity from civil jurisdiction generally the views of Grotius, compared to those of other jurists of the sixteenth and seventeenth centuries, are 'to the modern mind . . . the soundest, because he keeps to the main principle of allowing such immunity as is necessary for the due performance of an ambassador's functions', *Exterritoriality*, p. 76; he was also well in advance of practice in this regard, pp. 90, 252.
73. What Grotius had to say on asylum remains essentially the same today, though the entirely unqualified statement of the VCDR (which is silent on 'diplomatic asylum' itself) on the inviolability of mission premises (Art. 22.1) clearly strengthens asylum in practice; see *Satow's Guide to Diplomatic Practice*, 5th edn, 14.17–23.
74. Though not unknown, it was unusual for an ambassador to be accompanied by his wife and children until the second half of the seventeenth century, Young, 'The development of the law of diplomatic relations', p. 163.
75. *De Legationibus*, p. 104.
76. It was common, not least in England, for an ambassador to be left to appoint *all* of his subordinates, Adair, *Exterritoriality*, pp. 103–4.
77. Though it should be remembered that Gentili's own prescription had less serious implications since he had a very restricted notion of immunity from criminal prosecution, Young, 'The development of the law of diplomatic relations', p. 155.
78. This had begun with Richard Zouche, who published not long after Grotius; see Young, 'The development of the law of diplomatic relations', p. 155.

79. Though Adair says that 'this might possibly be inferred from the security which he maintains the ambassador, his suite and his goods enjoy', *Exterritoriality*, p. 201.
80. Young, 'The development of the law of diplomatic relations', pp. 155–6. See for example Wicquefort, *The Embassador and His Functions*, Book I, ch. 28: 'The House and Domesticks of an Embassador are inviolable'; and Vattel, *Le Droit des Gens*, vol. 3, ch. 9.
81. Cahier, 'Vienna Convention on Diplomatic Relations', *International Conciliation*, no. 571, Jan. 1969, pp. 24–6.
82. Compare *HGIR*, p. 27: 'He did discuss embassies and the institutions of diplomacy, but without adding a great deal to the existing literature in that field . . .'.
83. Young, 'The development of the law of diplomatic relations', p. 150.

Further reading

Works by Grotius in English translation

De Jure Belli ac Pacis Libri Tres (Three Books on the Law of War and Peace), trans. Francis. W. Kelsey (1646 Latin edition), Classics of International Law (Oxford, 1925); repr. New York and London, 1964. See also M. G. Forsyth, H. M. A. Keens-Soper and P. Savigear (eds), *The Theory of International Relations: Selected Texts from Gentili to Treitschke* (London, 1970).

Historical background

New Cambridge Modern History, vol. III, ch. 6 (Mattingly), and vol. IV.
Carter, C. H. (ed), *From the Renaissance to the Counter-Reformation: Essays in Honour of Garrett Mattingly* (London, 1966), ch. by Carter – 'The ambassadors of early modern Europe: patterns of diplomatic representation in the early seventeenth century'.
Carter, C. H., 'Gondomar: ambassador to James I', *The Historical Journal*, Fall 1964.
Hill, David Jayne, *A History of Diplomacy in the International Development of Europe* (London, 1905), vol. II, ch. 7.

Biography

Clark, 'Grotius' East India mission to England', *Transactions of the Grotius Society*, vol. 20, 1935, pp. 45–84.
Dumbould, E., *The Life and Legal Writings of Hugo Grotius* (Norman, 1969).
Gellinek, C., *Hugo Grotius* (Boston, 1983).
Knight, W. S. M, *The Life and Works of Hugo Grotius* (New York and London, 1962).
O'Connell, D. P., *Richelieu* (London, 1968), chs 17 and 18 [Grotius in France].

General

Adair, E. R., *The Exterritoriality of Ambassadors in the Sixteenth and Seventeenth Centuries* (London, 1929).
Berridge, G. R., *Diplomacy: Theory and Practice*, 2nd edn (Leicester, 1999), ch. 1.
Bozeman, Adda B., 'On the relevance of Hugo Grotius and *De Jure Belli ac Pacis* for our times', *Grotiana*, NS I, pp. 65–124.

Bull, Hedley, B. Kingsbury and A. Roberts (eds), *Hugo Grotius and International Relations* (Oxford, 1992).

Butterfield, H. and M. Wight, *Diplomatic Investigations: Essays in the Theory of International Politics* (London, 1966), ch. 2 (Bull, 'The Grotian conception of international society').

Bynkershoek, Cornelius van, *De Foro Legatorum Liber Singularis (The Jurisdiction over Ambassadors in both Civil and Criminal Cases)*, first publ. 1721, trans. of the 1744 edn by G. J. Laing, with an introduction by Jan de Louter, repr. in London 1964 in the 'Classics of International Law' series.

Cahier, Philippe and Luke T. Lee, 'Vienna Conventions on Diplomatic and Consular Relations', *International Conciliation*, no. 571, Jan. 1969.

Cutler, A. C., 'The Grotian tradition in international relations', *Review of International Studies*, vol. 17, no. 1, 1991 [comments on his experiences at hands of Richelieu in Paris].

Denza, Eileen, *Diplomatic Law: Commentary on the Vienna Convention on Diplomatic Relations, 1961*, 2nd edn (Oxford, 1998)

Edwards, C. S., *Hugo Grotius, the Miracle of Holland: a Study of Political and Legal Thought* (Chicago, 1981).

Gentili, Alberico, *De Legationibus libri tres* (1585), trans. G. L. Laing, Classics of International Law (Oxford and New York, 1924), repr. New York and London, 1964.

Holk, L. E. von, and C. G. Roelofson (eds), *Grotius Reader* (The Hague, 1983).

Lauterpacht, H., 'The Grotian tradition in international law', *British Yearbook of International Law*, 1946; repr. in H. Lauterpacht, *International Law: collected papers*, ed. E. Lauterpacht, vol. 2, part I (Cambridge, 1975).

Lyons, A. B., 'Immunities other than jurisdictional of the property of diplomatic envoys', *British Yearbook of International Law*, vol. 30, 1953.

Mattingly, Garrett, *Renaissance Diplomacy* (Harmondsworth, 1965), chs. 4, 27 and 28.

Murphy, C. F., 'The Grotian vision of world order', *American Journal of International Law*, vol. 76, 1982, pp. 477–98.

Suarez, Francisco, *De Legibus ac Deo Legislatore* (1612), in *Selections from Three Works of Francisco Suarez*, Classics of International Law (Oxford, 1944).

Vattel, Emmerich de, *Le Droit des Gens (The Law of Nations, or the Principles of Natural Law Applied to the Conduct and to the Affairs of Nations and of Sovereigns)*, first publ. 1758, trans. of this edition by C. G. Fenwick, with an introduction by Albert de Lapradelle, repr. in London in 1964 in the 'Classics of International Law' series.

Young, E., 'The development of the law of diplomatic relations', *British Yearbook of International Law*, vol. 40, 1964, pp. 141–82.

4
Richelieu

G. R. Berridge

An almost exact contemporary of Grotius, Armand Jean du Plessis, Cardinal and Duke of Richelieu, was born in 1585 in Paris. However, it was while he was an energetic and successful bishop in the impoverished diocese of Luçon in Poitou, close to the Huguenot redoubt of La Rochelle, that he developed his political and administrative skills and built his power base. In this vocation, which he pursued from 1608 until 1616, he had shown a toleration for contrary religious views and a general inclination to favour reason over force. [1] Nevertheless, despite doubts both at the time and since, and despite the unquestioned fact that *raison d'état* always took precedence in his political decisions, the consensus among historians is that he remained until his death a pious Catholic.

Following an impressive performance in the States General in 1614, [2] which drew the favourable attention of the embattled Regent, Marie de Medici, [3] Richelieu gravitated more and more towards Paris in search of a political career. Early in 1616 he was made a member of the council of State and shortly afterwards was employed on embassies to the Prince of Condé and the Duke of Nevers; this was his only personal diplomatic experience, and that within France itself. [4] In November he was made a secretary of state (war and foreign affairs), though he only enjoyed the position for five months, falling from office as a result of a palace revolution against his patrons, Marie de Medici and her favourite, Concini, in April 1617. [5] However, Marie gradually rebuilt her influence and with it that of Richelieu was also restored. In 1622 he was elevated to the cardinalate. In 1624 he was appointed Chief Minister to King Louis XIII, and this post he held until his death in 1642. [6]

In office once more, Richelieu found himself confronting massive problems. Domestically, the overriding one was weak monarchical authority: the princes of the kingdom were a law unto themselves, while the Huguenots were virtually a state within a state. On top of this, the economy was in poor condition and his personal enemies were legion. If this was not bad enough, the international position of France was also serious. The conflict subsequently known as the Thirty Years' War had broken out in 1618 and Richelieu feared encirclement by a Spain which, assisted by its Habsburg cousins in Austria, he feared was bent on universal empire. But there were Spanish sympathizers at court, and in any case the Cardinal knew that he could not rely on French military strength alone: 'This was because of the country's economic situation, because of its internal tensions, and not least because Richelieu believed that France was, basically speaking, not a warlike nation.'[7] It was against this background that Richelieu conceived and pursued his two great objectives. The first was to forge unity within France and increase the authority of the crown. The second was to create a peace of Christendom, by which he meant, according to Hermann Weber's convincing interpretation, not any peace but one which provided a 'durable framework...that preserved all the powers of Christendom in untroubled coexistence and liberty'.[8]

What were Richelieu's methods? First, to increase the military and naval strength of France. Secondly, to create a balance of power within Christendom resting on an alliance of Protestant as well as Catholic states with France at its centre; this would serve as a counterpoise to the (Catholic) Habsburgs[9] and was, of course, the 'realism' for which Richelieu was condemned by the '*dévots*' within as well as outside the country. Thirdly, to weaken his Habsburg enemies by a combination of subversion, indirect and limited war until their defeat of the Swedes at Nördlingen in 1634 made it unavoidable that France declare open war; for Richelieu, general war was a last resort.[10] Above all, however, Richelieu's methods turned on diplomacy, or what he called 'continuous negotiation', which was the most significant corollary of his desire to stabilize an equilibrium between the states of Europe.[11] Indeed, even after he had declared open war on the Spanish in 1635 he was constantly putting out secret feelers for peace.[12]

The Relevant Writings

Richelieu wrote thousands of official documents and letters and many of them survive.[13] We also have his *Mémoires* and, above all, his *Testament Politique*. This was conceived as a handbook of political advice for the private guidance of Louis XIII should Richelieu's own death precede that of the king, and did not find its way into the hands of the public until 1688. It is true that the books are not all the Cardinal's own work and that until the late nineteenth century the *Testament Politique* was still widely believed to be either a deliberate forgery or as good as a forgery. [14] Nevertheless, it is now generally agreed that, while both this and the *Mémoires* were compiled by others after his death, the work was done by people who had been close to him and was based substantially on Richelieu's own papers. In short, they are authentic. [15]

The key work for an understanding of Richelieu's contribution to diplomatic theory is his *Testament Politique*, and the best version of it the critical edition published by Louis André in Paris in 1947. [16] In 1961 the American historian, Henry Bertram Hill, produced an English translation of 'the significant chapters' together with 'supporting selections' which was based on this edition, and it is Hill's translation on which this chapter relies. The *Testament Politique* is divided into two parts, the first dealing chiefly with the earlier part of the reign of Louis XIII and with French institutions and the second with more general questions of political strategy and tactics. While heavily abridging Part I, Hill's translation presents virtually complete the more theoretically interesting Part II, which includes what is for us the key chapter on 'The Need for Continuous Negotiation in Diplomacy'.

The Concept of 'Continuous Negotiation'

What is immediately impressive about Richelieu's account of the value of *négociation continuelle* is his quite extraordinary emphasis upon it. He begins the chapter dealing with this subject by saying that 'States receive so much benefit from uninterrupted foreign negotiations...that it is unbelievable unless it is known from experience'. Then, after admitting that he did not immediately understand this, only two sentences later drives home the point once more: 'But I am now so convinced of its validity that I dare say emphatically that it is absolutely necessary to the well-being of the state.' He ends the paragraph by calling in the witness of history: 'I can truthfully say that I have seen in my time the nature of affairs *change completely* for both France and the rest of Christendom as a result of my having...put this principle into practice – something up to then completely neglected in this realm' (emphasis added). [17] No doubt, too, it was his perfect grasp of the potential of continuous negotiation which led him to be fearful of its use by others. [18] What, however, does Richelieu mean by 'continuous negotiation'?

It seems clear that by 'continuous negotiation' Richelieu has two separate if related ideas in mind. In the first place, he means having diplomatic agents everywhere and at all times: '. . . it is absolutely necessary to the well-being of the state to negotiate ceaselessly, either openly or secretly, and in all places, even in those from which no present fruits are reaped and still more in those for which no future prospects as yet seem likely.' [19] Again, a little further on, he says that 'It is necessary to act everywhere, near and far, and above all at Rome.' [20] Thus 'continuous negotiation' means at a minimum continuous *representation*: permanent diplomatic representation in all states, remote as well as neighbouring and hostile as well as friendly, albeit with some courts deserving of more attention than others.

In the second place, 'continuous negotiation' also signifies Richelieu's belief that it is insufficient for this comprehensive network of representatives to confine itself to gathering information, ceremonial functions, and so on. Instead, it should be ceaselessly pursuing achievement of agreement on all outstanding questions, that is, negotiating in the narrower, more modern sense, though Richelieu is aware that negotiations cannot always proceed at the same speed and same intensity (see below).

The Value of 'Continuous Negotiation'

Richelieu's justification of the need for 'continuous negotiation' contains no real surprises, though it is interesting for its emphases. In the main chapter on diplomacy he notes almost as an afterthought that it enables the state to keep 'abreast of events in the world' and says that this 'is not of little consequence in the lives of states'. [21] However, apart from adding that 'common sense teaches us that it is necessary to watch our neighbours closely, because their proximity gives them the chance to be bothersome', [22] this is all he has to say about what has customarily been regarded as the chief function of resident missions, especially in early modern Europe. This is probably because he thought its importance self-evident and because he had in any case devoted an earlier chapter in Part II of the *Testament Politique* to emphasizing the point that 'nothing is more necessary in governing a state than foresight . . .', in which full and accurate information is an indispensable ingredient. [23] However, the scant attention paid to information gathering is perhaps also further evidence of his determination to emphasize the importance of engaging foreign governments in discussion, in *pourparlers*. Why is this so valuable?

Richelieu thought that his ambassadors should debate with foreign governments because of his profound belief in the general power of reason and language. 'Authority constrains obedience,' he writes in another chapter of the *Testament Politique*, 'but reason captivates it. It is much more expedient to lead men by means which imperceptibly win their wills than, as is more the practice, by those which coerce them.'[24] It was Richelieu, after all, who in 1631 had grasped the importance of extending his protection to Renaudot's infant *Gazette de France* and turning it into a propaganda machine for the court,[25] and who four years later had founded the *Académie Française* – 'an explicit recognition of the power of language, of the superiority of eloquence and reason over naked force ... '.[26] The chief prize of this kind of 'continuous negotiation' was obviously to secure agreements congenial to one's interests, not least on marriage alliances and leagues.[27] As already noted, agreements would sometimes take a long time to secure but continuous discussion would make their eventual attainment more likely. Even if this seemed unlikely or even undesirable, continuous discussion, provided it was visible, might have great propaganda value, demonstrating to those citizens at home and allies abroad who favoured peace that the Cardinal was himself sincere in its pursuit and that its achievement remained a possibility.[28] This could at the least, in a distinct echo of the Florentines, buy time: 'Even if it [negotiation] does no other good on some occasions than gain time, which often is the sole outcome, its employment would be commendable and useful to states, since it frequently takes only an instant to divert a storm.'[29]

Providing the capacity to persuade other states to favourable agreements with eloquence and reason, as well as the ability to observe them closely and so avoid unpleasant surprises, were strong arguments for continuous negotiation. Richelieu, however, does not by any means rest his case here. It is also important for the prestige or *réputation* of the state, which in his chapter on 'The Power of the Prince' in the *Testament Politique* Richelieu lists as the first of the four chief sources of a monarch's power (the others are soldiers, money and 'possession of the hearts of his subjects').[30] It is true that Richelieu is thinking at this point chiefly of the moral components of the prince's reputation, above all godliness and honesty, but in the chapter on diplomacy he has in mind also reputation for power. Elliott sums up the relationship between the two in Richelieu's thinking: 'Prestige brought power; power brought prestige; and prestige, if skilfully exploited, could sometimes make it unnecessary to resort to arms.'[31] Where does 'continuous negotiation' fit in here? Broad and permanent diplomatic representation in itself sustained a state's prestige by testifying to its wealth in human and material resources but it would do this even more effectively if the quality of what today would be called its 'news management' skills was high. In Richelieu's time this was important everywhere but above all at the papal court, since Rome had 'long been the diplomatic and geographical center of the world' and the standing of ambassadors there was accepted as an unusually accurate barometer of the power of the state which they represented. Richelieu almost labours this point: 'the respect rendered there to ambassadors of princes rises and falls day by day accordingly as the affairs of their masters wax or wane. Indeed, it often occurs that ministers receive two contradictory treatments on the same day if a courier who arrives in the evening carries different news than the one who came in the morning.' [32] Ambassadors, however, were not merely barometers whose treatment registered the unmediated reception of news of external events. At a time when other sources of foreign news were extremely limited, an ambassador who was agreeable, eloquent, energetic, well informed by couriers from home (as well as by correspondence with colleagues abroad and gossip within the diplomatic corps), and above all known to be honest could himself affect the reading: he could maximize the impact of good news from home and at the least cast doubt on the veracity of bad news. This was not the least of the reasons which led Richelieu to attach such importance to broad and permanent diplomatic representation.

Is Richelieu right, nevertheless, to maintain that it is necessary for all states 'to act everywhere, near and far'? It is true that the *Testament Politique* was conceived in general as advice to the French king in the circumstances in which France found itself in the early seventeenth century, and presumably not as advice to all kings in all circumstances. Nevertheless, there is a clear suggestion in the presentation of the argument in the chapter on diplomacy that Richelieu believed that his advice held good for all states, and – whether this is true or not – there is a common assumption that this was his view, and also that he was right. [33] In reality, however, a qualification must be added to Richelieu's argument since some states have survived for long periods with only the most rudimentary of diplomatic services and some have survived with none at all. It all depends on circumstances – and ambitions. Richelieu's France certainly did need continuous negotiations. It was internally divided and militarily and economically weak; it had powerful enemies on its borders and unpredictable allies; and yet it had grand ambitions. Insecurity plus ambition equals frantic diplomacy. It is hardly the same for states which are secure, self-reliant, introspective and convinced that they are in sole possession of the moral mountain-top, for example Manchu China, the Ottoman Empire until the reign of Selim III at the end of the eighteenth century, and the United States during its long 'isolationist' period. Albeit for more than one reason a problematical example, at the time of its invasion by the Chinese Communists in 1950, Tibet did not even have a diplomatic vocabulary.[34] It is true nonetheless that there have always been far more states like early seventeenth-century France than states like these, and that this is particularly true today.

Negotiating Method

It was Richelieu's view that negotiations would never be effective unless they were directed from home by a single mind, which had not hitherto been the tradition in France.[35] No doubt aware that *continuous* negotiation made this even more essential, as it multiplied the possibilities of contradiction and inconsistency, by a Decree of 11 March 1626 the Cardinal had given all responsibility for foreign policy to the Ministry of External Affairs.[36] Though often more honoured in the breach than in the observance, and not always assuming the same form in different regimes,[37] this idea gradually became a central feature of European diplomatic method and remains cogent today, despite the spread of summitry and direct discussions between other ministries of different states.

A second theme emphasized by Richelieu in his account of negotiating method is that different circumstances require different approaches. 'He who negotiates continuously', we are told, 'will finally find the right instant to attain his ends . . . ',[38] but this may be later rather than sooner in dealings with republics, which in their nature are slow-moving. 'For this reason it is wise to negotiate painstakingly with them in order to give them time, and to press them only when they are ready for it.'[39] In any event, and contrary to Guicciardini, do not remain immobile if the 'right instant' is not yet at hand but probe gently, listen carefully, plant ideas in influential quarters, stimulate support, and thus be in the best position to spot the 'right instant' when it develops, at which point only should the attempt be made to move the negotiation into a higher gear. If it is an important negotiation it is vital that its momentum should not be lost. 'Important negotiations', Richelieu informs us, 'should never be interrupted for a moment. It is necessary to pursue what one has undertaken with an endless programme of action so ordered that one never ceases to act intelligently and resourcefully, becoming neither indifferent, vacillating, nor irresolute.'[40]

There are other differences which need to be taken into account in the conduct of negotiations. Men of genius need to be tackled with strong and convincing reasons, while the sympathies of lesser men – unable to grasp the complexity of public affairs – may be captured by concessions on things which seem important to them but are in fact trivial. Sometimes negotiators should put on a bold face when confronted with 'imprudent remarks', and sometimes – 'having an ear only for those remarks leading toward the end in mind' – they should adopt a more forbearing attitude. However, in no circumstances, at least in dealing with 'honorable men', should negotiators bluster. [41] Secrecy is essential because the *faits accomplis* which are impossible without it suggest decisiveness and nullify opposition. [42]

Since he believed that negotiation required great shrewdness, it is not surprising that Richelieu also believed that the qualifications for the work should be exacting. Negotiators should be well informed and intelligent. On the other hand, they should not have 'minds so finely drawn and delicately organized as to . . . become overly subtle about everything'. [43] 'Toujours la théorie de la modération: n'être ni sot ni fin et délicat', comments André in a footnote to his critical edition at this point. [44] Since words could also have different meanings, it was necessary for negotiators also to 'know the weight of words and how best to employ them in written documents'. [45]

While famously eloquent in his belief in *raison d'état*, [46] it is most interesting that Richelieu – unlike Machiavelli – goes out of his way to emphasize that this does not apply to keeping promises. In this matter, says the Cardinal, echoing the customary seventeenth-century view that international treaties were personal compacts between monarchs, [47] there is no autonomous political morality: the prince should keep his promises to other princes in the same way that his subjects should keep their promises to each other. This was critical to his *réputation*, which in turn was critical to his power. On this point – and in a document, let us recall, which was not designed for public consumption – the Cardinal was utterly unambiguous. 'Kings', he writes, 'should be very careful with regard to the treaties they conclude, but having concluded them they should observe them religiously. I well know that many statesmen advise to the contrary, but without considering here what the Christian religion offers in answer to such advice, I maintain that the loss of honour is worse than the loss of life itself. A great prince should sooner put in jeopardy both his own interests and even those of the state than break his word, which he can never violate without losing his reputation and by consequence the greatest instrument of sovereigns.' [48]

The corollary of requiring the prince to keep his promises to other princes at all costs, was, of course, that these promises should only be made after very careful consideration, as Richelieu had already made clear in the lines quoted in the preceding paragraph. Highlighting the importance he attached to this, he immediately goes on to spell out its practical implications, and this in the final paragraph of the chapter on diplomacy in the *Testament Politique*. 'It is absolutely necessary', he stresses, 'to be discerning in the choice of ambassadors and other negotiators', [49] who could, after all, if operating with 'full powers', bind their sovereigns by any agreement they made in their name, even if they exceeded their instructions. [50] The whole of the following chapter is devoted to 'The need to appoint suitable men to public offices' and, not surprisingly, the office of ambassador is the first example he cites. [51] No doubt with himself and his *éminence grise*, the Capuchin monk Father Joseph, especially in mind, Richelieu concludes this chapter with the observation that 'churchmen are often preferable to many others, particularly when the highest offices are considered'. This is because they have neither wives nor children and thus have fewer 'personal interests' clamouring for attention before their public duties. [52]

If careful choice of ambassadors was the first practical corollary of the need to give the most watchful consideration to international agreements involving the reputation of princes, the second was that the utmost severity should be employed 'in punishing those who exceed their authority, since by such misdeeds they compromise the reputation of princes as well as the fortunes of states'. Speaking with the weariness of a man who had 'had so many experiences with this truth', [53] Richelieu points out that it is not only weakness or corruption that can lead negotiators to overstep their instructions. Some men, he writes, have such 'a consuming ambition ... to accomplish something' that they 'allow themselves to be drawn into the making of a bad treaty rather than none at all'. [54] It is a pity that Richelieu remains silent at this point on what to do when ambassadors overstep the mark, either by concluding negotiations without 'full powers' or by exceeding their substantive 'instructions'. In fact, as a statesman, Richelieu risked his sovereign's reputation for good faith by advising him to repudiate the Treaty of Regensburg with the Emperor in 1630, on the grounds that his agents exceeded their instructions rather than their powers. However, it seems that he only did this because *honouring* the treaty would also have compromised the reputation for good faith of Louis XIII, and this would have been more serious in its political consequences since it would have suggested a breach of faith with his allies. [55]

Are Negotiations 'Innocuous Remedies Which Never Do Harm'?

Richelieu presents a persuasive argument for 'continuous negotiation' or for what we would now call continuous diplomacy, and it is a sophisticated theory since it is qualified by the suggestion that negotiation narrowly conceived should not be *intensively* pursued until the 'right instant', as already noted in this chapter. Despite this, perhaps Richelieu gets a little carried away in his enthusiasm for continuous negotiation and falls into the trap of overstating his case.

It has already been noted that certain kinds of state have survived for long periods without continuous diplomacy. It is now necessary to ask if it is in fact true that, as the Cardinal claims, even if negotiations fail, the government which instigated them has 'at least...lost nothing'? Is it true that (appearing to hold the view so firmly that he repeats the point in the very next sentence) 'negotiations are innocuous remedies which never do harm'?[56] In reality, even if we go along with Richelieu's assumption that negotiations are conducted with 'prudence',[57] this claim is manifestly false, and some of the reasons for this where negotiation narrowly conceived is concerned have already been noted in the earlier discussion of Guicciardini's view of 'premature' negotiations (see page 40 above). Indeed, the list of costs associated with a hyperactive diplomacy is almost endless, even if some of them are regarded as nothing more than normal expenses and routine occupational hazards.

Even if continuous negotiation means only maintaining permanent ambassadors abroad and continually despatching special envoys, this costs money, so at the least it harms the national exchequer. If envoys are sent to insecure countries or politically unstable ones, they are also literally hostages to fortune. In this connection it is worth noting that until the early nineteenth century it was customary for the Ottoman government to imprison the ambassadors of states with which the Porte found itself at war. Richelieu may have been complacent on this score because of France's traditionally good relations with the Turks but subsequently even French diplomats proved vulnerable to this treatment.[58] In this century diplomats have become targets of violent opposition groups, while in Tehran in 1979 a most dangerous situation was created when, with the connivance of the government, the occupants of the US embassy were seized and held hostage for 444 days. States with far-flung diplomatic networks and thus far-flung communications also make their thinking more vulnerable to penetration.

Richelieu may have been unwise to overlook these costs of continuous negotiation but they must be admitted to be relatively minor. More important are two additional ones, the first of which derives from the fact that the doctrine of *raison d'état* has never been universally accepted. First of all, then, there is the obloquy which states generally attract – both from home and abroad – as a result of being seen to keep the diplomatic company of states which in the religious or ideological spheres are regarded as beyond the pale. Indeed, the reputation of the French monarch, who had long claimed to be 'the most Christian King', suffered as a result of Richelieu's dealings with the Protestant states and Muslim Ottoman Empire. All of this provided the *dévots* within France, as well as the Papacy and the country's Catholic Habsburg enemies outside, with much ammunition for their propaganda. [59] As a result, the Cardinal had to devote considerable energy and resources to counter-propaganda. [60] In this century, examples of the damaging publicity attracted by the maintenance of diplomatic relations with widely detested regimes are legion; it will serve to note merely that which followed the decision of most Western states to preserve their relations with South Africa despite the increasingly strident calls for it to be boycotted which began to be made at the United Nations in the early 1960s as a result of its race policies.

The second risk entailed by negotiation, where this means negotiation in the modern sense, is the risk of being committed to bad agreements by corrupt, incompetent or simply exhausted ambassadors. When negotiation in the modern sense is continuous this risk is even greater, since agreements may be concluded which judged on their own merits might be considered to serve the national interest but which nevertheless contain inconsistencies when compared. [61] A notorious twentieth-century case is provided by the contradictory promises made by Britain to the Jews and the Arabs during the First World War. With first-class training and adequate rewarding of ambassadors, efficient procedures for coordination, and good communications perhaps none of these problems is insurmountable. However, in Richelieu's times, and despite his own exceptional efforts, diplomacy served in this way was only in its infancy, [62] and it is certain that even today there are many diplomatic services which do not reach these standards. In the *Testament Politique*, with the costly Regensburg fiasco no doubt chiefly in his mind, Richelieu himself admits that 'it sometimes happens that the wisest undertakings produce unhappy results', adding, of course, that this is the fault of the 'maladroitness' of the diplomats concerned rather than of 'the mode of conduct I have proposed'. [63]

It thus emerges that Richelieu's doctrine that 'negotiations are innocuous remedies which never do harm' is really the doctrine that negotiations *should* be innocuous remedies. In reality, two conditions are added: first, that *raison d'état* must be universally accepted; and secondly, that the diplomatic machine must run like a Rolls-Royce. It is true that Richelieu does not conceal the second condition but it has to be said that he is inclined to lose sight of it. André's brief footnote to this doctrine is apposite: 'Optimisme exagéré'. [64]

Conclusion

For Richelieu, 'continuous negotiation' meant a broad and permanent network of diplomatic agents. These persons, he believed, should be charged before other tasks with seeking accommodations whenever opportunities presented themselves and making their princes appear as powerful as possible at the most important courts. Though Richelieu had more to say directly on the tactics required by the first of these tasks than the second, the emphasis on the importance of honouring treaty obligations was rooted in his belief in the need to guard at all costs the *réputation* of the prince. In his enthusiasm for *négociation continuelle* Richelieu may have overlooked, or simply been uninterested in noting, both its costs and hazards and even in some circumstances its very limited relevance. Nevertheless, for his circumstances and his time his emphasis was right and his insights were shrewd. Richelieu's *Testament Politique* is the clear and authentic voice of the diplomatic system of early modern Europe.

Notes

1. J. H. Elliott, *Richelieu and Olivares* (Cambridge, 1984; Canto edn., 1991), pp. 11, 22–3.
2. Richelieu had been elected as one of the representatives of the clergy from Poitou to sit in the first estate. He achieved great prominence, both at the meetings of the first estate and in the plenary sessions of the States General as a whole, and won the affection of the Regent by championing her position before the second estate (the nobles).
3. Louis XIII was only eight when his father, Henri IV, was assassinated in 1609, and was not declared to be of age until the autumn of 1615.
4. It had been intended to send him as an ambassador to Spain to resolve a difficulty which had developed in Italy with the Duke of Savoy but 'affairs at home soon became too critical for him to be spared', Richard Lodge, *Richelieu* (London, 1896), p. 32.
5. King Louis XIII was still only fifteen years old at this juncture and a regency was held by the queen mother.

6. Louis himself died in the following year.
7. Hermann Weber, ' "Une bonne paix": Richelieu's foreign policy and the peace of Christendom', in J. Bergin and L. Brockliss (eds), *Richelieu and his Age* (Oxford, 1992), p. 50. For Richelieu's famous account of the inadequacies of the French soldier, see H. B. Hill, *The Political Testament of Cardinal Richelieu* (Madison, 1961), pp. 121–3, which begins uncompromisingly: 'There are no people in the world so little suited to war as ours'.
8. Weber, ' "Une bonne paix" ', p. 48.
9. Weber, ' "Une bonne paix" ', p. 48.
10. Weber, ' "Une bonne paix" ', p. 60; D. P. O'Connell, *Richelieu* (London, 1968), p. 195.
11. Keith Hamilton and Richard Langhorne, *The Practice of Diplomacy: Its Evolution, Theory and Administration* (London and New York, 1995), p. 71.
12. Elliott, *Richelieu and Olivares*, p. 129.
13. For an account of Richelieu's surviving papers, see Elliott, *Richelieu and Olivares*, pp. 3–5.
14. In an Appendix on the *Testament Politique* in his book on *Richelieu* in Macmillan's 'Foreign Statesmen' series (London, 1896), Richard Lodge, Professor of History at the University of Glasgow, revealed that his doubts on the book's authenticity remained so serious that he had 'carefully abstained – in spite of obvious temptations to the contrary – from making any use of the *Testament* as a guide to the real aims of Richelieu's policy', p. 235.
15. For an account of the controversy over this subject, see *The Political Testament of Cardinal Richelieu: The significant chapters and supporting selections*, translated by Henry Bertram Hill (Madison, 1961) [hereafter *TP*], intro. pp. xi–xii.
16. *Testament Politique du Cardinal de Richelieu*. Édition critique publiée avec une introduction et des notes par Louis André et une préface de Léon Noël (Paris, 1947).
17. *TP*, p. 94.
18. Among other new measures against rebellion submitted by Richelieu to the Assembly of Notables in December 1626, all of which swiftly became edicts, was a prohibition on all communications between French subjects and foreign ambassadors, including the papal nuncio, *The Cambridge Modern History*, vol. IV (Cambridge, 1934), p. 131.
19. *TP*, p. 94.
20. *TP*, p. 95.
21. *TP*, p. 95.
22. *TP*, p. 96. Of course, he had in mind chiefly Spain.
23. *TP*, p. 80, and pp. 81–2: 'It is necessary to sleep like the lion, without closing one's eyes ... '.
24. *TP*, p. 72.
25. Howard M. Solomon, *Public Welfare, Science, and Propaganda in Seventeenth Century France: The innovations of Théophraste Renaudot* (Princeton, NJ, 1972), chs 4 and 5.
26. Elliott, *Richelieu and Olivares*, p. 134.
27. *TP*, pp. 99–101.
28. *The Cambridge Modern History*, vol. IV, pp. 145–6.
29. *TP*, p. 99.
30. *TP*, p. 119.

31. *Richelieu and Olivares*, p. 85; see also p. 105.
32. *TP*, pp. 95–6. The strength of Richelieu's belief in the political importance of representation at Rome is underlined by the fact that he had no personal affection for the methods of the Curia, D. P. O'Connell, *Richelieu* (London, 1968), p. 13.
33. For example, Adam Watson, 'Russia and the European states system', in H. Bull and A. Watson (eds), *The Expansion of International Society* (Oxford, 1984), p. 65.
34. Robert Ford, *Captured in Tibet* (Hong Kong, 1990), pp. 25, 87.
35. Hamilton and Langhorne, *The Practice of Diplomacy*, p. 72. Of course, Richelieu also believed that the king should have a 'prime mover' among his councillors, that is, a prime minister; see *TP*, p. 61.
36. This is one of the aspects of Richelieu's doctrine picked out for emphasis in Harold Nicolson's short but admiring account in his *Evolution of Diplomatic Method* (London, 1954), p. 53. See also Orest A. Ranum, *Richelieu and the Councillors of Louis XIII* (Oxford, 1963), pp. 91–9.
37. For example, at the height of his powers as National Security Adviser to the US President at the beginning of the 1970s, Henry Kissinger provided the mind of American foreign policy, while the State Department was sidelined.
38. *TP*, p. 95. On the importance of timing in domestic politics as well, see *TP*, p. 74.
39. *TP*, p. 97.
40. *TP*, p. 99.
41. *TP*, pp. 96–8.
42. *TP*, p. 75.
43. *TP*, p. 98.
44. *Testament Politique* (1947), p. 351, n. 3.
45. *TP*, pp. 98–9.
46. See especially *TP*, part II, ch. 5.
47. J. Mervyn Jones, *Full Powers and Ratification: A study in the development of treaty-making procedure* (Cambridge, 1946), p. 12.
48. *TP*, pp. 101–2.
49. *TP*, p. 102.
50. In the seventeenth century, full powers normally meant full powers, and the prince could not refuse to ratify his ambassador's handiwork even if he disliked it; if 'ratification' was provided for it was understood that this was empty of legal, though not, of course, symbolic significance. However, some so-called 'full powers' indicated that the diplomatic agent bearing them only had the power to negotiate a provisional agreement and that this would have no effect until it was ratified. A 'conditional' full power of this kind was condemned by de Wicquefort as a contradiction in terms; see *The Embassador and His Functions*, pp. 117, 406, 408. See also Jones, *Full Powers and Ratification*, pp. 1–12, and D. P. O'Connell, *Richelieu* (London, 1968), p. 209.
51. *TP*, p. 104.
52. *TP*, pp. 109–10. Richelieu's preference for clergymen in diplomacy and other public offices was not shared by Abraham de Wicquefort, who appealed for support both to the Bible and to the practice of his much-admired Venice. From the first he drew the argument of Jesus that 'his Kingdom is not of this World; that those who will follow him, must renounce all things, and cast off

all Solicitude for temporal Goods, that they may with less Incumbrance travel on in the Path they are to follow during the whole Course of their Lives.' From the second he drew the argument that 'they who live in the State of Celibacy, not being sensible of that Tenderness marry'd Men have for their Children and Families, cannot have that natural Affection for a Countrey, which they cannot be succeeded in by their Posterity, as having none; and that those who take to the Church, become as it were Strangers, and subjects to a foreign Power', *The Embassador and His Functions*, p. 57.

53. For example, with the Comte de Fargis, French ambassador in Madrid, shortly after he came to office but most famously with Brulart de Léon, French ambassador to the Swiss, and his own éminence grise, Father Joseph, both of whom were sent by Richelieu to negotiate certain matters with the Emperor at Regensburg in 1630. Richelieu felt that he had to repudiate the treaties negotiated by both of these French missions. See D. P. O'Connell, 'A *cause célèbre* in the history of treaty-making: the refusal to ratify the peace treaty of Regensburg in 1630', *British Yearbook of International Law 1967*, vol. 42, pp. 71–90.

54. *TP*, p. 102; and O'Connell, 'A *cause célèbre*', pp. 82–3.

55. O'Connell, 'A *cause célèbre*', pp. 83–4; and O'Connell, *Richelieu*, pp. 218–19. De Wicquefort, interpreting Richelieu's motives less charitably, condemned this decision, *The Embassador and His Functions*, p. 413.

56. *TP*, p. 95.

57. *TP*, pp. 94, 99.

58. Outraged by Bonaparte's invasion of its most precious province of Egypt and emboldened by news of Nelson's destruction of the French fleet in Abukir Bay, on 2 September 1798 the Porte imprisoned the French chargé d'affaires in Istanbul; see J. Christopher Herold, *Bonaparte in Egypt* (London, 1962), pp. 129–34.

59. M. S. Anderson, *The Rise of Modern Diplomacy, 1450–1919* (London and New York, 1993), pp. 160–1.

60. Nicolson, *The Evolution of Diplomatic Method*, pp. 51–2; Elliott, *Richelieu and Olivares*, pp. 99, 111, 123, 128–9; Solomon, *Public Welfare, Science and Propaganda in Seventeenth Century France*, chs 4 and 5; and Church, *Richelieu and Reason of State*, part 4.

61. In Richelieu's own diplomacy, see for example O'Connell, *Richelieu*, pp. 216, 260, 265.

62. Hamilton and Langhorne, *The Practice of Diplomacy*, p. 72.

63. *TP*, p. 99; see also p. 102.

64. *Testament Politique* (1947), p. 352, n. 4.

Further reading

Works by Richelieu

The Political Testament of Cardinal Richelieu: the Significant Chapters and Supporting Selections, trans. H. B. Hill (Madison, 1961), from the Louis André edition, *Testament Politique* (Paris, 1947).

Mémoires du Cardinal de Richelieu, ed. Société de l'Histoire de France, 10 vols (Paris, 1907–31).

Lettres, instructions diplomatiques at papiers d'état du Cardinal de Richelieu, 8 vols (Paris, 1853–77).

Historical background

Briggs, R., *Early Modern France* (Oxford, 1977).
Faber, Richard, *The Brave Courtier: Sir William Temple* (London, 1983), ch. 4.
Hill, David Jayne, *A History of Diplomacy in the International Development of Europe* (London, 1905), vol. II, ch. 7.
Mandrou, R., *Introduction to Modern France 1500–1640* (London, 1975).
New Cambridge Modern History, vol. IV, chs 11 and 16.
O'Connell, D. P., 'A *cause célèbre* in the history of treaty-making: the refusal to ratify the Peace Treaty of Regensburg in 1630', *British Yearbook of International Law 1967*, vol. 42, pp. 71–90.
Parker, D., *The Making of French Absolutism* (London, 1983).
Ranum, Orest A., *Richelieu and the Councillors of Louis XIII: A Study of the Secretaries of State and Superintendents of Finance in the Ministry of Richelieu, 1635–1642* (Oxford, 1963), ch. 4.
Solomon, Howard M., *Public Welfare, Science and Propaganda in Seventeenth Century France: the innovations of Théophraste Renaudot* (Princeton, N. J., 1972).
Tapié, Victor-Lucien, *France in the Age of Louis XIII and Richelieu*, new edn (Cambridge, 1984).

Biography

Bergin, J., *Cardinal Richelieu: Power and the Pursuit of Wealth* (New Haven and London, 1985).
Burckhardt, Carl J., *Richelieu and his Age*, trans. in 3 vols. (London, 1940–71).
Knecht, Robert, *Richelieu* (London and New York, 1991).
O'Connell, D. P., *Richelieu* (London, 1968).

General

Bergin, J. and L. Brockliss (eds), *Richelieu and his Age* (Oxford, 1992), ch. by Weber, 'Une bonne paix': Richelieu's foreign policy and the peace of Christendom'.
Church, William F., *Richelieu and Reason of State* (Princeton, NJ, 1972).
Cutler, A. C., 'The Grotian tradition in international relations', *Review of International Studies*, 17(1), 1991.
Elliott, J. H., *Richelieu and Olivares* (Cambridge, 1984).
Hamilton, Keith and Richard Langhorne, *The Practice of Diplomacy* (London and New York, 1995).
Hauser, Henri, *La Pensée et l'action économiques du Cardinal de Richelieu* (Paris, 1944).
Kissinger, Henry A., 'The white revolutionary: reflections on Bismarck', *Daedalus*, Summer 1968.
Kissinger, Henry A., *Diplomacy* (New York and London, 1994), ch. 3.
Meinecke, Friedrich, *Machiavellism*, ch. 6: 'The doctrine of the best interest of the state in France at the time of Richelieu'.
Nicolson, Harold, *The Evolution of Diplomatic Method* (London, 1954), chs 3 and 4.
Thuau, Etienne, *Raison d'état et pensée politiques a l'époque du Richelieu* (Paris, 1966).

Treasure, G. R. R., *Cardinal Richelieu and the development of absolutism* (London, 1972), ch. 19.
Wollenberg, Jörg, *Richelieu* (Bielefeld, 1977).

5
Wicquefort

Maurice Keens-Soper

Abraham de Wicquefort is not a name to reckon with in the history of early modern Europe. In a long life (1606–82) spent in and around the courts of Europe the highest office he held was as a diplomatic envoy of the second rank.[1] Although a close and fascinated observer of negotiations at the Congress of Westphalia which brought the Thirty Years War (1618–48) to an end, he seems not to have influenced their outcome. In the historiography of Europe he is somewhat better known for works on the German Empire and the United Provinces.[2] His interests spread as far as Persia and include translations of memoirs of European travellers. Throughout his life he was a voracious letter writer and his weekly gazettes (1647–53) on the convulsions of the Fronde are valued by historians of seventeenth century France. Wicquefort seems to have earned his living not so much as a diplomatist as a purveyor of political intelligence[3] and on at least two occasions his proximity to events landed him in serious trouble. In 1659 Cardinal Mazarin, Richelieu's successor as first minister at the French court, had him first briefly imprisoned in the Bastille (despite his diplomatic status) and then summarily expelled from France;[4] and in 1675 he was given a life sentence in his native Holland and incarcerated, like Grotius before him, in the castle of Loevestein.[5] His large library was confiscated and sold but it was as a prisoner that Wicquefort wrote *L'Ambassadeur et ses Fonctions*. 'I lived in terrible isolation', he recalled, 'for eight months...with only the company of owls, the jailor's family, and plenty of rats and bats, which although cheeky enough were also rather inconvenient.'[6]

It is upon this work, first published in 1681, and republished at intervals over many years that his reputation now rests. In 1716 it was translated into English as *The Embassador and His Functions* and it is on this version that this chapter is based.[7] If Wicquefort remains no more than an occasional footnote in the histories and historiography of Europe, he enjoys a more instructive position in the history of the European diplomatic system. He belongs to the handful of writers who identified the resident ambassador as the principal institutional device for the conduct of foreign affairs. Wicquefort provides the most densely recounted profile of the ambassador ever composed.

A Guide to Diplomatic Practice

Wicquefort's absorption in the actions and reactions of public life is evident in all he wrote. His interest spanned 'domestic', 'federal' and 'foreign' affairs and his delight in the virtuosity of human conduct is reminiscent of Machiavelli, whose realism he applauded. [8] Like Machiavelli he was not merely content to observe how politics documented human nature. Amid the flux of events not everything turned in circles. New developments arose from the age-old wilfulness of rulers vying with one another for power and prestige, wealth and possessions. In seventeenth-century Europe no ruler or subject could ignore the incidence of war and the troubles it caused to sovereigns accustomed to regarding it as the sport of kings as well as their decisive instrument of policy. The innovation that attracted Wicquefort however, had to do not with the increased turmoils of war but with peace. Or rather, with how over the previous two centuries the peacetime relations of states gradually came to be organized around the novel practice of *resident* diplomacy. [9] The sending and receiving of ambassadors is of course as old as the interactions of separate political entities, but what Wicquefort found striking was the extent to which among most, though not all the states of Europe, envoys were now expected to remain in their postings for several years at a time. [10] Their presence within other states had ceased to be governed by exigencies of policy. Only in time of war was it now the practice to entertain no permanent diplomatic relations. Wicquefort did not claim to be the first to notice a development that had already become a commonplace in the conduct of foreign affairs. Indeed, what seems to have spurred him to write *The Embassador and His Functions* were shortcomings of an already abundant literature.

Wicquefort seems to be the first writer on diplomacy aware that its recent history already included inadequate attempts at self-explanation. Near the beginning of his treatise he mentions two earlier writers, the Italian Carlo Pasquale and the Spaniard De Vera. It was the latter who served as his foil. Published in 1620 De Vera's *El Embajador* was translated into French as *Le Parfait Ambassadeur* and in that form

became the best-known manual of its kind. [11] Although De Vera treated
the resident ambassador as an established fact, Wicquefort dismissed his
portrait as worthless and was surely right to do so. One of the favoured
themes of the Renaissance had been the 'Mirror of Princes' depicting the
qualities deemed desirable in a virtuous ruler, and as this literature
grew so it produced a subdivision dealing with the ambassador. [12] Wicquefort's criticism is that in describing an ideal of conduct, the special
and increasingly specialized demands of a particular activity become
lost in moral disquisition. Between 1625 and 1700 some 153 books on
'diplomacy' were published, of which 114 were new titles. Not all of
these were worthy of scorn, although many were. Apart from being the
first to be written in French since Jean Hotman de Villiers' treatise of
1604, *The Embassador and His Functions* was a conscious attempt to
ignore speculation in favour of an account of what, in practice, makes
for a successful envoy. The last chapter of his book is a commentary on
diplomats he most admired, many of whom he seems to have known.
His method is to establish the figure of the envoy not by reference to
standards set by moral reasoning but on the basis of accomplishment.
This is often a ploy of those who rate success above principle, but in
Wicquefort's case the opposite of a 'perfect ambassador' is not a guileful
opportunist but rather someone steeped in a knowledge of the long-
term interests of his and other states, and possessed of honesty, loyalty,
prudence and good judgement.

A hefty portion of the literature on the ambassador which Wicquefort
rejected was the work of jurists, a breed for whom he expressed little
admiration. They too had succeeded in stifling the subject in discussion
of an envoy's legal status with the result that his 'functions' were left
unexplored. Wicquefort wished to alter the focus of interest in suggesting that the purpose of diplomacy, the reason for having resident ambassadors and for surrounding them in legal safeguards, had to be sought
beyond the law. [13] In making secure the necessary interchanges of international relations, the *droit des gens*, or 'law of nations', served a political
purpose. Perhaps because his anti-Catholic and anti-Spanish sentiments
are pronounced, Wicquefort does not mention either Vitoria or Suarez.
In contrast he acknowledges the towering figure of his fellow country-
man Grotius, whose son was a friend. Even here he noted reservations.
Grotius had remained unconvinced that the shift from fitful to resident
diplomacy was either desirable or inevitable (see p. 57 above), a scepticism that questioned the central proposition of *The Embassador and His
Functions*. Their differences, however, went deeper and included quite
contrary casts of mind. Although subsequently hailed as the 'father of

International Law' Grotius's outlook was in fundamental respects turned towards the past. As with many Renaissance writers, the sources he cited as evidence of a *jus inter gentes* were overwhelmingly from Latin and Greek writers of classical times. It is also far from clear what his multiple references are designed to establish. If they are used in support of laws of right reason this only compounds well known difficulties associated with natural law thinking; how can reason establish law between states when the only reason states habitually follow is *raison d'état*?

What is impressive in Wicquefort's thinking is that he does not even bother to take issue with this standpoint. As with Machiavelli, whose writings he admired, rather than argue against opinions he found wrongheaded, he ignored them. He preferred to find evidence of a law of nations not in the purported laws of nature but in the manifest conduct of states. In this connection, his observations on treaty observance and the doctrine of *raison d'état* adopted by the princes of his day speak for themselves: 'The wax and parchment do not bind faster than a chain of straw, and they seem to glory in outdoing the Florentine politician, in all he says, concerning the most pernicious maxims of the worst of men.' [14] Explaining why princes only observe treaties while this remains in their interest, Wicquefort states with clear approval that 'princes have an obligation to their subjects, which is beyond comparison much stronger, than that they enter into by any alliance, how strict soever it may be'. [15] He is quick to stress nevertheless that only 'necessity' can excuse a prince who throws over a treaty, since to do this out of caprice is 'to offend the publick faith, and to subvert the foundations of all the commerce princes are oblig'd to entertain among themselves'. [16]

This preoccupation with the world about him helps to explain why he so rarely used classical writers as authorities, and went out of his way to reason in a vernacular language. States were more and more coming to use French rather than Latin in the conduct of their affairs. Whereas Grotius was suspicious of resident envoys, partly because he could find no support for them in classical literature, what mattered to Wicquefort was that they had come into existence in 'modern' times in response to the demands of public life. More generally these demands were the pedigree and raison d'être of the entire law of nations. It was issued from the consent of states. In contrast to Bodin, whose work he knew, Wicquefort treated the law of nations as prevailing over civil and canon law precisely because no set of judges and no single sovereign could alter it to fit their purposes. In that sense it was a law above as well as between states because all states – or all civilized states – share an interest in sustaining the 'civil society' that exists among them.

Wicquefort's method is therefore inseparable from his message. *The Embassador and His Functions* is a long, dense but direct treatise composed for the most part in casting backwards and forwards over two centuries of history in order to substantiate the claim that a particular practice has become established as a rule, as part of the law of nations. [17] He is on firmest ground when recalling the events of his own century, his knowledge of which is astounding. His intellectual achievement is no less noteworthy. It is to fill the gap between the hitherto largely unformulated peacetime practices of states and the speculative and antique reasoning of so many other publicists. With the title of Ernest Satow's book of 1917 in mind (see Chapter 7), one can say that *The Embassador and His Functions* is the first guide to the diplomatic practice of the European states-system as it emerged from the Congress of Westphalia.

One of Wicquefort's ambitions, which imprisonment made impracticable, had been to compile a collection of recent treaties. Even so, two chapters in Book Two of his own treatise contain a survey of those he considered most important. Presumably done from memory it is quite an achievement, but its importance to us lies in his reason for wishing to undertake such a Herculean project. Bibliophile though he was, his reasons were less historiographic than practical. He believed that the content of treaties between states supplied the best record of their interests and therefore the best instruction for statesmen and envoys seeking guidance in the conduct of foreign affairs. Treaties presented a digest of the terms under which states were willing, or forced, to coexist. It is therefore notable that the great collections of treaties associated with the names of Dumont and Leibniz began to appear in print soon after Wicquefort's death. At the same time the publishing houses of Europe were busy issuing huge numbers of biographies, histories, as well as diplomatic correspondence, all of which were grist to the mill of those, like Wicquefort, who wished to ground their knowledge of the states-system on state practice. He would surely have found consolation of sorts that his more famous successor in the genre of books on diplomacy, François de Callières whose *De la Manière de négocier avec les souverains* appeared in 1716 (see Chapter 6), owned a copy of his work. Perhaps as much to the point, when the French foreign minister Torcy established the first Political Academy for the training of diplomats in the closing years of Louis XIV's reign, the syllabus (which included *The Embassador and His Functions*) was organized around the study of treaties.[18] By that time French diplomatic method had become the model for all Europe, and to the extent that between them Wicquefort and Callières formulated its outlook, their treatises represent the diplomatic theory of the *ancien régime*.

Rules of Conduct

If Wicquefort's treatment of topics is less systematic than his method of enquiry, that in itself is of interest. For those familiar with discussing diplomacy by reference to 'maintaining channels of communication', negotiating, political intelligence, economic interests, protection of nationals and taking part in formal occasions, *The Embassador and His Functions* may suggest that nothing much has changed over the last several centuries. Although most of these topics receive attention, the book is not arranged under such headings. Book One, which runs to almost 300 pages of small, double-column print in the English version and is more than twice the length of Book Two, deals with what self-styled realists in the study of foreign affairs treat too cavalierly as matters of marginal importance. But it is because he is a painstaking observer, determined to give due attention to the daily preoccupations of Europe's sovereign rulers, that Wicquefort focuses for so long on the *representational* significance of diplomacy. An ambassador is first of all the representative of a sovereign, and what he calls 'the right of embassy' is the most illustrious mark of sovereignty.[19] An embassy is a prized political possession attesting to the independence of a state and its desire to conduct its own affairs on a wider stage. The ability to act externally vis-à-vis other states is conditional upon their recognition. The sending and receiving of accredited envoys with the rank of ambassador is thus a powerful symbol of statehood. Although seventeenth-century monarchs were sensitive and combative over matters of honour and rank, Wicquefort was too much a son of the bourgeois United Provinces, and too great an admirer of the Venetian Republic, to be taken in by the display of regal vanities. Nevertheless, the observer in Wicquefort also recognized that no matter what their principles of political organization, monarchical or republican, states of all kinds stand on their dignity. Some have little else to stand upon. Most political bodies who claim sovereign jurisdiction do so for the realistic reason that status is a humanly persuasive component of power. Once recognized, status confers privileges. Wicquefort also had ample first-hand experience of the diplomatic pretensions of German would-be states at the Congress of Westphalia and the lengths to which they were prepared to go in order to assert their standing in the eyes of recognized sovereign rulers. He noted that more attention was paid to issues of representation, recognition, rank, precedence, ritual and ceremony than over striking the bargains that eventually resulted in the terms of Münster and Osnabrück.

On closer inspection many of the 'substantive' issues in dispute at the close of the Thirty Years War were less about shifts of territory, population and resources, than over which political entities were to enjoy the right to participate, if not as equals, then at least as recognized members in what Wicquefort calls 'civil society'. In the chapter on Westphalia he firmly distinguishes between matters associated with diplomatic procedure (especially representation and proposals for mediation) and those that had divided France and Sweden, Spain and the Austrian Habsburgs during a generation of warfare. Of the elaborate attention devoted to matters of ceremonial representation, he wrote, 'but it was all an opera'. [20] The force of his commentary, however, is that where states – that is political bodies composed of men – are concerned no such neat or categorical distinction can be made between form and substance, appearance and reality. Wicquefort illustrates rather than escapes a difficulty faced by all those wishing to subscribe to a 'realistic' account of diplomacy and politics while doing justice to those matters on which their proponents spend much of their energies and time. He holds fast to the view that what governs the relations of states is the clash of 'interests' without wishing to underplay customary rules and individual habits that constitute their all-too-human setting. In perhaps the most illuminating passage of the book, to be found at the beginning of the second volume, Wicquefort writes:

> The Embassador... ought to have a tincture of the comedian, and I must here add, that perhaps in the whole commerce of the world, there is not a more comical personage than the Embassador. There is not a more illustrious theatre than a court; neither is there any comedy, where the actors seem less what they are in effect, than Embassadors do in their negotiation; and there is none that represents more important personages. [21]

The moral of this can be easily misjudged. We are not being told that because public life occurs on a stage of human make-believe we are to discount its forms and rules of conduct as mere show designed to fool the unwary and amuse the gullible. It is being suggested that to act at all in public, whether in war or peace, at both the highest and lowest elevation of power implies the assumption of prescribed parts. How else, for example, can an ambassador re-present his sovereign than by 'playing up', acting in accordance to a part he has temporarily been given? Being worldly-wise, Wicquefort was impatient with the extent to which courts and nobles became absorbed in the play-acting at the expense of the scripts. In a scathing aside on the diplomatic practice of the papal court, he wrote that it 'is composed only of ceremonies'. [22] Yet the 'script' of Europe's seventeenth-century foreign affairs was written by monarchs notorious for 'standing upon their dignity'. And it is perhaps worth reminding ourselves that although the twentieth century rejected monarchism and its panoply of aristocratic manners, the diplomatic representatives of liberal and peoples' democracies are no less punctilious in upholding the dignity of nations. Wicquefort's desire to do justice to both the representational side of diplomacy and its employment in the pursuit of state interests extends to the very structure of the book: volume one concentrates on the former while the second part dwells on an envoy's 'functions'. If the distinction does not quite work this is perhaps true to life, but the attempt does lend a somewhat static feel to the argument as a whole. Greater minds than Wicquefort have of course also failed to elicit precisely how 'appearances' are blended with 'reality'. Or indeed how the distinction can be drawn without separating – and therefore distorting – what is experienced as a seamless whole.

Wicquefort is more sure-footed in describing the distinctive character of a diplomatic envoy. [23] An ambassador is neither a deputy nor a delegate and his duties require a combination of knowledge, skill and prudence that a good training can help to form. Except for ceremonial occasions Wicquefort does not think the nobility make good diplomats. They are prone to be too full of themselves and too taken with a liking for war. As for clergymen, because the knowledge called for is this-worldly, because it is not easy to punish them, and because – as the wise Venetians point out – the natural affection for a country and concern for its future provided by children is denied them by their celibacy, they should *not* be good at diplomacy. For the first of these reasons bookish men are also unsuitable. A dogmatic or disputatious temperament goes ill with the search for accommodation. Great minds and common sense seldom go together. Grotius made a better scholar than ambassador. In the same vein business provides a poor schooling in the necessary arts because the love of profit has little to do with representing a sovereign and attending to his interests. Unsurprisingly the best formal preparation is a knowledge of recent rather than classical history. It is difficult to avoid noticing how Wicquefort tumbles into many of the same errors he is quick to pounce upon in others. The attempt to list qualities uniquely appropriate to an envoy produces truisms and he wisely prefers on occasion to rely on the *Maximes* of La Rochefoucauld for axiomatic reflections on human nature. Wicquefort does succeed in highlighting that in diplomacy as in politics there is no substitute for trust. Without some measure of settled belief that words are to be believed, and hence can be used as safe guides to deeds, there could hardly be anything called purposive action involving interaction with others. An envoy, Wicquefort pertinently notes, who has the trust of his own sovereign as well as the ruler to whom he is accredited, is uniquely placed to sustain the 'civil society' of European states. [24]

Useful Knowledge and the Limits of Exposition

The Embassador and His Functions presents an exhaustive as well as orderly account of the procedures that constitute the public life of envoys. If the chapters concerned read like a conducted tour through the professional life of a dutiful diplomat, it is well to remember that that is what they were designed to be. The book is aimed at would-be practitioners of an exposed and increasingly exacting department of officialdom, and one which was by no means well staffed in the Holland of Wicquefort's day; [25] and it is intended not for amusement but for instruction and use. If students of diplomacy now turn to Wicquefort as a piece of historical evidence that is not the audience for which he wrote. Apart from giving him something to do in prison and the chance to air some of his personal grievances, what he wanted to leave behind was a digest of the common experience of the states of Europe that would be of practical value.

Whether or how far a body of experience can be compressed as a handbook or manual raises several interesting philosophical questions. In *Rationalism in Politics* for example, Michael Oakeshott examines the errors of seeking to formulate experience in the manner of techniques. [26] Among the misunderstandings to which this is said to give rise is a false idea of human action. To act can never be a question of following rules stored up in books of reference, because what can be foreshortened into an abridged version of experience, and placed between the hard covers of a book, is always misleadingly unlike the real McCoy. More directly, the extent and manner to which a public and professional activity such as diplomacy can be made the subject of instruction raises matters of policy that reach into the very heart of education.

How far are envoys born and not made? Is their training to be like that of, say, a musician or chef where natural aptitude is of the essence, or more like that of a soldier or merchant where the raw material may be of less importance? On more than one occasion Wicquefort offers reminders that he was no philosopher. But at the beginning of his work he voices an ambition which echoes both the Baconian belief that the purpose of 'science' was *useful* knowledge for the practical enlightenment of mankind, and Descartes' principle that no reasoning can be better than the assumptions on which it is based:

> I know very well, [writes de Wicquefort] all that I can say will never be able to make it a science that has its mathematical principles, or that is founded on demonstrative reasons, upon which certain and infallible rules may be made; but however, I think I can reduce all my discourse to maxims, wherein will be found something that comes very near to a moral infallibility. [27]

Bacon's *esprit systématique* and Descartes' *esprit de système* both influenced the intellectual habits of the seventeenth century, and *The Embassador and His Functions*, which carries references to both authors, shows traces of their ambitions. Even if it is true that Wicquefort's exposition often groans under the burden of historical references, it remains true that like no previous author on the subject, his aim was to make explicit the 'functions' of the ambassador. Perhaps even more noteworthy is the extent to which, in spite of his yearning to compose a treatise worthy of systematic and analytical reason, he did *not* believe that the conduct of diplomacy could dispense with what only exposure to the experience of foreign affairs was able to provide. 'But neither birth... nor study,' he wrote, 'can form an accomplished Embassador without experience; which consummates what the others only began.' [28]

Political Necessity and Diplomatic Immunities

The personal insecurity of an envoy derives from his occupational position. He is the missive of one sovereign and dependent for his well being upon the whims of another. Authorized by one state he is vulnerable to the power of another. Wicquefort chose to describe the risky and suspect position of an ambassador as that of 'an honourable spy'. [29] This predicament is as old as the exchange of ambassadors and so has been the remedy. The safety of envoys is founded on the 'necessity' of unhindered and reliable 'commerce' between rulers. The dangers of having 'honourable spies' nearby are outweighed by the greater liability of having no contacts with other states, and so being left in the dark. Only the most isolated (and usually small) states can afford the risks of ignorance. This inescapable fact of obligatory coexistence – with the need to be well informed as its lasting consequence – was universally recognized except among those states who hankered after (what the seventeenth century called) universal monarchy. Where numbers of states exist they are condemned to live cheek by jowl, and sooner or later find means by which they can share the advantages of continuity of settled expectations. Law is a favoured method of achieving continuity on the basis of regulation. In the case of willfully independent states, however, law is the product of consent among sovereigns. Hence according to Wicquefort the 'law of nations' is grounded in the general consent of those who expect to gain from its provisions. In keeping with this line of understanding, the legal inviolability of envoys (together with their suites and their mission premises), which is the antidote to their insecurity, is secured not by the civil laws of states but by international laws directly binding on their otherwise sovereign jurisdictions. Although for the most part implicit, the political sense Wicquefort brings to the discussion of diplomatic immunities is refreshing. [30] In contrast to Bodin whom he criticizes for reserving too much to the domestic jurisdiction of states, he gives a broad interpretation of their scope. In this there is no doubt a touch of special pleading, as in 1675 Wicquefort was gaoled by the civil authorities of Holland even though he claimed legal exemption as the envoy of another state. In his view the fact that he was a Dutchman was irrelevant to his juridical standing under the law of nations. [31] In any case, the argument for the autonomy of international law could hardly be put with greater vigour. Even when envoys directly foment civil strife, the authorities should, he says, resist the urge to act and ask instead for the suspect's withdrawal. The reason given is once more the standing of an envoy: his actions are not those of a private person. Diplomatic agents are public officials able to fulfil their tasks only when immune from local jurisdiction. He finds support in Grotius for the opinion that to tamper with this rule, the fruit of 'a kind of agreement or tacit contract' made by a prince's acceptance of the diplomat's credentials, [32] is short-sighted and at odds with the long-term interests which states have in common. The laws of diplomatic immunity are buttresses which allow the system of states to function in regular, if not orderly, fashion.

Diplomacy and the Constitution of a States-system

Wicquefort is well acquainted with the limited powers of diplomacy. Political reasoning is unlike mathematics where force of logic leads to unavoidable conclusions. In relations between states all the resourcefulness of reasoned persuasion may be to no avail. The final arbiter is force of arms. Even though the interests of states are largely unsusceptible to reason it does not follow that they cannot be rationally explained or pursued with moderation. The lesson here for an envoy who grasps the scope of diplomacy is to guard his temper and exercise patience. If a certain phlegmatism does not come naturally, Wicquefort counsels that it should be cultivated or at least assumed. The impersonation of virtues is not to be confused with deceit. Like present day capitals and international organizations, seventeenth-century courts were rife with intrigue but Wicquefort believed that an envoy should use his wits not to become party to dealings which he must nevertheless observe and faithfully report. In the pursuit of political information it is permissible to use presents, subsidies and other inducements but a prudent envoy will not expect too much from soliciting that amounts to bribery. In general the use of guile in negotiation can too easily lead to confusion and eventually undermine the trust essential to winning agreements designed to last. Mazarin, for whom Wicquefort once worked, [33] is criticized for engaging in such Byzantine dealings that he succeeded in misleading himself. The 'functions' of an ambassador are summarized in the following way:

> His chief function consists in his entertaining a good correspondence between the two Princes; in his delivering the letters his master writes to the Prince with whom he resides; in soliciting an answer thereto; in his observing all that passes at the court where he negotiates; in protecting the subjects, and in preserving the interest of his master. [34]

The Embassador and His Functions conveys the institutional density of diplomacy as well as its necessity as an instrument of statecraft. Through first-hand knowledge of the administrative curriculum of ambassadorial life Wicquefort provides an actualized concept of the seventeenth-century European states-system. As we have seen, he believed that in formulating its rules, practices and precepts in the form of a manual, his work would be of use. It is difficult to know how far it achieved that purpose but its value today rests on the analysis it provides of the states-system at the time of the Congress of Westphalia. Wicquefort wrote of the Congress that not for many ages had there been a gathering 'where so many different and opposite interests met'. [35] It set the seal on the transformation of a long divided Christendom into the states-system of the *ancien régime*. The treaties of Münster and Osnabrück make explicit the claims of states and would-be states against one another, but what Wicquefort's comments on the negotiations reveal is how, as the means of protecting their interests when exhausted by war, the rulers of Europe found themselves obliged to cultivate the arts of diplomacy as the condition of tolerable coexistence. Wicquefort was well aware that before as well as after Westphalia, diplomacy was used sometimes to mitigate, sometimes to prosecute and sometimes to conclude the endemic conflicts of Europe's bellicose rulers.

Unlike other writers of the *ancien régime*, who observed the states-system only to reject it as morally defective or ineffectual, Wicquefort is content to provide a detailed guide to its peacetime routines. Although not always successful in holding to it, he values Machiavelli's favoured distinction between what is and what ought to be. There is much however about the foreign affairs of this time that he found distasteful. The waste of war appalled him, especially when spiced with religious intemperance. Wicquefort did not see that Descartes could be used to uphold theological dogma, much of which he treats as superstition. He also clearly found the excesses of human vanity ludicrous. Nonetheless he uses his considerable powers of memory and observation, not to catalogue human defects but to elaborate, if only by implication, a distinction central to the existence of diplomatic theory.

For surely what marks off a *diplomatic* system from a *political* one, is that whereas a 'body politic' is a unity with a common good or common will as its essential principle of existence, a diplomatic system of states proclaims no such principle of substantive unity. The idea of sovereignty, so much discussed at Westphalia, with its claims to acknowledge no authority higher than its own, precludes this. What therefore distinguishes a diplomatic system is the existence of rules of procedure and not common policies. A states-system is systematic only in the sense of being a system of diplomacy. War by comparison is haphazard. [36]

Many publicists, Puffendorf above all but including Wicquefort, were fascinated by the German Empire as it emerged from the Thirty Years War. Part of the attraction was that it was ceasing to be a body politic and becoming an association of states. Although still attached by ties of common inheritance, its principal members were increasingly incorporated in the wider European order of independent states. It is true that the well-known recognition at Westphalia of the right of German princes to conduct their own relations with states outside the Empire was circumscribed by the proviso that in doing so the interests of the Empire were to prevail. It soon became clear, however, how little this limited their freedom of action. Once states have successfully asserted their title to conduct an independent foreign policy this places insuperable obstacles in the way of saying anything systematic or theoretical about the substance of interstate relations. Wicquefort has the merit of being forthright about this. Whatever can be specified about the rules of diplomacy not much of general significance can be said about the content of policy.

> But as for the essence [of negotiation], there is neither precept nor example to be given, because it changes with the affairs the Embassador has to negotiate, which are innumerable, and almost all of a different nature. [37]

If true this acute observation has implications for the study of international relations. Foreign policy for example can be described and analysed but hardly theorized. It is a historical enquiry. In contrast, the rules of procedure which constitute the states-system, and without which foreign policy could not proceed or be intelligible, can be theorized in the manner of constitutional theory. Despite the prominence of war, the post-Westphalian states-system was not a Hobbesian state of nature, a *bellum omnium contra omnes*. The rules of diplomatic conduct, which lent coherence and a modicum of continuity to the conduct of foreign affairs are no more ephemeral than those that constitute constitutional government. The rules of parliamentary procedure are not some anodyne 'framework of reference' of merely incidental significance to the character of lawful government and its furtherance of policy. In their absence talk of good government would be meaningless. The speaker of the British House of Commons is the linchpin of orderly government but says not a word about what policies government should adopt. In a somewhat similar vein diplomatic theory is the constitutional theory of a states-system. Its focus of interest cannot be foreign policy for the reasons already suggested; there is nothing consistent enough to be theorized. One of the merits of *The Embassador and His Functions* is the attention it rivets on what can be adumbrated in systematic form and by means of an inductive, historical, method.

At the close of the Thirty Years War a new order of foreign affairs took shape in Europe, whose cardinal, and increasingly explicit, axiom was *raison d'état*. This in turn evoked the need for greater regulation in the relations of states, in both war and peace. What this produced was not international organization in the modern sense. The manifold spider's web of diplomacy did however equip the states-system of the *ancien régime* with a rudimentary institution, the work not of rational design but of necessity born of experience. If this was a rickety principle of order which failed to keep the peace of Europe, it had the subsidiary merits of providing a buttress against some of the excesses of war, and of preserving most, though not all, states from extinction.

Notes

1. From 1626 until 1658 he served in Paris as the Resident of the Elector of Brandenburg-Prussia, and from 1674 until 1675 was among other things Resident of the Duke of Brunswick-Luneburg-Celle: *Biographie Universelle, Ancienne et Moderne* (1827); Phyllis S. Lachs, *The Diplomatic Corps under Charles II & James II* (New Brunswick, NJ, 1965); Herbert H. Rowen, *John de Witt, Grand Pensionary of Holland, 1625–1672* (Princeton, NJ, 1978); C. van Bynkershoek, *De Foro Legatorum* (1721; repr. New York, 1964), introduction by Jan de Louter.
2. *Discours historique de l'élection de l'empereur et des électeurs de l'empire* (Paris, 1658); *L'Histoire des Provinces Unies des Pays-Bas, depuis le parfait établissement de cet état par la paix de Münster* (The Hague, 1719).
3. Rowen, *John de Witt*, pp. 147, 275–6.
4. Rowen, *John de Witt*, p. 276.
5. Following his expulsion from France, Wicquefort was invited to The Hague by John de Witt, who was the Grand Pensionary of Holland, or what today we would call its 'foreign minister'. He had already been providing de Witt with intelligence from France since 1656 and was now formally employed as a translator for the States General but chiefly as the Grand Pensionary's special secretary for French correspondence. De Witt was assassinated in 1672 and in 1675 Wicquefort's enemies accused him of selling state secrets to the English. He was tried and on 20 December the Court of Holland imprisoned him on the grounds that although he was a public minister (diplomat) he remained a Dutch national and in the paid service of the States, to whom he had taken an oath of secrecy. From his prison cell Wicquefort wrote the *Mémoires touchant les Ambassadeurs et les Ministres Publics* (see 'Further reading'), which he addressed to the peace congress which assembled at Nimegen in 1676. In this work – which was the precursor to *The Embassador and His Functions* – he sought to prove that his position as a diplomat in the service of a foreign prince rendered him immune from prosecution under Dutch law. However, his appeal fell on deaf ears and he remained in prison until he escaped to Celle in 1679: *Biographie Universelle, Ancienne at Moderne* (1827); Bynkershoek, *De Foro Legatorum*, esp. pp. xvi, 57, 98; Lachs, *The Diplomatic Corps under Charles II and James II*, p. 125; Rowen, *John de Witt*, pp. 275–6.
6. Quoted in M. L. Lending (ed.), *Histoire des Provinces-Unies* (Amsterdam, 1861) I, p. xxi, translation supplied.

7. All subsequent references to *The Embassador and His Functions* are to this English translation by John Digby in 1716. A facsimile edition (minus the account of the German empire) was published by the Centre for the Study of Diplomacy at the University of Leicester, Leicester, England in 1997, with an Introductory Essay by Maurice Keens-Soper. This book was also translated into German. The present essay is a revised version of the Introductory Essay to the facsimile edition. I am grateful to G. R. Berridge for helpful comments and suggestions.
8. *The Embassador and His Functions*, pp. 52, col. 2; 53, col. 2; 90, cols 1–2; 372, col. 1. Wicquefort's regard for Machiavelli may also have been influenced by the fact that they were both 'ministers of the second order', which made them in the Dutchman's view the most valuable of all diplomats. There is a striking passage in *The Embassador and His Functions* (p. 34, col. 1) where Wicquefort describes how, unencumbered by the cautions and formalities imposed upon them by the 'representative' character of an 'embassador', ministers of the second order can the more readily conduct intrigues and negotiations.
9. Garrett Mattingly's *Renaissance Diplomacy* (Harmondsworth, 1965) remains the most scholarly account of the advent of resident diplomacy, at least in English.
10. *The Embassador and His Functions*, p. 6, cols. 1–2.
11. See Mattingly, *Renaissance Diplomacy*, pp. 201–2.
12. C. H. Carter, 'Wicquefort on the Ambassador and his Functions', in *Studies in History and Politics*, vol. 11, 1981/1982.
13. It remains true that *The Embassador and His Functions* contains a persuasive and particularly vigorous argument for diplomatic immunity on the basis of customary law, and is acknowledged as such even by eminent international lawyers who disapproved of Wicquefort's role as an intelligencer for hire. In *De Foro Legatorum*, Bynkershoek, for example, described this as 'a definitive work, which in our opinion is inferior to none' (p. 57).
14. *The Embassador and His Functions*, p. 372, col. 1.
15. *The Embassador and His Functions*, p. 372, col. 1.
16. *The Embassador and His Functions*, p. 372, col. 1.
17. This, of course, appealed to the lawyers. Bynkershoek in particular defended Wicquefort's method of piling example on example in order to confirm customary practice. He added, too, that while a counsel of perfection would have had Wicquefort citing the authorities for his examples, this was no longer the fashion for those writing in French. More to the point he said: 'I should be unwilling to refute the testimony of Wicquefort as a witness, since I have found that a great many of the examples which he reports are actually recorded in the annals, and about a few others I myself am sure', *De Foro Legatorum*, pp. 46, 101–2.
18. H. M. A. Keens-Soper, 'The French Political Academy, 1712: A School for Ambassadors', *European Studies Review* vol. 2, no. 4 (1972).
19. *The Embassador and His Functions*, pp. 1, col. 1; 6–7.
20. *The Embassador and His Functions*, p. 385, col. 1.
21. *The Embassador and His Functions*, p. 294, col. 1. In the seventeenth century, of course, a 'comedy' was a light play with a happy ending, as opposed to a 'tragedy'.

22. In this rare instance, Digby provides a mistranslation. The original French reads 'La court de Rome, qui n'est composée que de ceremonies', whereas Digby's translation omits the important negative. See *The Embassador and His Functions*, p. 128, col. 1.
23. *The Embassador and His Functions*, Book One, chs 7–9.
24. *The Embassador and His Functions*, Book One, ch. 12, esp. p.90.
25. Rowen, *John de Witt*, pp. 243–7.
26. Michael Oakeshott, *Rationalism in Politics* (London, 1962).
27. *The Embassador and His Functions*, p. 2, col. 1.
28. *The Embassador and His Functions*, p. 53, col. 2.
29. *The Embassador and His Functions*, p. 86, col. 2. This expression already enjoyed a wide currency by the late seventeenth century; see Sir Ernest Satow, *A Guide to Diplomatic Practice*, 2nd edn (London, 1922), vol. I, pp. 183–4.
30. See *The Embassador and His Functions*, Book One, chs 27–9.
31. This was actually one of the two cases which provoked Bynkershoek, appointed President of the Supreme Court of Holland in 1721, to write *De Foro Legatorum*, and on this point he could not entirely agree with Wicquefort: ch. 11.
32. *The Embassador and His Functions*, p. 257, col. 2.
33. *Biographie universelle, ancienne et moderne* (1827).
34. *The Embassador and His Functions*, p. 296, col. 1.
35. *The Embassador and His Functions*, p. 385, col 1.
36. For further discussion, see my 'The Practice of a States-System' in Michael Donelan (ed), *The Reason of States: A study in international political theory* (London, 1978).
37. *The Embassador and His Functions*, p. 315, col. 2.

Further reading

Works by Wicquefort

The Embassador and His Functions, trans. into English by John Digby in 1716, repr. by the Centre for the Study of Diplomacy, University of Leicester, Leicester, UK, 1997. This was first published in The Hague in two volumes over the years 1680 and 1681 under the title *L'Ambassadeur et ses Fonctions*.

Mémoires touchant les Ambassadeurs et les Ministres Public (1676/7). This has not been translated into English and is not readily accessible. On the somewhat complicated history of its appearance, see: *Biographie universelle, ancienne et moderne* (below); Bynkershoek, *De Foro Legatorum*, p. 41; and *The Embassador and His Functions*, p. 2, col. 1. Nevertheless, the *Mémoires* are mentioned here because this is the only other work of Wicquefort's which is wholly dedicated to diplomacy. The author is described on the title page simply as 'L. M. P.' but there has never been any doubt that 'Le Ministre Prisonnier' was Wicquefort. For background, see footnote 5 to this chapter.

Historical background

Anderson, M. S., *The Rise of Modern Diplomacy* (London and New York, 1993), chs 2 and 4.

Faber, Richard, *The Brave Courtier: Sir William Temple* (London, 1983). This is worth looking at because Wicquefort regarded Temple as the most successful British diplomat of his day.

Hamilton, K. and R. Langhorne, *The Practice of Diplomacy* (London and New York, 1995), ch. 3.

Hill, David Jayne, *A History of Diplomacy in the International Development of Europe* (London, 1905), vol. III, pp. 52–5, 240–2, 500–2.

Horn, D. B., *The British Diplomatic Service, 1689–1789* (Oxford, 1961).

Lachs, Phyllis S., *The Diplomatic Corps under Charles II & James II* (New Brunswick, NJ, 1965).

The New Cambridge Modern History, vol. 5, ch. 9; vol. 6, ch. 5 (esp. p. 168ff.).

Roosen, W. J., *The Age of Louis XIV: the rise of modern diplomacy* (Cambridge, Mass., 1976).

Rowen, Herbert H., *John de Witt, Grand Pensionary of Holland, 1625–1672* (Princeton, NJ, 1978).

Wolf, John B., *Louis XIV* (London, 1968).

Wolf, John B., *Towards a European Balance of Power, 1620–1715* (Chicago, 1970).

Biography

There is no biography of Wicquefort in English, though interesting entries on him are to be found in various dictionaries of biography, for example:

Biographie universelle, ancienne et moderne, vol. 50 (Paris,1827); nouvelle édition (1854), vol. 44; and this edn repr. (Graz, Austria, 1970).

Nouvelle Biographie Générale (Paris, 1877), vol. 46.

There is also a fair amount of biographical detail on Wicquefort in Herbert H. Rowen's massive biography of de Witt, his latter day Dutch patron: *John de Witt, Grand Pensionary of Holland, 1625–1672* (Princeton, NJ, 1978), esp. chs. 12 and 14.

General

Belcher, G. L., *Politics and Protocol: the Ambassador in the Age of Louis XIV* (Lafayette, 1975).

Bynkershoek, Cornelius van, *De Foro Legatorum: The Jurisdiction over Ambassadors in both Civil and Criminal Cases*, first publ. 1721, trsl. of the 1744 ed. by G. J. Laing, with an introduction by Jan de Louter, repr. in 1964 in the 'Classics in International Law' series by Oceana of New York and Wildy & Son of London.

Carter, Charles H., 'Wicquefort on the Ambassador and his Functions', in *Studies in History and Politics*, 1981–2, pp. 37–59.

Galardi, P. Ferdinand, *Réflexions sur les Mémoires pour les Ambassadeurs, et Reponse au Ministre Prisonnier*, first published anonymously in Ville-Franche in 1677; repr. to accompany the edition of *L'Ambassadeur et ses Fonctions*, etc. published by Janssons & Waesberge in Amsterdam in 1730.

Keens-Soper, Maurice, 'The practice of a states-system', in Michael Donelan (ed.), *The Reason of States: A study in international political theory* (London, 1978).

Mattingly, Garrett, *Renaissance Diplomacy* (Harmondsworth, 1965).

Oakeshott, Michael, *Rationalism in Politics and Other Essays* (London, 1962).

Osiander, Andreas, *The States System of Europe, 1640–1990: peacemaking and the conditions of international stability* (Oxford, 1994), chs. 2 and 3.

6
Callières

Maurice Keens-Soper

François de Callières (1645–1717) was a diplomatic envoy and man of letters who in 1716 published *De la Manière de négocier avec les souverains*. [1] A Normand of literate and noble, but modest ancestry, he lived for many years in various parts of Europe before securing somewhat late in life a position in the service of Louis XIV. [2] Although he won admission to the French Academy for a panegyric on the King and published several other books including a notable contribution to the 'Battle of the Ancients and Moderns', the high point in his sombre but determined life came during the Nine Years War (1688–97) when as a secret envoy he negotiated the crucial terms with the Dutch which led to the Congress of Ryswick and a short-lived peace. Callières was one of the three French ambassadors at Ryswick. Thereafter he held the sensitive position of *secrétaire du cabinet* at Versailles and supplied the secretary of state for foreign affairs with a flow of memoranda on the conditions of peace. Callières left only a pale mark on the history and letters of his country. Since the publication of *The Art of Diplomacy* his name has however been secure in the history of European foreign affairs, considered less as the succession of events than as the elaboration of a diplomatic system of states articulated and mediated by the activities of resident envoys. [3]

Reputation

Callières's treatise was greeted with immediate acclaim. Two French editions appeared in 1716 and were accompanied by an English translation. Though subsequent sales proved disappointingly meagre, his work enjoyed a European reputation throughout the eighteenth century, becoming one of the standard references on diplomatic practice. Indeed, along with Wicquefort's *The Embassador and His Functions* (see Chapter 5) and to a lesser extent Antoine Pecquet's *Discours sur l'art de négocier* of 1738, Callières was considered essential reading for prospective diplomatists. During the nineteenth century, however, he was largely neglected and it is not until the First World War that renewed interest can be detected. This revival began with the publication of Satow's *A Guide to Diplomatic Practice* (1917) which called Callières's book 'a mine of political wisdom', and was furthered two years later when A. F. Whyte produced an abbreviated 'English rendering' under the title *The Practice of Diplomacy*. [4]

A member of the British delegation at the Paris peace conference of 1919, Whyte was disturbed by the new trends in diplomacy evident at Paris and particularly disliked diplomacy by conference, that is, the idea of conducting negotiations within public view where extraneous influences such as the press and public opinion, threatened to distort the search for agreement between the official representatives of states. To arrest these trends, Whyte returned to the methods of traditional diplomacy and to what he considered most instructive in its approach. He urged that recent innovations in diplomacy, such as the 'open covenants of peace, openly arrived at' advocated by the American President Woodrow Wilson, should be resisted. Whyte used Callières as a guide to the maxims and techniques of European diplomacy which he denied had been superseded or indeed could, with safety, be put aside so long as foreign affairs were dominated by growing numbers of independent states. This view was largely shared by Harold Nicolson who regarded Callières's work as 'the best manual of diplomatic method ever written'. [5]

Satow, Whyte and Nicolson, all diplomats, viewed their profession in a similar light, as a specialized activity endowed with its own repository of precepts that may be imparted to novices in such a way as to be of practical and regular use – even in a field where first-hand experience counts for so much. Circumstances and manners may alter with the time but the substance of sound diplomacy and the need for training as well as experience, do not. One can distinguish two further currents of more recent interest in Callières: first, among historians of diplomacy who see him as representative of a uniquely French standpoint and to a large extent reformulating the opinions of Richelieu; and secondly, among diplomatic historians who regard *The Art of Diplomacy* as 'a classic text'. [6]

What these varying approaches fail to supply is sufficient appreciation of *The Art of Diplomacy* from the viewpoint of the setting in which foreign affairs occur. They overlook how Callières, in seeking to make explicit the terms of the emerging European diplomatic tradition, is raising a prime feature of a uniquely complex states-system to the level of thought.

The Focus of Attention

The starting point for a fuller appraisal of Callières's essay is the institution of recognizably modern diplomatic method: the transition from temporary or *ad hoc* to regular representation, generally fixed by historians as occurring among the city-states of Italy during the second half of the fifteenth century.[7] What would now be called diplomatic missions were, of course, familiar long before then and the practice of sending agents abroad for specific purposes, sometimes for lengthy periods, is as old as commerce, suspicion, rivalry and war. The seminal difference is that throughout earlier times, which reach back thousands of years to ancient Mesopotamia, envoys did not occupy their posts at the courts of foreign rulers on a continuous, regularized or reciprocal basis. Once his particular task was completed, an envoy – unless held as a hostage – returned home. Sporadic or fitful negotiations of this kind proved inadequate among the princely states of Renaissance Europe, who increasingly ignored the twin authorities of Empire and Papacy around whom the affairs of Christendom had for long received at least a simulacrum of order. As the external affairs of secular rulers became increasingly enmeshed in alliances of shifting interests, military enmities and denser commercial dealings, so the defects of occasional diplomacy became increasingly costly.

Permanent embassies which first appeared in the 'subsystem' of Italian states between 1454 and Charles VIII's invasion of Italy forty years later, were slowly adopted in a similarly competitive setting north of the Alps from where they gradually spread to other parts of the continent. A by-product of this development was the emergence of a specialized literature dwelling on the changes in the conduct of foreign affairs. As already noted in Chapter 5, in the sixteenth century the literary portrait of 'the perfect ambassador' became a favoured theme frequently found alongside treatment of an envoy's legal position. Together these two kinds of account crowd discussion of the ambassador until the second half of the seventeenth century. Casting over the literature of Renaissance diplomacy Mattingly concludes that 'the essential substance' of what all these authors have to say 'boils down to the same scanty residue of what seem like the tritest platitudes', only to add 'so do the simple and difficult rules of any enduring human art'. [8] Yet Mattingly's account of the formative stages in European diplomacy concludes with the Thirty Years War (1618–48) and is surely wrong to imply that the literature on diplomacy spawned by the Congress of Westphalia is of little account. More was at stake in the affairs of Europe after 1648 than reiteration of issues long debated by lawyers and moralists. Grotius, for example, wrote an early contribution to and not the last word on the exterritoriality of embassies (see Chapter 3). There was expansion of the literature on the immunity of envoys and continuing reflection on the ethics of war. Above all, intellectual interest came to focus on the form and workings of the states-system that emerged from Westphalia and which led Puffendorf to call the German Empire a 'political monstrosity'. [9]

The powers and claims of independent states were furthered by improvements in governmental, fiscal and military organization while these developments in turn prompted a large increase in the numbers of resident ambassadors throughout Europe. Like the military, clergy and judiciary, diplomats gradually acquired their own distinct character and methods of work. At a time when the absolute monarchy of France dominated the affairs of Europe and French language and culture enjoyed a similar pre-eminence, it is not surprising to see the emergence of a distinctively French view of diplomacy that served as a compelling example to other rulers. One feature of this was to infuse the literature of diplomacy with the forthright political content hitherto absent. In moving the centre of attention in this direction the discussion of diplomacy became less ephemeral. It is here that Callières, and to a lesser degree Abraham de Wicquefort, succeeded in producing diplomatic theory out of an age-old literature hitherto the preserve of jurists and guides to good conduct.

Past Events and Present Understandings

Callières owned a copy of *The Embassador and His Functions* [10] and, though he nowhere mentions its author by name or indeed refers to earlier writers of diplomatic manuals, there are passages in his own account which suggest he had Wicquefort in mind when he wrote his own, as far as can be told in the year 1697. Between them these two authors span the seventeenth century. As befitted intelligent diplomatic ne'er-do-wells they shared a critical attitude towards the nobility, believing that excepting embassies of ceremony the 'real' work of negotiations was accomplished by envoys of the second order. Both men also

possessed a solid grounding in recent history and asserted the significance of the Congress of Westphalia. Holland, admiration for the Dutch
statesman de Witt and service under the French Crown provide further
personal links between the two men, but otherwise the Frenchman's
experience of European foreign affairs carries a different stamp from that
of the cosmopolitan Dutchman.

Callières was most active as an envoy during the years after 1689,
when French military ascendancy was more and more effectively
resisted. Notions of hegemony gave way to a view where France figured
as but one eminent power among a number of others who, allied in
combination, were able to counterbalance the ambitions of even the
greatest states. In Callières's view the occasion for diplomacy arises only
when this initial condition is met. 'Universal monarchy' is seen by him
as an alternative to Europe's constitution as it emerged from Westphalia
as a plurality of legally independent states. This initial condition is not
however sufficient. At the other extreme from the mastery of a single
great power, the haphazard coexistence of several states also falls short
of conditions which allow rivalries, including war, to be managed. For
diplomacy to flourish, those engaged in foreign affairs must first recog-
nise what they need to have in common. The essential presupposition
which is stated early in *The Art of Diplomacy* sets the tone for all that
follows.

'In order to know truly the usefulness of negotiations,' Callières
writes, 'we ought to consider that all the States of Europe have
necessary ties and commerces one with another, which makes them
to be looked upon as members of one and the same Commonwealth.
And that there can hardly happen any considerable change in some
of its members, but what is capable of disturbing the quiet of all the
others.' [11]

History provides the detailed evidence of how bound up with each
other are the willful rulers of Europe's states. Although he shared with
Wicquefort a taste for contemporary affairs, Callières is not interested in
past events solely for themselves. Their usefulness is to point a lesson. A
practical man of the world, he calls on historical knowledge covering
two centuries of foreign affairs to drive home and illustrate the abiding
predicament of states. This is the unswerving centre of his interest.
Whereas Wicquefort seems drawn to the study of events as possible
evidence for the existence of settled rules of diplomatic practice,
Callières turns to them in order to indicate the principal elements of

interstate relations. The political angle of his outlook which depicts Europe as a field of diplomatic forces, serves as a filter which prevents the detail of particular occurrences from obscuring the more lasting features of the setting in which they take place. Callières's ability to distinguish the wood from the trees is impressively firm. In his estimate, a single theme reverberates through the modern history of Europe, governing the flux of events and acting as their principle of interpretation. The membrane of foreign affairs is formed by the rivalry of France and Austria. He counsels a young diplomat to study

> all the public treaties, both general and particular, which have been made between the Princes and States of Europe; and he may look upon the treaties concluded between France and the house of Austria as those which give the principal form to the affairs of Christendom, because of the dependance which other sovereign Princes have on these two great monarchies.... he should inform himself of all the treaties that have been made since that time [the fifteenth century]; but more especially of those which have been concluded between the chief potentates of Europe, beginning from the treaties of Westphalia, down to the present time. [12]

Understanding of this kind has a clear and present object in mind: to illuminate the configuration of Europe's public affairs by reference to what lends coherence to them. For all his sympathy with the 'ancients' in matters of literature and taste, Callières (unlike Machiavelli) ignores the attractions of antiquity as a guide to the world about him. In this sense he was free from an appeal which condemned much of Renaissance writing on the functions of the ambassador to obscurity. He also brought more personal predilections to the reading of contemporary affairs. He well appreciated that the position of eminence bequeathed to Louis XIV by Richelieu and Mazarin, and implicit in the settlement of Westphalia, was endangered by the Sun King's thirst for *gloire*. Dutiful subject and instrument though he was, Callières regarded war as an expensive and wasteful pursuit, a 'hideous goddess'. He wrote privately that France should resist the temptation to seek conquests beyond the 'natural' frontiers of the kingdom. 'I would prefer', he confided to a lady friend, 'that our kings never dreamed of going beyond the limits that God and nature have given them; the Alpes, the Pyrenees, the two seas and the Rhine, were we able to go that far.' [13] He believed that French invasions of Italy had always proved ruinous and concluded that a moderated sense of French power and interests was the hallmark of true policy. 'God who has set limits to the sea', he mused, 'desires the same for the powerful of the earth.'[14]

Terms of Art: Language and Diplomacy

At the beginning of *The Art of Diplomacy* the author describes his early fascination with 'the strength, the rights, and pretensions of every one of the chief Princes and States of Europe; of their different interests, the forms of their government; the causes of their friendships, and of their differences, and the treaties which they have made one with another'.[15] In a long life this interest in foreign affairs seems never to have flagged, yet even a professional's pride in his calling does not entirely explain how he came to write the book he did.

In the period spanning the years from 1625 until 1700, 153 titles on diplomacy have been discovered, of which 114 were new contributions to the literature.[16] It is easy to distinguish *The Art of Diplomacy* from the hundred or so Latin expositions of the law relating to the ambassador. Most of them deal either with the special problems which arose within the Empire as German Princes asserted independent powers and the corresponding right to accredit ambassadors, or with the fraught issue of exterritoriality. The merit of Callières's essay is also quite different from the handful of treatises which appeared in modern languages. Without exception they rehearse a range of comment long familiar, the gist of which is to be found expressed in the fifteenth century by Bernard du Rosier.[17] The appearance of Wicquefort's *The Embassador and His Functions* struck a fresh note and showed that other treatments of the subject were at least possible. From the success it came to enjoy, his vast monument evidently fulfilled a need. Yet the design of *The Art of Diplomacy* could not have been less like that of an encyclopaedia, and perhaps this very dissimilarity is in some way a tribute to his predecessor. To succeed in the *genre* the Frenchman had to avoid being compared with the Dutchman. By contrast, Callières's choice of a schematic form and modest volume of words established diplomatic theory not only with its indispensable frame of reference but as a branch of literature in which clarity and economy of expression became important virtues.

If *The Art of Diplomacy* lacks Bossuet's thunderous power, Fénelon's taught passion and the efficient beauty of Saint-Simon's writing, Callières's prose is sufficient to its subject. It presents the issues in a readable, measured way, unclogged with overweighty references, yet well illustrated from European history. In one respect, however, the pleasures of literature threatened the author's account of diplomacy. A particular weakness for ruminating on worldly success led him to construct the portrait of an envoy as gentleman and hence to distract attention from his central purpose. At times Callières follows the path which Wicquefort condemned in earlier writers and which is the bane of sixteenth-century books on 'the perfect ambassador'. In the event, however, a firm awareness of the distinctive character of diplomacy saved him for the history of international thought. The professional in him restrained the fashionable author. In return Callières salvaged the literature of diplomacy from pedantry.

In another sense too the author's ear for his own language may be relevant to a full understanding of his conception of diplomacy. In the second half of the seventeenth century French language and power reached their apogee together. The French Academy, which was officially charged with safeguarding the purity of the language, was also the highest school of state propaganda. Callières was implicated in both; he served the ambitions of a sovereign who demanded men of letters to attest his deeds, while also belonging to a body charged with policing standards of verbal expression. As an author he contributed to the latter by acting as a sort of watchdog of taste, while the 'gentleman' and businessman in him were alive to the element of conversation present in all forms of regular and polite bargaining. At the same time his political sense concerning the limitations of power led Callières to place special emphasis on the written and spoken word as vehicles for fostering agreement and formulating terms. In writing about the conduct of foreign affairs he was thus unusually placed to establish, in language well attuned to public affairs, the character of French diplomacy.

The Art of Diplomacy reveals a view of diplomacy as an essentially moderating influence. It may be summarised as follows: the pursuit of interests in relation to other states is taken to be compatible with civilized behaviour. Intelligence with respect to one's own interests and that of others must however inform the conduct of foreign policy. Without intelligence prudence is impossible, and in the absence of prudence men habitually come to rely on force. From another of his writings, Callières's conception of prudence can be seen to compose three 'principal functions'. [18] It is a combination of 'knowledge, foresight and dextrous action'. [19] Hence the management of external relations requires technical competence, mental energy and a reliable understanding of men and events. He insists that diplomacy is a necessary, unavoidable, activity essential to the well-being of a state and deserving of recognition as a separate profession. Perhaps this is a tactful swipe at the prestige attached to making war rather than maintaining peace. Besides the assertion that public service as an envoy is honourable, *The Art of Diplomacy* conveys the conviction that under circumstances that are always likely to be unstable, relations among a multiplicity of states can nevertheless be mediated by honest dealing and awareness of where the 'real' interests of rulers lie. The virtues of polished manners are at no time of more practical importance than when foreign affairs are problematical and haunted by the risks of war. For the same reasons, dignified conduct between sovereigns is considered to be conducive to orderly habits. The forms demanded in official aspects of diplomatic procedure possess a logic of their own, and, though open to abuse, the disciplines of an envoy's routine provide a measure of continuity in circumstances where order of a more substantial kind is frequently absent.

The benefits of professional diplomacy cannot however be imparted or absorbed in the abstract. Nor can they, to take the other extreme, be acquired by untutored exposure to events. The schooling of a diplomat is a lengthy affair. The essential principle is nevertheless easily grasped: to intelligence, character and temperament, of sorts demanded by the *métier*, must be added an instruction which stresses modern history and a noviciate which educates through example. Diplomacy involves the detailed appreciation of varied and unstable circumstances, and the kind of intelligence necessary is the ability to place particular events within their widest setting. By its nature, therefore, diplomacy cannot hope to elucidate or apply infallible precepts of action. Rationalism and empiricism are therefore equally defective guides. But although the exact configuration of events issuing from the enforced coexistence of numerous states is unpredictable, useful knowledge of the diplomatic system is for all that obtainable. The unexpected need not take the trained eye of the practised envoy by surprise because, in spite of appearances, an adept of foreign affairs is able to see how all events 'are connected in a single development'. Hence to bring to the 'art' of diplomacy only a common sense unfamiliar with the general predicament of states and the grain of individual conflicts, is a recipe for failure. In war and in peace, to wait upon events for instruction is to 'dream of acquiring arms when it is time to fight'.

Callières does not express his conception of diplomacy in the form of a system. That was not his method. Unmistakably he derives his themes, language and style, and above all his 'reading' of Europe's foreign affairs, from experience digested in thought. *The Art of Diplomacy* was the only book on that topic published by a French diplomat between 1603 and

1737, and Callières's standpoint is perhaps therefore indicative of a tradition that by the end of Louis XIV's long reign was approaching maturity. In a manner of speaking, *The Art of Diplomacy* is the French tradition of diplomatic thinking under the *ancien régime* become aware of itself.

The Precepts of Practice

Callières belongs to French history, where his attainments are curiously ignored. Yet from its subject *The Art of Diplomacy* also belongs to European thought. It is by his replies to questions arising from the elaboration of a diplomatic system of states that his essay has finally to be judged. Firmly and without commotion he redirects attention away from the ambassador as an officer of state and brings it to bear on the *activity* of diplomacy. This is a simple but telling adjustment of perspective from which Callières seldom departs. The move is one from exclusive focus on the actor to a view which brings the public stage of foreign affairs to the forefront. As a result his account of diplomacy is thoroughly – if not always systematically – political. Time and again he reiterates that no matter how absorbed states are with their individual interests, the rulers of Europe are bound together in so many ways that each depends on the others for the successful pursuit of its own interests. As with Machiavelli, Callières's view of the dilemmas of statecraft is notable partly for what it chooses to omit from lengthy discussion. According to *The Art of Diplomacy* it is the state of relations among Europe's principal political bodies, rather than their responsiveness to the constraints of natural or positive law, that constitutes the measure of order that exists. Beyond occasional references to the protection afforded to envoys, there is little emphasis on the *droit des gens*. In this Callières stands in contrast to juristic literature and also to Wicquefort, part of whose interest was to establish international law on the basis of the diplomatic practice of states.

Callières's political point of view is made clear in other ways. Domestically the 'authority of the state' may vary in practice and by design, but in principle the phrase is a tautology. Other authors, at whose head stands Machiavelli, had commented on the ways in which foreign affairs impinged on the *powers* of states, but Callières is to be particularly credited with the observation that Machiavelli does not make: that a plurality of states condemned to coexistence of some kind, and where none has *authority* to direct the affairs of others, constitutes a unique and restricted setting. Grotius had done no more than sense this. In keeping with his concern to assert the legal community of mankind, his 'great society of states' is neither geographically nor historically specific. More importantly, it is a moral rather than a political or diplomatic conception. In comparison *The Art of Diplomacy* is a testament to the persistence of Europe as a 'Commonwealth' ('*une même république*') in spite of being composed of self-assertive states. It is what these previous components of the *respublica christiana* continue to have in common that makes their external relations capable of order and adjustment by civilized means. The independence demanded by states does however ensure that they are surrounded by uncertainties posed by their neighbours. This fact stimulates men's ambitions in ways that both Callières and Wicquefort recognized and Machiavelli had accurately analysed. To the 'constitutional' uncertainties implicit in a diplomatic system one has therefore to add a wilful element of mutual rivalry. Hence insecurity is no accidental feature of transitory disagreements, much less the product of misunderstandings which better communications, more information and moral exhortation can once and for all resolve. The addition of better techniques of diplomacy thus offers no final release from a want of security endemic among states. The importance Callières attaches to trustworthiness in diplomats, and of honest dealings among sovereigns, is a recognition not only of how fraught relations are in their absence, but of how problematic diplomacy remains even when states do trust each other. Small wonder that one of his favourite metaphors to describe a setting where 'there are no foolproof rules' adopts the image of the diplomat as a pilot 'in a sea always rough'. Hence in ungovernable waters, 'one has to navigate according to the wind'.

Confidence between states is a scarce commodity in whose absence the prospects of order in foreign affairs remain flimsy. Systematic distrust, in the sense, for example, of failure to believe in *pacta sunt servanda* (the principle that treaties are binding on the parties to them) would condemn all states to mutual incoherence. Even war would lose its rationale as an instrument of policy. In a literal sense trust has therefore to be created, above all by resident envoys able to empathise with the interests and understand the follies of other rulers. Yet the reasons which explain the scarcity of trust also demonstrate why it is so difficult to sustain, even among allies. Once again *The Art of Diplomacy* points to the difficulties of maintaining civilized relations with other states even when all are agreed on their necessity if war is to be confined. Reliance on force may be costly and risky, and calculated to inflame rather than appease, but one of its attractions is that it gives full vent to men's passions. Perhaps the 'diplomatic' expression of this viewpoint is enough to explain why *The Art of Diplomacy* was published only after the death of Louis XIV. Only on his deathbed did the Sun King admit that he had 'loved war too much'.

The character of Europe's diplomatic system made itself felt in every department of diplomatic effort. Even the representational side of foreign affairs can be traced to, and justified by, the demands of a civilized understanding of how best to promote a country's interests. A diplomat has to 'bear the person' of his sovereign before he can claim to act on his behalf. An envoy's performance as a 'comedian', with which Wicquefort makes such play, is misunderstood by actors and audience alike through lack of knowledge of the *milieu* in which they are obliged to operate. The same applies to seeing why such importance is attached to the 'mechanism' of diplomacy as the source of political information. As with confidence, moderation, and dignified behaviour, intelligence is important just because it is usually in scarce supply. States have no authority to demand information from their opposites, and in consequence are obliged to rely on the loyalty and competence of their diplomatic agents to acquire it. Unable to command the news of other states they need, or do without it altogether without forfeiting their interests, resident diplomacy once again stands out as a general imperative in which all states reciprocate.

Wicquefort makes great play with the notion that diplomats are 'honourable spies', and the phrase reappears in *The Art of Diplomacy*. The difference in their treatment is that, by dwelling on the predicament that gives rise to the need for diplomacy, Callières's discussion contains an explanation of why states are willing to tolerate 'honourable spies' within their sovereign territories, and to license their intelligence gathering activities. Where so many of his predecessors in the *genre* were jurists who treated the issue of territoriality solely as a legal issue, Callières's assumptions are refreshingly different and, more to the point, instructive. He naturally condemns the exploitation of the *droit de franchise* which caused celebrated scandals in seventeenth-century Rome, and briefly mentions the *droit des gens* as the customary rules in terms of which envoys enjoy the protection of immunities and privileged liberties. It was the least he could do. Considerations of this kind are however of secondary interest to his account. He makes clear that the true basis for the immunities of envoys is necessity of state. Once a sovereign takes it upon himself to punish the excesses of another's agents, his actions threaten an institution in which he, along with other rulers, has a vital stake. Where diplomats fear their conduct in countries to which they are sent may expose them to personal dangers, their efficiency and reliability is likely to be cramped.

Europe as a Diplomatic System

Historical knowledge and experience of public affairs were not enough to produce a view of seventeenth-century Europe's warring states as nevertheless constituting a 'Commonwealth'. Some imaginative force was also needed to see beyond the variety and inequality of states and beyond their incessant conflicts, to the perception that Europe persisted as a unity of sorts – as a diplomatic system and not a mere anarchy. Callières's achievement should not be underestimated by the supposition that at the close of the century his formulation of diplomacy was already established comment. It was not. Some thirty titles dealing with the ambassador have been listed for the period between 1681, when Wicquefort's major treatise was first published, and 1700. [20] Of these, all but Carlos Maria Carafa's *El Embaxador politico-christiano* appeared in Latin. [21] Most would seem to lack the kind of politically attuned insight which is the hallmark of *The Art of Diplomacy*. [22]

Perhaps of greater relevance than the writings of long-forgotten German lawyers are French writers who, despite personal experience of foreign affairs, failed to share the progress of understanding embodied in Callières's essay. In 1697 a minor French diplomat who had served in Stockholm and later represented Louis XIV at the German diet at Ratisbon, wrote a pamphlet with the title *L'Idée du parfait Ambassadeur*. [23] Designed for the instruction of a general about to be sent as ambassador to London, Chamoy's tract is in many ways an interesting document. It was not intended for publication and is therefore perhaps more nearly a manual for the guidance of a practitioner than either Wicquefort's encyclopaedic treatment or Callières's exercise in political literature. Chamoy cites no examples and is wholly concerned with describing the administrative machinery of diplomacy, which he assumes is definite enough to allow precise and systematic exposition. His profile breathes the spirit of professionalism that had taken root among Louis XIV's hard pressed envoys. Some of his comments, such as the importance attached to the secretary in a well-ordered embassy are of considerable interest. In France, one might recall, secretaries were still chosen by the ambassador rather than, as had been the case in Venice for hundreds of years, appointed and maintained by the state. Nevertheless, from the standpoint of diplomatic theory Chamoy's manual has little to offer. Following Wicquefort, he says only that ambassadors are necessary as intermediaries between sovereigns who cannot conduct their external affairs in person. [24]

Twenty years after the appearance of *The Art of Diplomacy* Antoine Pecquet, an official with long experience of foreign affairs, published his *Discours sur l'Art de Négocier*. [25] Pecquet was familiar with Callières's work and his choice of title suggests that he might have absorbed his predecessor's advance towards a fuller conception of diplomacy. This is not the case. Pecquet dissolves the particular character of negotiations between states in the wider argument that all social life is a matter of bargaining. Whatever the force of this truism it does nothing to determine the specific character of diplomacy. Pecquet also criticizes Callières for not having dwelt longer on the personal qualities needed in an envoy. Pecquet's conception of 'the perfect ambassador' is hardly to be distinguished from sanctity, and marks in this, as in other respects, a relapse in the literature on diplomacy. His manual is however saved by a single important insight, which, though hinted at in both Wicquefort [26] and Callières, [27] he was the first to make plain. He expressly draws attention to the manner in which diplomats throughout Europe maintained among themselves a sense of cultural but also professional solidarity.

> The body of envoys in a particular country form among themselves a sort of independent society. They live closely together and treat each other politely and with honesty even when their sovereign masters are at war. Led by different interests and often opposed, envoys nevertheless share a common objective which is to know the country to which they are assigned and promote the viewpoints they are charged with. They are at the same time bound together by a community of privileges, whose loss by one of their number becomes a cause of complaint by all. Sovereigns are all damaged when the representatives of one are threatened, even when the rulers they serve are at loggerheads. [28]

This forthright testament to the existence of a *corps diplomatique* marks a stage in the elaboration of the European system of states, later but no less important than the development of the *esprit de corps* already to be found among officers serving in different armies. The community of ambassadors resident at a court or assembled in congress, was both a miniature and an embodiment of the diplomatic society of Europe's rulers. It is one of Europe's more lasting legacies to a universal diplomatic system incorporating states with markedly different cultures, in which, of course, the states of Europe have long since ceased to have pride of place.

Chamoy, Pecquet, and the assemblage of ideas to be found in the short-lived experiment of the Political Academy – which is perhaps the first 'school for ambassadors' [29] – all confirm the increasing importance attached in official quarters to cultivating more professional standards in diplomacy. Only Callières's essay, which does not however appear to have received official sponsorship or to have enjoyed special credit in the royal administration, is of lasting value to the history of diplomatic thought.

Callières's conception of a uniquely constituted association of unequal states does not envisage alternative arrangements. Nowhere does *The Art of Diplomacy* bring into the reckoning schemes of radical reform which abounded in the early years of eighteenth-century Europe. [30] Callières left no comment on the schemes of his fellow Academician the abbé de Saint-Pierre whose *Projet de Paix Perpetuelle* was first published in 1713. He was not sympathetic to the belief that a transformation of Europe's diplomatic regime was necessary and he therefore does not bother to enquire whether it was possible. In his view European states already composed an order. War and endemic insecurity could be finally overcome only by suppressing the independence of states – an aim which he maintained the Habsburgs had not altogether abandoned and which many attributed to Louis XIV. The spectre of Charles V haunts *The Art of Diplomacy* without any direct hint that the Emperor was intended to serve as a code for His Most Christian Majesty. Callières is averse to the prospect of 'universal monarchy' whatever its provenance. All his reasoning derives from the belief that a more administratively cogent and intelligent cadre of diplomats could improve the existing order. These proposals may appear modest to the point of serving as a justification of the *status quo*, from which of course France benefited so long as royal ambitions were kept in check. Intellectually his sticking point was the assumption, (perhaps nowhere made explicit but manifest in all he wrote) that conflicts of interest between states could not, and perhaps should not, be terminated. Adroit diplomacy might mitigate clashes of interest but should not aim to dissolve the dilemmas upon which the precarious independence of armed states ultimately rests.

Placed on the stage with the likes of Machiavelli, Callières would have found much to admire in the Florentine diplomat's stress on the mutability of events though he explicitly parts company with him over the matter of deceit. *The Art of Diplomacy* is critical of lying and double-dealing because even where it brings short-term rewards, undermining trust between states sooner than later makes it more difficult to promote a country's interests. Whereas Machiavelli relies on the *virtù* of rulers to overcome the waywardness of events, Callières, with perhaps a surer sense of the connectedness of even the most determinedly independent states, advocated the generation of confidence as the highest achievement of diplomacy. In another direction, Callières lived too close to foreign affairs to find credible the idea of Grotius that laws serving the interests of states were at the same time capable of restraining their actions. While no doubt in sympathy with the Dutchman's appeal for moderation in the conduct of peace and war, he must have found the assertion of a 'great society of states' too general and imprecise, and above all too dismissive of the wilfulness of Europe's states, to look to its elevated ideas as precepts capable of directing the actions of their rulers.

Power Politics and Civilized Behaviour

The Art of Diplomacy is a valuable work. It is surely not, as Nicolson would have it, 'a great book'. Its author was not an incisive thinker or wholly consistent. Many of the ideas on which he draws are uncritically deployed and stunted in growth. Callières does not, for example, make clear in what sense the notion of 'interest' is to be taken. It never quite becomes the principle of *raison d'état*. An undoubted belief in an equilibrium of power distributed among a plurality of states fails to break surface and become an exposition of the balance of power. In view of the Anglo-Spanish treaty of 1713, which for the first time declared the securing of peace through the balance of power as one of its purposes, this absence is perhaps noteworthy. [31] His views on the morality of a diplomat's calling and conduct are similarly shallow to the point of banality. Perhaps most serious of all is the refusal to relate his belief in the fecundity of diplomacy to any systematic discussion of the prevalence of war. He at no time considers the issue raised half a century later by Frederick the Great when the latter observed that diplomacy without armed force is like trying to play music without instruments. Tantalizingly, ideas of great interest lie just beneath the surface of *The Art of Diplomacy*. One catches only a glimpse of the presiding role he attributes to great powers and of the limitations to which they are nonetheless subject. He notices only in passing that small states are not thereby virtuous and frequently play havoc with relations between their stronger neighbours. Whether intentionally or by default, a literary complaisance hampers the full development of much of Callières's account of diplomacy. Even so, it is among the best we have.

Some years after the Congress of Westphalia Samuel Puffendorf described the Holy Roman or German Empire as 'several states that are so connected as to seem to constitute one body but whose members retain sovereignty'. [32] This has often been taken as a good description of the entire diplomatic system of the *ancien régime* of Europe. Two years before the outbreak of the French Revolution, Edmund Burke wrote about Europe's 'civil, diplomatique, and mercantile affairs'. [33] In doing so he helped the verbal identification of a distinct public activity that until then had usually been referred to as 'negotiating' or what ambassadors and envoys did. When a few years later the same author inveighed against the 'double diplomacy' [34] of revolutionary France, the 'honourable spies' who for generations had come to regard their 'art of negotiating' as worthy of professional recognition, were at last released from the vague company of 'public ministers' and 'negotiators'. The right word had finally been coined to capture a long-practised activity.

Writing between the end of the Thirty Years War and the Wars of the French Revolution, François de Callières's achievement was to provide the discussion of diplomacy with a focus of political interest, around which its precepts and practices could acquire fuller coherence. In *The Art of Diplomacy*, diplomacy emerges as a principle and institution of order. Perhaps it took a Frenchman of the *grand siècle*, steeped in the foreign affairs of Europe, to express a view of his art in which power politics and civilized behaviour are conceived in unison.

Notes

1. In the same year an anonymous translation appeared in English and this was used in the critical edition *François de Callières. The Art of Diplomacy*, ed. H. M. A. Keens-Soper and Karl W. Schweizer (Leicester, 1983). In 1994 this was reprinted in paperback by the University Press of America. All references are to the 1983 edition, hereafter *The Art of Diplomacy*.
2. *The Art of Diplomacy*, pp. 3–18.
3. This essay is a revised version of my 'François de Callières and diplomatic theory', *The Historical Journal*, XVI, 3 (1973), pp. 485–508.
4. François de Callières, *The Practice of Diplomacy*, with an Introduction by A. F. Whyte (London, 1919).
5. Harold Nicolson, *The Evolution of Diplomatic Method* (London, 1954) p. 62.
6. For example, Gordon Craig, 'On the nature of diplomatic history – the relevance of some old books', in P. G. Lauren (ed.), *Diplomacy: New Approaches in History, Theory, and Policy* (New York and London, 1979), pp. 22–8.
7. Still the most accessible as well as scholarly account is Garrett Mattingly, *Renaissance Diplomacy* (London, 1965).
8. *Renaissance Diplomacy*, p. 108.
9. For a fuller discussion, see my essay 'The practice of a states-system' in Michael Donelan (ed.), *The Reason of States* (London, 1978).
10. First published 1681; trans. into English by John Digby in 1716; reprinted by the Centre for the Study of Diplomacy, University of Leicester, Leicester, UK, 1997.

11. *The Art of Diplomacy*, p. 68.
12. *The Art of Diplomacy*, pp. 91–2.
13. Quoted by Keens-Soper and Schweizer in *The Art of Diplomacy*, pp. 30–1.
14. *The Art of Diplomacy*, p. 31.
15. *The Art of Diplomacy*, p. 57.
16. Vladimir E. Grabar, *De Legatis et Legationibus Tractatus Varii* (Dorpat, 1905), pp. 229–304.
17. On Rosier's *Ambaxiator Brevilogus* (Short Treatise about Ambassadors), see Mattingly, *Renaissance Diplomacy*, pp. 26–7.
18. François de Callières, *De la Science du Monde* (Paris, 1717), p. 204.
19. Ibid.
20. Grabar, *De Legatis et Legationibus Tractatus Varii*, pp. 303–4.
21. Ibid.
22. I have been unable to consult all the treatises, many of which are to be found only in Rome and other continental centres. Grabar produces abstracts of many of the documents as well as full references.
23. Rousseau de Chamoy, Louis, *L'Idée du parfait Ambassadeur*, ed. L. Delavand (Paris, 1912).
24. Ibid., p. 11.
25. (Paris, 1737).
26. *The Embassador and His Functions*, ch. 21.
27. *The Art of Diplomacy*, p.182.
28. *Discours sur l'Art de Négocier*, p.134. Of course, Pecquet excluded from the general body of Europe's diplomats those employed from time to time by the Ottoman Empire – none of whom, in any case, became residents for another 50 years. However, it is an interesting possibility that the very gap between the Ottoman world and European diplomacy which contributed to this ostracism may have in some small measure fostered the emergence of the *corps diplomatique* by forcing those of its members posted in Istanbul to close ranks on matters of common professional interest to an unusual degree.
29. H. M. A. Keens-Soper, 'The French Political Academy, 1712: a School for Ambassadors', *European Studies Review*, vol. 11, no. 4. (Oct. 1972).
30. E. V. Souleyman, *The Vision of Peace in Seventeenth and Eighteenth Century France* (Columbia, 1942); F. H. Hinsley, *Power and the Pursuit of Peace* (London, 1963), ch. 11.
31. M. S. Anderson, 'Eighteenth-century theories of the balance of power', in Ragnhild Hatton and M. S. Anderson (eds), *Studies in Diplomatic History: Essays in Memory of David Bayne Horn* (Harlow, 1970), pp. 183–98.
32. *De jure naturae et gentium libri octo*, trans. J. Simmons (Washington, 1934), pp. 22, 1043.
33. *The Annual Register*, 1787, p.1.
34. Edmund Burke, *Letters on a Regicide Peace* (Oxford, 1907), vol. VI.

Further reading

Callières, François de, *The Art of Diplomacy*, ed. H. M. A. Keens-Soper and Karl W. Schweizer (Leicester, 1983). In 1994 the University Press of America published a paperback of this critical edition.

Historical background

Anderson, M. S., *The Rise of Modern Diplomacy* (London, 1993), especially chs 1 and 2. This includes a lengthy bibliography.

Baillou, J. (ed.), *Les Affaires Étrangères et le Corps Diplomatique Français*, 2 vols (Paris, 1984).

Hamilton, Keith and Richard Langhorne, *The Practice of Diplomacy* (London and New York, 1995), ch. 3.

Hatton, Ragnhild (ed.), *Louis XIV and Europe* (London, 1976), especially chs 1 and 11.

Mattingly, Garrett, *Renaissance Diplomacy* (Harmondsworth, 1965).

The New Cambridge Modern History, vol. 5, ch. 9; vol. 6, ch. 5 (esp. p. 168ff).

Sonnino, Paul (ed.), *The Reign of Louis XIV* (New Jersey and London, 1990), ch. 9.

Picavet, C.-G., *La Diplomatie française au temps de Louis XIV (1661–1715)* (Paris, 1930).

Roosen, W. J., *The Age of Louis XIV: the Rise of Modern Diplomacy* (Cambridge, Mass., 1976).

Rule, John C. (ed.), *Louis XIV and the Craft of Kingship* (Columbus, Ohio, 1969), especially chs by Rule and Hatton.

Biography

Kertesz, Stephen D., Introduction to *On the Manner of Negotiating with Princes*, by François de Callières, trans. by A. F. Whyte (New York, 1963).

Schweizer, Karl W., *François de Callières: Diplomat and Man of Letters, 1645–1717* (Mellen, Canada, 1995).

Schweizer, Karl W., Introduction to *The Art of Diplomacy* (see head of 'Further reading').

General

Bull, Hedley, *The Anarchical Society: a Study of Order in World Politics* (London, 1977), ch. 7.

Butterfield, Herbert, *Christianity, Diplomacy and War* (London, 1953), chs 6–8.

Forsyth, M. G., H. M. A. Keens-Soper and Peter Savigear (eds), *The Theory of International Relations: Selected Texts from Gentili to Treitschke* (London, 1970).

Gilbert, F., 'The new diplomacy of the eighteenth century', *World Politics*, vol. 6 (1951), pp. 1–38.

Keens-Soper, H. M. A., 'François de Callières and diplomatic theory', *Historical Journal*, vol. 16, no. 3 (1973), pp. 485–508.

Keens-Soper, H. M. A., 'The French Political Academy, 1712: A School for Ambassadors', *European Studies Review*, vol. 11, no. 4 (Oct. 1972), pp 329–55.

Keens-Soper, H. M. A., 'The practice of a states-system', in Michael Donelan (ed.), *The Reason of States* (London, 1978).

Nicolson, H., *The Evolution of Diplomatic Method* (London, 1954), chs 3 and 4.

Schmidt, J. D., 'The establishment of "Europe" as a political expression', *Historical Journal*, vol. 9, no. 2 (1966), pp 172–8.

7
Satow
T. G. Otte

'mentis subtilitate curiosa sicco lumine ingenii praestitit.' [1]

'Tradition', Gustav Mahler is reported to have remarked, 'is *Schlamperei*'. Whatever the validity of this remark in matters of music, in the often cacophonous political life tradition is certainly a factor to be reckoned with; none more so than in diplomacy. Indeed, reflecting on the nature of diplomacy, Harold Nicolson identified several markedly different national traditions of European diplomacy. Of the British version he observed that its representatives abroad

> display little initiative, take no pains to impress others with their intellectual brilliance, and are to all appearance unimaginative, uninformative, lethargic and slow. On the other hand . . . the British diplomatist is exceptionally well informed, manages to acquire and to retain the confidence of foreign governments, is imperturbable in times of crisis, and almost always succeeds. [2]

What Nicolson omitted in this impressive list is the one strand of British diplomatic tradition of which he himself was a prominent representative: its literary tradition. In this, British diplomacy is probably unrivalled.

Unlike old elephants, British diplomats rarely simply withdraw from the herd to die a solitary death on their retirement. Instead they turn to what they were trained to do: writing. Many write their memoirs. These form by far the largest section of the literary outpouring of retired diplomatists. [3] Since the mid-nineteenth century each new generation of former diplomats has contributed to it. Perhaps one of the most exceptional representatives of the literary tradition of British diplomacy was Sir Ernest Satow. His literary *oeuvre* encompassed his own memoirs, historical, cultural and philological studies, as well as writings on the nature of diplomacy and diverse questions of international law. [4] Satow was by any standards an outstanding figure in the diplomatic service of his time. Of partly Swedish and north German extraction, he was born into a Nonconformist family in 1843. [5] Mill Hill School and University College London completed his strictly puritanical, Lutheran education, though the latter institution widened his outlook. Satow's professional career began in 1861, when the excellent linguist won the first place in a Foreign Office competition for student interpreterships in China and Japan. [6] At his own wish he was assigned to the Japanese consular service. Laurence Oliphant's *Narrative of the Earl of Elgin's Mission to China and Japan* had kindled his lifelong fascination with Japan and East Asia; an account of Commodore Matthew Perry's expedition deepened it. [7] Later Satow was claimed to have been Britain's greatest ever Japanophile. Indeed, his most important commitment to Japan, albeit one shrouded in the strictest and long-kept secrecy, was to start a family with a Japanese 'common-law wife', with whom he had two sons. [8] Undoubtedly, Satow was one of the best informed British diplomats in the East. [9] His old friend and colleague at the Tokyo legation, Lord Redesdale, later paid tribute to his academic and diplomatic skills:

> [Sir Harry] Parkes [, the British minister in the 1860s,] had at his elbow a man of extraordinary ability in the person of Mr. Satow. He it was who swept away all the cobwebs of the old Dutch diplomacy, and by an accurate study of Japanese history and of Japanese customs and traditions, realized and gave true value to the position of the Shogun ... Nor was this all. His really intimate knowledge of the language, combined with great tact and transparent honesty, had enabled him to establish friendly relations with most of the leading men in the country; thus, young as he was, achieving a position which was of incalculable advantage to his chief. [10]

The 1860s were exciting times for the young Satow. He arrived in Japan at a crucial turning point in the country's history. The process of the opening of Japan to the West had only just begun. But these years were also dangerous ones for foreigners. More than once, Satow himself narrowly escaped attacks by the dreaded Japanese swordsmen. He rendered his own account of this period in his memoirs, *A Diplomat in Japan*, and in his earlier contribution to the *Cambridge Modern History*. [11]

The 1870s were the decade when Satow acquired the reputation of an outstanding Japanese scholar and noted Orientalist with a series of studies on different aspects of Japanese and south east Asian culture, history and philology. Among his contemporaries, his knowledge of Japanese was 'practically unrivalled'. [12] Indeed, he has been called 'one of the Founding Fathers of modern Japanology'. [13]

Throughout his career, which also took him to Bangkok, Montevideo, Tangier, and finally, as minister plenipotentiary, back to Tokyo and Peking, Satow maintained his scholarly interests. These were by no means confined to Asian affairs. In 1876, he spent his home leave attending lectures on the history of Roman law at the University of Marburg in Germany; in 1883, again on home leave, he passed a law examination in London; and three years later, he qualified as a barrister-at-law. Satow's other interests were in matters of Christianity, European history and literature, and questions of international law. [14] Above all, Satow was an exceptional linguist. At one stage or another of his career, he had studied Latin, Greek, German, Dutch, French, Japanese, Mandarin Chinese, Spanish, Korean, Italian, Portuguese, Manchu, Siamese, and Russian. [15] His diaries are sprinkled with foreign expressions and literary quotations. Recording, for example, his first meeting with his retirement friend, the historian Harold Temperley, he noted that 'history [was] his *Fach* [i.e.his subject].' [16] He also had a fine understanding of music and the arts. [17]

The catholicity of his interests, his erudition and learning, as well as his diplomatic tact and skill did not fail to impress Satow's contemporaries. Baron d'Anethan, his Belgian colleague at Tokyo, described him as 'a tall, slight, rather careworn-looking man, with an intellectual face and the stoop of a student'. [18] Sir Eyre Crowe, a Foreign Office official who accompanied Satow to the second peace conference at The Hague in 1907, was distinctly less impressed, though he acknowledged the former's scholarliness. In the course of the conference proceedings Crowe confessed to having

> completely given up Satow. I can only suggest that his mind has become completely Chinese so soon as it is taken off books and studies and gardens and flowers, on all of which subjects he is a delight to talk to. But when it comes to understanding the laws of contraband or the rights and duties of neutrals and such like dry matters of business, the twist in his mind is such that no one can understand him. [19]

The Guide: Satow and Diplomatic Practice

Crowe's remarks were somewhat unfair to Satow, the man, but certainly
to Satow, the scholar of diplomacy. The latter is now mostly associated
with the title of his most famous work, the *Guide to Diplomatic Practice*. [20]
The *Guide*, often simply referred to as 'Satow', acquired for its author the
reputation as the leading English language authority on the practice and
theory of diplomacy. When first published in 1917, the *Guide* received
wide and immediate acclaim. [21] Eighty years later, and by now in its fifth
and much revised edition, the *Guide* is still regarded as one of the classic
expositions of diplomacy.

Satow's most famous work owed much of its enduring success to the
absence of comparable literature on the subject in English at the time of
its first appearance. It is true there were smaller works by Montague
Bernard, Spencer Walpole and J. W. Foster as well as Hill's monumental
history of European diplomacy. [22] But in nineteenth-century English
language literature there was nothing comparable in scale or erudition
to Charles de Martens' *Guide Diplomatique*, the Comte de Garden's *Traité
Complet de diplomatie*, Pradier-Fodéré's *Droit Diplomatique*, or Alt's *Europäisches Gesandtschafts-Recht*, to name but a few of the standard works of
contemporary diplomatic literature. [23]

In writing the *Guide* Satow intended 'to produce a work which would
be of service alike to the international lawyer, the diplomatist, and the
student of history'. [24] In consequence, he placed special emphasis on the
practical and international law aspects of diplomacy; similarly, he treated in some detail the different kinds of international compacts. The
manner of conducting international conferences and congresses is also
analysed at great length; as is the framing of treaties and other legal
instruments. The practical merits of his work were indeed of particular
concern to Satow. He had always intended it to be a 'manual of diplomacy, a monograph on the position, rights and duties of the diplomatic
envoy', a 'Diplomatist's Guide' or a 'Handbook of Diplomatic Practice'. [25]
So imbued was he with his desire to impart practical advice to budding
diplomats that he originally planned the book as something resembling
a guided tour through diplomacy. In the first draft of his manuscript the
chapters were laid out in accordance with the normal pattern of a diplomatic mission, starting with the presentation of credentials and, having
traversed the whole range of diplomatic activity, ending with the termination of the mission. [26] When finishing the manuscript of the *Guide* in
July 1916, Satow was also hopeful that the work would 'prove a useful
work of reference' for the peace conference after the war. [27]

Still, neither the *Guide* nor indeed Satow's complete diplomatic *oeuvre* are exclusively concerned with the mechanics of diplomacy. His erudition, though conspicuous and profound, did not convert him into a 'dry-as-dust' peddler of diplomatic *minutiae*. Above all, Satow was not the 'invariably discreet' and over-cautious authority on the form rather than the substance of diplomacy, as has often been suggested. [28] The *Guide*, when read carefully and in conjunction with his other writings, offers valuable insights into the evolution of European diplomatic traditions, the nature of international politics and the importance of diplomacy as an instrument of statecraft.

Diplomatic Theory and the Reality of International Politics

The essential presupposition which underlies all of Satow's writings is that international politics is based on the principle of the independence and sovereignty of states. In this he followed closely the precepts of François de Callières's *De la Manière de Négocier*. Satow had discovered Callières rather late in life, but he valued his small treatise on diplomatic negotiations as 'a mine of political wisdom'. [29]

Diplomacy, in Satow's famous and often quoted definition, 'is the application of intelligence and tact to the conduct of official relations between the governments of independent states'. [30] A number of inferences can be drawn from this statement. The independent states which maintain mutual relations, Satow contended, are part of a 'society' of 'civilized nations'. They are, therefore, on a footing of equality, their relations being regulated by the rules of International Law. [31] It is adherence to the principles of International Law which distinguishes the 'civilized nations' from the uncivilized ones. [32] Diplomacy is thus the civilized pursuit of state interests; as such it is a moderating influence. Like all 'public policy [it is] directed to the defence of the national welfare'. [33] By implication, it is an inevitable aspect of modern statehood; it is a precondition as well as the principal consequence of state sovereignty. The practice of diplomacy therefore deserves special attention and recognition. In this respect Satow's views on the evolution and nature of international diplomacy were strongly Eurocentric, his Far Eastern experience notwithstanding. But Japan and China, of course, had not contributed to the evolution of diplomatic methods as established by the nineteenth century. Both had been new- or indeed late-comers to the world of international diplomacy; and their eventual adoption of established diplomatic procedures had been a slow and often difficult process, as Satow himself witnessed, sometimes at great personal danger. [34]

Though he devoted some of his writings to specific aspects of International Law, Satow remained sceptical about the universal applicability of the rule of law to international politics. '[T]he rulings of jurists', he quoted Palmerston approvingly, 'prove facts of law but have no value whatever in relation to policy.'[35] He insisted that 'diplomats are not lawyers'.[36] Sovereign states are equal in theory but not in practice. Satow repeatedly elaborated on this dichotomy between the theory and reality of modern European diplomacy:

[T]he theory of the political equality of independent States...is recognized by the Doctrine of International Law. It is not derived from equality of extent, population, wealth, military or naval power, or any other feature in which States differ among themselves. It is a consequence of their independent sovereign character.... But in actual practice a distinction cannot but exist between Great Powers and secondary and minor Powers, as regards the weight to be attached to their expression of will.[37]

The fundamental premise of Satow's conception of the international society of civilized nations is that it is an ordered or 'hierarchical society'. All independent states are equal in terms of International Law, but:

[i]n practice...it has been found convenient, as far as the affairs of Europe are concerned, for the Great Powers to form a kind of committee which assumes to direct the more important international affairs of that continent. Their authority rests upon their predominant military and naval strength, which might conceivably be called into action against any minor State that refused to bow to the decision of the Concert of Europe.[38]

Satow's conception of international politics was remarkably modern. Although the idea of a 'hierarchical society' remained implicit, Satow's writings anticipated the so-called Grotian school of thought in international relations theory.[39] Hugo Grotius and his work, indeed, were fixed points of reference for Satow; and he repeatedly acknowledged his intellectual debt to that great Dutchman.[40] His views on international politics mirrored his general political convictions. Satow was a firm believer in the virtues of a moderate, Westminster-style parliamentary monarchy, which he regarded as the best guarantee of individual liberties. Republics he suspected of tending to degenerate into dictatorships.[41]

Diplomatic Practice and the Importance of History

The underlying approach of Satow's work is descriptive and analytical. He had little interest in quasi-Cartesian, logically deduced systems of politics.[42] His preferred method in dealing with matters related to diplomacy was essentially an historical one.[43] He shared this taste for history with previous writers on diplomacy such as Wicquefort or Callières.[44] As a trained lawyer and experienced diplomatist, however, he was not interested in the past for itself. He viewed diplomacy as a highly specialized activity, subject only to its own rules and precepts. Whilst diplomatic manners and techniques may change with time, the essence of sound diplomacy does not. The history of European diplomacy after the Peace of Westphalia provided Satow with illustrations of the fundamental elements of the relations between states. Satow turned to history in the search for precedents for diplomatic rules and procedures; for illumination of the basic problems of statecraft; and for guidelines for sound diplomacy. It should also be noted in this context that Satow's *Guide* and his only other full-length monograph were intended for publication in the same series, Oppenheim's *Contributions to International Law and Diplomacy*. The latter book, under the provisional title *The Silesian Loan: A Chapter of Diplomatic History*, was planned as the first volume in this series, to be followed by the *Guide*.[45] War-time paper shortage prevented the plan from being carried out, so that only the *Guide* was published in Oppenheim's series.[46] Satow was above all a pragmatic historian, more interested in practical conclusions concerning the conduct of diplomacy than in the academic study of the past:

> If, in the interest of historical knowledge, it is desirable that the inner secrets of diplomacy should be unveiled, prudence would suggest a measure of delay, at least until the political events related have become so completely a portion of the past that no harm can result from the facts being disclosed.[47]

On the basis of such convictions Satow rejected specialist historical literature as 'invented in the laboratory'. He preferred historical narratives in the tradition of Lord Macaulay; for only such general histories could provide instructive examples of the workings of the modern states system.[48] The concluding paragraph of Satow's 1908 *Rede Lecture* renders eloquent testimony to his pragmatic and utilitarian understanding of history:

The study of history... is an endeavour to trace the causes and ante-
cedents of the political events in the past, with the object of forecast-
ing the future – near or remote – in short, it may be regarded as
resembling the science of meteorology. If it does not teach us what
are the signs of bad [political] weather, it is difficult to see in what its
practical utility consists. [49]

For Satow history was the school of prudent diplomacy and farsighted
statecraft. [50] But knowledge of the past, though useful as an illumination
of the structure and techniques of international politics, is only one
indispensable factor of successful diplomacy. Diplomacy is not a
mechanical activity; it cannot be reduced to a mathematical equation.
Diplomacy, in the definition of the *Guide*, is 'the application of intelligence and tact to the conduct of [international] relations'; it is 'the
manner of carrying on international relations, not by the use of force,
but by discussion and agreement'. [51] Diplomacy, to be successful, therefore requires a modicum of prudence and judgement. As a professional
diplomat, Satow was scornful of 'amateur' diplomacy; and he distrusted
the assumed 'innate genius' of the dilettante diplomatist. '[W]ithout
diligently acquired knowledge and practical experience of the art', no
successful diplomacy is possible. [52]

Sense and Sensitivity: The Ideal Diplomatist

Knowledge, general precepts and practical advice, of course, can be
imparted to diplomatic novices; but they are no substitute for the
other essential qualities of a diplomat. These cannot be imparted, nor
can they be learned or acquired simply by exposure to diplomacy in
action. The education of young diplomats is a lengthy affair. Satow had
very definite views on these necessary qualities. But he was also well
aware of the general misconception of the diplomat's role:

Since Sir Henry Wotton perpetrated for the amusement of his Augsburg friend the well known witticism which is popularly believed to
describe the conduct characteristic of international agents, [53] the
general view has been that the weapons of the diplomatist are con-
cealment, artifice, evasion, and systematic falsehood. [54]

Though, needless to say, Satow refuted such popular views, he did not
offer his own, positive definition of a diplomat's essential qualities. The
Guide follows largely Callières's counsel to diplomatists. In Satow's view,

the observations of this seventeenth-century Frenchman had still much to commend them to notice. To a firm character, civil manners and a patient and well-tempered disposition must be added a subtle and perceptive mind. [55] What is required is a highly trained and highly sensitive political intelligence. The function of diplomats abroad

> is chiefly to watch over the execution of treaties, to make representations on behalf of their countrymen who complain of injustice, and to smooth over difficulties and adjust disputes arising between the Governments to which they are accredited and the Government which appoints them. [56]

In the *Guide* Satow gave a further, more specific description of the diplomat's role:

> The duty of the diplomatic agent is to watch over the maintenance of good relations, to protect the interests of his countrymen, and to report to his government on all matters of real importance, without being always charged with the conduct of a specific negotiation. At the more important posts, the agent is assisted in furnishing reports of a special character by military, naval and commercial attachés. [57]

Diplomacy is an ongoing process; it is characterized by complex and intangible, yet inherently unstable and continuously changing circumstances. A diplomatist, therefore, needs to possess the capacity to appreciate a developing situation; to distinguish the essential from the ephemeral; and to identify potential threats to the interests of the government he represents. [58] Diplomatic intelligence entails the constant reassessment of events and developments with a view to these interests, based on the accurate gathering and relaying of relevant information. Satow identified a pentad of qualities which, together, form diplomatic intelligence: 'prudence, foresight, intelligence, penetration, wisdom'. [59] They are indispensable qualities; without them diplomacy can not fulfil its function as the principal moderating institution of international politics.

In addition to these qualities Satow pointed out further necessary qualifications for the diplomatic career:

> Good temper, good health and good looks. Rather more than average intelligence, though brilliant genius is not necessary. A straightforward character, devoid of selfish ambition. A mind trained by the

study of the best literature and by that of history. Capacity to judge of evidence. In short, the candidate must be a *gentleman*. ... At some posts it is useful to have had a legal training ... Science is not necessary. Geography, beyond elementary notions, is not of great value. [60]

Diplomatic intelligence, in the dual meaning of the word, is also indispensable to the formulation of foreign policy as well as to the diplomat's chief activity of accommodating rival claims. Satow repeatedly argued that 'tact and intelligence' and the art of 'discussion and agreement' are at the core of all diplomacy. [61] It replaces the use of force, the primeval manner of conducting international politics, with persuasion, thereby civilizing international affairs. Diplomacy is the constant search for mutually acceptable terms and conditions. In order to identify what is mutually acceptable an atmosphere of confidence and understanding has to be created between the two sides. Satow, not unlike other diplomatic writers before him, accepted the need for secrecy. He remained consistent in his rejection of all notions of the beneficial nature of new and open diplomacy: 'Nothing is to be gained by taking the world prematurely into the confidence of governments in regard to matters of high policy.' [62]

Secrecy is not the only prerequisite of confidence. Satow acknowledged that, like all human contrivances, diplomacy has an ethical dimension. In this he followed once more Callières's observations: honesty is the best policy; it is the only sound policy. [63] Satow's other authority on this matter was the first Earl of Malmesbury:

> no occasion, no provocation, no anxiety to rebut an unjust accusation, no idea, however tempting, of promoting the object you have in view, can *need*, much less justify, a *falsehood*. Success obtained by one, is a precarious and baseless success. Detection would ruin, not only your own reputation for ever, but deeply wound the honour of your court. [64]

On an earlier occasion, Satow concluded that the word of a diplomat, be he a minister for foreign affairs or a diplomatic agent, 'is binding in honour on the Government and the nation which he represents'. [65]

Steadfast though he remained on the question of honesty in diplomatic transactions, Satow was less unambiguous on another aspect of diplomatic ethics. He was too much of a professional to discard the importance of secret intelligence. The history of European diplomacy provided him with an abundance of examples of the considerable importance of such information. He conceded that obtaining through bribery, and using, secret intelligence raises moral questions. At the same time, his lawyer's mind and his own professional experience made him bow to well-established precedents and practices. There was after all enough evidence of the fact 'that the practice of purchasing secret information is more or less universal'. [66] As a minister Satow had himself frequently used 'private agents' to obtain secret information. [67]

In so far as the more outward qualities of a diplomat are concerned Satow concurred with the observation of the mid-nineteenth century Austrian diplomat Count von Hübner, whose diplomatic career formed the subject of his *Rede Lecture*:

> What a trying profession is that of the diplomatist. I know of none which demands so much self-denial, so much readiness to interest and duty, so much patience, and at times so much courage. The ambassador who fulfils the duties of his office never betrays fatigue, boredom nor disgust. He keeps to himself the emotions he experiences, the temptations to weakness that assail him. He has to remain silent regarding the bitter disappointments to which he is subjected, as well as the unexpected successes which chance sometimes, but rarely bestows on him. While jealous of his own dignity, he is constantly mindful of others, is careful not to fall out with anyone, never loses his serenity, and in great crises, when it is a question of peace and war, shows himself calm, unmoved and confident of success. [68]

A further quality, not listed by von Hübner, but one which the polyglot Satow himself stressed repeatedly, is the thorough knowledge of foreign languages. Diplomacy as the institution through which relations between sovereign states are carried out 'by discussion and agreement' is at its core a highly developed system of communication, aimed at identifying and accommodating different, and often conflicting interests. [69] Both to discuss and accommodate these interests linguistic abilities are a distinct advantage. To study the language of the country to which a minister is accredited is '[t]he surest way to gain admission to the heart of a nation'. [70]

International Assemblies and Great Power Diplomacy

Alongside the emergence of the resident ambassador, the establishment of the practice of holding international assemblies is arguably the most distinct feature in the development of modern diplomacy since the later seventeenth century. [71] The importance of this practice was fully recognized by Satow. He had himself taken part in two such international gatherings, the ambassadorial conference at Peking in 1900-1 and the Second Peace Conference at The Hague in 1907. Congresses and conferences as functions of modern diplomacy continued to occupy his academic studies until the end of his life. The precise distinction between these two forms of international assemblies was of particular interest to him; as was their respective functions in diplomatic practice. In consequence, his writings on international congresses and conferences form a substantial part of his entire diplomatic *oeuvre*.

The dichotomy between the theory of the equality of sovereign states and the reality of Great Power dominance in international affairs has already been noted. [72] The practice of holding international congresses and conferences is a corollary to the 'hierarchical' nature of the modern states system. It is undoubtedly one of Satow's achievements to have made explicit the link between Great Power dominance and the institution of international assemblies. In this respect, his legal training and his historical interests proved a fruitful combination. As was shown before, in Satow's view the major powers form some 'kind of committee' which directs international affairs. [73] With regard to international assemblies Satow, the diplomatic historian, noted, that they 'have frequently been limited to representatives of the [Great Powers]'. [74] In other words, congresses and conferences are therefore the meetings of this exclusive committee.

In contemporary international law no distinction was made between the two types of international assemblies. Satow observed that '[b]oth are meetings of plenipotentiaries for the discussion and settlement of international affairs. The presence of sovereigns at the place where they have been carried on does not alter their character'. [75] Always primarily concerned with precision and clarity of expression, the rulings of international law left Satow dissatisfied. At closer, historical inspection, he argued, modern diplomatic practice does reveal a distinction between congresses and conferences. The former were convened to deal with territorial readjustments in the aftermath of wars; conferences, by contrast, were assembled for the discussion of questions arising between nations who are at peace. [76] He explained that it was a well-established diplomatic practice that

> [w]henever belligerents begin to desire a resumption of peaceful intercourse arrangements are made for the meetings of representat-

ives duly authorized to negotiate and conclude terms of peace, such meetings being usually preceded by the conclusion of an armistice.... It was the use of the Latin word *congressus* in the preamble of the two treaties of Münster and Osnabrück [in 1648] that caused this term to be adopted to denote a gathering of plenipotentiaries for the conclusion of peace. The actual meetings for discussion were denominated 'conference'. [77]

Satow later specified the function of the two forms of international assemblies:

Congresses have usually been convoked for the negotiation of a peace between belligerent Powers and the redistribution of territory which in most cases is one of the conditions of peace. At a Congress, as a rule, more than two Powers have been represented...Ordinarily Congresses have been held at a neutral spot, or at some place expressly neutralized for the purpose of the meeting.... In the nineteenth century, Congresses...were mostly held at the capital of one of the Powers, and then the Chancellor or Minister for Foreign Affairs presided. [78]

Satow also noted that the term 'congress' 'is more frequently applied to assemblies of plenipotentiaries for the purpose of concluding peace, and is regarded as implying a specially important occasion'. [79] One of the authorities on which Satow rested his definition of the function of a congress was a semi-official article written by Prince Metternich at the time of the Congress of Vienna:

Les reunions antérieures qui ont porté le nom de Congrès, avaient pour objet, de vider un procès pour quelque sujet déterminé entre deux ou plusieurs puissances belligérantes ou prêtes à se faire la guerre, et dont l'issue devait être un traité de paix. [80]

The fact that the congress is an instrument of Great Power diplomacy circumscribes its function in a number of ways. As was noted before, the notion of the *de jure* equality of independent and sovereign states applies *de facto* only to the Great Powers. At congresses the representatives of the Great Powers, therefore, meet on a footing of equality. [81] Points of procedure, as Satow cogently argued, thus acquire great significance; and it was on these questions that he dwelt at great length in his various writings. [82] It will suffice to state two of these procedural points, the first one being the principle of unanimity. Since the Great Powers come together at international assemblies *inter pares*, no votes are taken; all proposals have to be approved unanimously by the congress. After careful analysis of the procedures followed at the international congresses after 1814, Satow concluded that the principle of unanimity was established by a series of precedents. In case of a difference of opinion the conflicting views had to be discussed privately by the parties concerned with a view to coming to a compromise solution. The second significant point of procedure, distilled by Satow from the history of past congresses, is the necessity of a prior agreement by all participants on the agenda of the congress and its eventual outcome. [83] The success of an international congress, like that of any diplomatic action, is thus dependent upon the political will of its participants.

His analysis of the purposes for which international assemblies were convoked and of the procedures adopted at them later gave Satow reason to reformulate his distinction between congresses and conferences in more abstract terms:

> [T]he former is defined as resulting in a bundle of common wills to which single wills would submit, and dealing with a complex of questions, while a conference would be limited to the consideration of a single question, and would have no power of enforcing its resolutions. [84]

Satow fully acknowledged the increased importance of congresses, attended by the principal ministers of the governments concerned, as instruments of diplomacy in the aftermath of the First World War. Still, on the basis of his historical research, he was able to argue that the underlying principles of congress diplomacy had not changed; and that the conduct of international relations through professional diplomats had not been superseded by some form of public or 'prime ministerial' diplomacy. [85]

Diplomacy and Statecraft: the Importance of Politics

Satow's understanding of diplomacy was not confined to the enumeration of a diplomat's necessary qualities; nor was it limited to the study of the procedural aspects of international congresses. His achievement lies in having shifted the focus of the traditional, 'ambassadorial' literature on diplomacy. Satow's concept of diplomacy was wider than that of other nineteenth-century writers. By placing diplomatic activity into a wider, political context, Satow's concept encompasses diplomacy in its entirety. Diplomatic agents, as Satow repeatedly stressed, fulfil chiefly executive functions. [86] Whatever their individual qualities and merits, all their efforts are bound to fail in the absence of a general guiding intelligence. The career of Count Hübner provided Satow with an illustration of the exacting business of diplomacy under such adverse conditions; it was 'the almost tragic spectacle of a devoted and public servant compelled to contend for a bad cause'. [87] Diplomacy is not simply the specialized and distinct activity of international negotiation; it is also an important aspect of statecraft.

Satow remained adamant that the success of diplomacy depends on what might be called the 'strategic outlook' of the policy-makers. Their firm understanding of the nation's interests; their 'knowledge of the past history of a question'; and their 'knowledge of men and how to deal with them' are indispensable factors. [88] By placing diplomacy into its wider, political context, Satow sharpened the focus on the responsibilities and obligations of the foreign policy decision-makers:

> We venture to suggest that a Minister of Foreign Affairs ought always to have a clear idea of the policy to be pursued in regard to each separate foreign state, and to seize every convenient opportunity of discussing it with the heads of the respective missions. [89]

Satow did not expect policy-makers to 'adopt ideas and theories in advance of the epoch in which their work is cast'. [90] But what he expected of them was foresight, a realistic appreciation of the problems of international politics and clear guidance. The policy of Napoleon III served him as an example of the absence of these elements of statecraft. His policy, Satow argued, was as amateurish as it was fatal; it 'imperilled the international status of France and weakened her position among surrounding nations by facilitating the rise of Italy and Prussia, and the waste of her resources in the ill-starred Mexican expedition'. [91] In Satow's judgement, Napoleon III had shown a mistaken preference for the use of military force over diplomacy. War, he contended, rarely, if ever, produces the intended consequences. Already the wars of Napoleon Bonaparte had given rise to German and Italian nationalism instead of consolidating France's dominance on the continent. [92] His nephew, the second Emperor of the French did not fare better in Satow's judgement:

Nothing is more certain than that Napoleon III was far from desiring the unity of the Italian people. Yet that was the outcome of the war of 1859. Its more serious consequences were the war of 1866, which brought about the exclusion of Austria from Germany, the consolidation of North and South Germany under the leadership of Prussia, and the war of 1870 which ended in the downfall of his dynasty and the dethronement of France from her position of predominance in Europe. [93]

A further, yet equally important factor which contributed to the failure of French foreign policy under Napoleon III was the latter's inclination towards secret diplomacy. For Satow, the professional diplomatist, the circumvention of established diplomatic channels and the exclusion of diplomatic agents from foreign policy formulation amounted to a cardinal sin. Diplomacy, Satow insisted, cannot be successful without constant communication between the diplomats abroad and the foreign minister. Yet, information must not flow in one direction only. The heads of the diplomatic missions abroad have an obvious duty to keep their government informed about the developments in the country to which they are accredited. At the same time, they cannot carry out their other duties effectively unless they are issued with detailed instructions and are kept informed about the government's assessment of the international situation. [94] Satow himself had had this experience in his own career. When transferring from Tokyo via London to Peking in August 1900, he was left without proper instructions until the beginning of 1901. [95]

Satow's understanding of diplomacy has a certain 'tragic' quality. There is a pessimistic tone in most of his diplomatic writings:

> The moral qualities...of statesmen and nations have not kept pace with the development of the means of action at their disposal: armies, ships, guns, explosives, land transport, but more than all, that of rapidity of communication by telegraph and telephone. These latter leave no time for reflection or consultation, and demand an immediate and often hasty decision on matters of vital importance. [96]

In an international system characterized by the absence of a 'supreme authority' diplomacy has to cushion the impact of crude power politics. [97] But Satow was realistic enough to concede that no nation, however peaceful its intentions, can exclusively rely on diplomacy and the doctrines of International Law. Love of domination, greed for territory, envy and jealousy between nations are strong motivating forces of state behaviour. Safety can only be ensured by 'strenuous, unremitting, and far-sighted preparations to resist attack'. [98] Still, like all human contrivances, efforts to secure peace are ultimately futile:

> [T]he utmost attainable by prudence and love of peace is the *postponement of the evil day*. The delay may be longer or shorter, for the precise moment of its termination cannot be predicted, owing to the incalculable effect of individual speech or action. What in our ignorance we call an accident may precipitate the catastrophe when we are hoping that it is still far off. But no confidence should ever be placed in the most elaborate assurances of pacific intentions...[99]

In light of such sentiments, diplomacy must appear an almost Sisyphusian labour. It requires of its practitioners rare qualities in a high degree. Yet success in diplomacy is elusive and depends upon circumstances beyond the individual diplomatist's control. Diplomacy, one is tempted to conclude, is the application of tact and intelligence to an inescapable, yet ultimately futile task.

Diplomacy and Coercion: Satow on 'Gunboat Diplomacy'

Satow had no pretensions at being, and indeed was, no philosopher. In consequence, he never elaborated on the 'tragic' nature of the business of diplomacy. But it would be inappropriate to accuse him of inconsistency in this regard. Indeed, Satow was remarkably consistent in his works on diplomatic theory and practice. Nonetheless, they are not entirely free from apparent contradictions, or at least significant qualifications.

The most important of these concerns the use of force in the furtherance of foreign policy objectives. As was shown above, Satow was a constant advocate against the application of military force to the conduct of international relations. A series of cases of nineteenth-century coercive diplomacy, cited in a number of his writings, provided him with powerful illustrations of the limited utility of this practice. [100] Still this applied only to the relations between 'civilized' states, i.e. states which adhere to the established principles of diplomatic practice. [101] Only in the relations between these states can diplomacy be the civilized pursuit of the national interest; and only then can diplomacy soften the naked aggressiveness of power politics. The relations of civilized states are based on the principle of mutuality. By implication, their relations with states, which do not adhere to the rules of International Law, are of an altogether different nature.

During the early stages of his own professional career in the Far East Satow gained first-hand experience of coercive forms of diplomacy. Though he was not uncritical of the often indiscriminate use of gunboats for the advancement of British or other foreign interests in China and Japan, he conceded the success with which such strong-arm tactics were employed. [102] In fact, in the cases of both these countries, the establishment of diplomatic relations was only accomplished by force of arms. [103] Satow was in no doubt as to the 'considerable moral effect' which the 'appearance of a gunboat' could produce on the government and people of a weaker country. [104] He was equally clear-sighted, however, about the implications of efforts to supplant diplomatic persuasion by forceful persuasion. As the 'moral effect' was easily produced, calm and prudent judgement on the part of the stronger power was always in danger of becoming the first victim of gunboat diplomacy: 'with a powerful, almost overwhelming squadron of men-of-war at one's back, the temptation to express one's feelings with frankness is not easy to resist.' [105] In Satow's judgement gunboat or coercive diplomacy was a double-edged sword. It required careful use; and only if handled carefully and applied to a limited extent was it likely to produce any results.

Throughout his career Satow maintained that the application of military pressure was a legitimate tool of Great Power diplomacy, especially in dealing with countries with a weak central government. Shortly before his retirement from the diplomatic service he gave expression to this view in a letter to his political master at the Foreign Office. The term 'gunboat diplomacy', he explained,

> was used to designate a habit that consuls had got into of calling in the aid of a gunboat whenever they had a dispute with the local officials. It was effective, but liable to abuse. Questions were settled promptly that, without the application of pressure on the spot, have a tendency to drag on for months and years. Properly applied, with the sanction of H. M. Government, it would often be useful in these days.... [106]

In the relations between the Great Powers diplomacy is the civilized discussion of contentious issues. Such behaviour is enforced by the adherence to commonly accepted general rules of conduct as much as by the fear of war. [107] In the relations of Great Powers and 'non-civilized', and often considerably less powerful, states diplomacy is the art of persuasion not only by oratorical means but occasionally also by military means. Such sentiments, of course, reflected very much contemporary thinking. Satow, when writing about the development of European diplomacy, pleaded for a more understanding attitude: *'il viso sciolto ed i pensieri stretti'*.[108] The same ought not to be denied to him; he could not be expected to 'adopt ideas and theories in advance of the epoch in which [his] work [was] cast'.[109]

Conclusion: Satow and Diplomacy

Posterity, Lord Salisbury once observed, does not treat kindly the achievements of a diplomat: '[a] diplomatist's glory is the most ephemeral of all the forms of that transient reward.'[110] The same may be said of Sir Ernest Satow, the commentator on the practice and theory of diplomacy. His reputation as a diplomatic writer rests entirely on the *Guide to Diplomatic Practice*. The work is often referred to and still widely held to be the classic twentieth-century English-language exposition of diplomatic practice.[111] Yet, as the preceding pages have shown, the *Guide*, though an important and invaluable work of reference, is not representative of Satow's entire *oeuvre*. The latter went far beyond statements of fact and law. When read in conjunction, Satow's writings reveal a richness of thought and insight into the nature of international politics and the workings of diplomacy, which has quite often been overlooked by later writers.

Satow was a pragmatic, historically informed writer in the positivist tradition of international law.[112] His academic work was primarily concerned with the reality of international politics; and Satow dealt with the world of international diplomacy as he found it. He was perhaps not an original thinker. His conception of diplomacy does not envisage any of the alternative arrangements, which were so widely discussed at the time of the publication of the *Guide*. Indeed, given the in essence unalterable substance of diplomacy, he deemed all forms of 'new diplomacy' unfeasible.[113] Satow conceived diplomacy as a civilizing influence, mitigating the conflicts implicit in the modern states system. Inevitably, this conception is linked with the notion of international law as a body of rules governing the relations between independent and sovereign states. Satow's understanding of international relations was not that of a Hobbesian state of nature; nor did he adhere to the notions of *Machtstaat* and *Realpolitik*, which had dominated political thinking in the late nineteenth century.[114] Yet, it is similarly true that as an active diplomat he had been exposed too much to unmitigated power politics in its crudest forms to place his trust exclusively in Grotius's notion of international law as a guiding influence of the actions of states. He fully acknowledged the military dimension of international politics. Indeed, as was noted above, Satow's conception of diplomacy had a certain 'tragic' quality. While it is the function of diplomacy to cushion the blows of power politics, Satow regarded the underlying conflicts between independent and sovereign states as often insoluble. There was no doubt in his mind as to the legitimacy of the *ultima ratio regum*.

Still, though he repeatedly emphasized the need for constant military preparedness, Satow relied mainly on the prudent judgement of professional diplomats and the guiding intelligence of statecraft to create stability and preserve peace. [115] In this respect, Satow's work was remarkably perceptive, perhaps more so than the works of previous writers on diplomacy. Indeed, the establishment of the political dimension of diplomacy is one of the main achievements of Satow's work. Of course, it also has its shortcomings. Satow was not an original and not always a consistent thinker. On occasions, his positivist bend of mind made him accept uncritically contemporary notions and concepts; and often he did not elaborate on the ideas which he did develop. It is equally true that his perspective on the practice and theory of diplomacy was conditioned by his own professional experience. His conception of diplomacy was very much that of Great Power diplomacy. Had he been the representative of a smaller power, he might well have written a different *Guide to Diplomatic Practice*. But all this should not detract from the merits of his work. It is a clear and precise exposition of the essence of diplomacy, and as such it has become by no means archaic. On a more practical level, the illustrations of diplomacy in action and the advice to practitioners offered by Satow deserve to be given due attention. One should be grateful for every bit of original, undiluted and unrevised Satow.

Notes

1. Memorial plaque in honour of Satow, erected first in the chapel of the British embassy at Peking, later re-erected in the Parish church of Ottery St Mary, Devon, where Satow lived after his retirement from the diplomatic service in 1907.
2. H. G. Nicolson, *Diplomacy* (London, 1939), p.131.
3. On this *genre* see: Z. S. Steiner, 'The diplomatic life: reflections on selected British diplomatic memoirs written before and after the Great War', in G. Egerton (ed.), *Political Memoir: Essays on the Politics of Memory* (London, 1995), pp. 167–87.

4. These have now been reissued as *The Collected Works of Ernest Mason Satow* (12 vols, Bristol and Tokyo, 1998).

5. See Satow diary, 11 February 1915, Satow MSS, Public Record Office, Kew, Surrey, PRO 30/33/17/2.

6. 'Obituary: Sir Ernest Satow, a Great Far Eastern Diplomatist', in *The Times* (27 August 1929), p. 12; H. W. V. Temperley, 'Sir Ernest Mason Satow', in *Dictionary of National Biography, 1922–1930* (London, 1932), p. 747; P. F. Kornicki, 'Ernest Mason Satow', in H. Cortazzi and G. Daniels (eds), *Britain and Japan, 1859–1991: Themes and Personalities* (London, 1991), pp. 76–7.

7. Sir E. Satow, *The Family Chronicle of the English Satows* (Oxford, 1925), p. 18; *A Diplomat in Japan: the Inner History of the Critical Years in the Evolution of Japan . . .* (London, 1921), pp. 4–5; B. M. Allen, *The Rt Hon. Sir Ernest Satow, GCMG: a Memoir* (London, 1933), p. 7; G. A. Lensen, *Korea and Manchuria Between Russia and Japan: the Observations of Sir Ernest Satow . . .* (Talahassee, FL, 1966), pp. 5–6. (Unless otherwise noted, all works quoted are by Satow.)

8. Lensen, *Korea and Manchuria*, pp. 19–21; N. Brailey, 'Sir Ernest Satow, Japan and Asia: the trials of a diplomat in the age of high imperialism', in *Historical Journal*, vol. XXXV, no.1 (1992), p. 118.

9. Allen, *Satow*, p. v; Z. S. Steiner, *The Foreign Office and Foreign Policy, 1898–1914* (London, repr. 1986), p. 178; D. C. M. Platt, *The Cinderella Service: British Consuls since 1825* (London, 1971), pp. 207–8.

10. Lord Redesdale, *Memories*, 2 vols, (London, 1915), vol. I, p. 377.

11. *A Diplomat in Japan*, pp. 54–5; 'The Far East (1815–1871): Japan', in A. W. Ward et al. (eds), *The Cambridge Modern History*, vol. XI, *The Growth of Nationalities* (Cambridge, 1909), pp. 802–23.

12. Sir M. Hewlett, *Forty Years in China* (London, 1943), p. 35.

13. G. Sansom, 'Annual address . . . ', in *Journal of Asian Studies*, vol. XXIV, no.4 (1965), p. 567; Allen, *Satow*, p. v.

14. Cf. Bishop Gore's letter to *The Times* (30 August 1929), p. 14.

15. Lensen's list is somewhat incomplete, *Korea and Manchuria*, p. 18.

16. Satow diary, 16 March 1916, PRO 30/33/17/3.

17. Cf. his talk on Bach and Handel, 9 November 1914, PRO 30/33/18/4B.

18. Baroness d'Anethan, *Fourteen Years of Diplomatic Life in Japan* (London, 1912), p. 121.

19. Crowe to Tyrrell (private), 6 August 1907, Grey Mss, PRO, FO 800/69; cf. also T. G. Otte, 'Communication: the Crowe–Satow correspondence (1907–1914)', in *Diplomacy & Statecraft*, vol. VII, no.3 (1996).

20. *A Guide to Diplomatic Practice* (2 vols, London, 1917; 2nd edn, 1922; 3rd rev. edn, 1931; 4th rev. edn, 1957; 5th rev. edn, 1979).

21. Cf. Anon., 'The Diplomat's Handbook', in *Times Literary Supplement* (3 May 1910, p. 206; A. W. Ward's review in: *English Historical Review*, vol. XXXII, no. 3 (1917), pp. 418–27; Anon., 'Diplomatic practice', in *Contemporary Review*, vol. CXII, no. 7 (1917), pp. 114–16; J. A. R. Marriott, 'Modern diplomacy', in *Quarterly Review*, vol. CCXXIX, no. 454 (1918), pp. 222–38; J. C. Ballagh in *American Journal of International Law*, vol. XII, no. 4 (1918), pp. 893–8; C. J. B. Hurst in *British Yearbook of International Law*, vol. IV (1923–4), pp. 193–4; D. Anzilotti in *Rivista di Diretto Internazionale*, ser. II, vol. VI, nos 3–4 (1917), pp. 446–7; Anon. in *Revue Générale de Droit Internationale Public*, vol. XXIV (1917), p. 259. The only critical, though avowedly non-expert, review is

Leonard Woolf's 'The Two Kings of Jerusalem', in *The New Statesman*, vol. IX, no. 212 (28 April 1917), pp. 85–7.

22. M. Bernard, *Four Lectures on Subjects Connected with Diplomacy* (London, 1868), esp. Lecture III, 'Diplomacy, past and present', pp. 111–61; S. Walpole, *Foreign Relations* (London, 1882), esp. chs iv and v; J. W. Foster, *The Practice of Diplomacy, as illustrated in the Foreign Relations of the United States* (Boston, 1906); D. J. Hill, *A History of Diplomacy in the International Development of Europe*, 3 vols, (London, 1905–14).

23. A. W. Ward to Satow, 4? February 1916, PRO 30/33/13/1; cf. also J. A. R. Marriott, *The European Commonwealth: Problems Historical and Diplomatic* (Oxford, 1918), pp. 19–20.

24. L. F. L. Oppenheim, 'Editorial Preface', in *Guide*, vol. I, p. v.

25. Satow diary, 3 February, 11 March and 25 July 1914, PRO 30/33/17/1, and 17/2; Satow to Oppenheim, 5 and 22 July 1916, PRO 30/33/13/3.

26. Satow to L. F. L. Oppenheim, 24 February 1915 (copy), and Oppenheim to Satow, 26 February 1915, PRO 30/33/12/11. At Oppenheim's suggestion Satow revised the arrangement of the chapters; cf. Oppenheim to Satow, 17 July 1916, ibid., PRO 30/33/13/3. The 'whimsicality' of the arrangement of which Lord Gore-Booth complained was therefore not at all Satow's work, 'Preface', in *Satow's Guide to Diplomatic Practice*, 5th edn (London, 1979), p. ix.

27. Satow to C. J. Longman, 22 July 1916, Satow Mss, PRO, PRO 30/33/13/3.

28. Temperley, 'Satow', p. 749; Kornicki, 'Satow', p. 85.

29. *Guide*, vol. I, p. x; A. Pearce Higgins to Satow, 1 June 1907, PRO 30/33/12/3; Satow notebooks, 'Books Read and Notes on Diplomacy from August 1906 to March 1913', and 'Notes on Diplomatic Matters II', PRO 30/33/22/4.

30. *Guide*, § 1, p.1.

31. *The Mutual Relations of Civilized Nations: a Paper Read at the Church Congress, Southampton, October 1913* (London, 1913), p. 4; *The Silesian Loan and Frederick the Great* (Oxford, 1915), pp. 5–6 and 113–14; ' "Pacta sunt servanda" or International Guarantee', in *Cambridge Historical Journal*, vol. I, no. 3 (1925), pp. 295–318; cf.Satow to Lord Reay, 19 September 1913 (copy), PRO 30/33/11/16.

32. *Mutual Relations*, p. 1.

33. Anon.[Satow], 'The immunity of private property at sea: II. theoretical', in *Quarterly Review*, vol. CCXV, no. 428 (1911), p. 22.

34. *A Diplomat in Japan*, pp. 84–7; 'Far East', pp. 803–8, 819–21, and 861–2.

35. 'Private property at sea in times of war: a reply to Lord Avebury', in *Nineteenth Century*, vol. LXXIII, no. 432 (1913), p. 303.

36. Review of A. H. Oakes and R. B. Mowat (eds), *The Great European Treaties of the Nineteenth Century*, in *English Historical Review*, vol. XXXIII, no. 3 (1918), p. 411.

37. *International Congresses* (London, 1920) (i.e. *Foreign Office Peace Handbook*, no.151), p. 2; Satow to L. F. L. Oppenheim, 22 March 1919 (copy), PRO 30/33/13/7.

38. *Mutual Relations*, pp. 4–5.

39. H. Bull, 'The importance of Grotius in the study of International Relations', in Bull et al. (eds), *Hugo Grotius and International Relations* (Oxford, 1990), pp. 65–93.

40. *Guide*, vol. II, p. 370; 'The treatment of enemy aliens', in: *Transactions of the Grotius Society*, vol. II (1916), pp. 1–10 (first published in: *Quarterly Review*, vol. CCXIV, no. 445 (1915), pp. 415–25). The only comparable, contemporary 'Grotian' work is: Sir W. Phillimore, *Three Centuries of Treaties of Peace and Their Teaching* (London, 1917).

41. 'The foundation of the Third Republic', in *Quarterly Review*, vol. CCX, no. 419 (1909), pp. 98–9; Temperley, 'Satow', p. 749.

42. 'Third Republic', p. 98; 'Private property II', pp. 17–18; draft note Satow, 3 February 1914, PRO 30/33/12/9.

43. Satow to L. F. L. Oppenheim, 5 July 1916, PRO 30/33/13/3; 'The immunity of private property at sea: I. historical', in *Quarterly Review*, vol. CCXIV, no. 426 (1911), pp. 1–23.

44. Marginal note by Satow, 3 February 1914, PRO 30/33/12/9.

45. Satow diary, 10 March 1914, PRO 30/33/17/1; Satow to Lord Reay, 6 July 1915, PRO 30/33/ 11/17; C. J. Longman to Satow, 15 May 1914, PRO 30/33/ 12/9.

46. L. F. L. Oppenheim to Satow, 6 August 1914, and Satow to C. J. Longman, 4 November 1914, PRO 30/33/12/10. *The Silesian Loan* was eventually published, under a slightly altered title, by the Clarendon Press in 1915.

47. *An Austrian Diplomat of the Fifties: the Rede Lecture, 1908* (Cambridge, 1908), p. 7; cf. *Guide*, vol. I, pp. x–xi. Satow later changed his views on this question, Satow to G. W. Prothero, 18 August 1920 (copy), PRO 30/33/13/10.

48. Anon. [Satow], 'Recent Napoleonic literature', in *Quarterly Review*, vol. CCVIII, no. 415 (1908), pp. 418–19. On Satow's authorship of this article see: Allen, *Satow*, pp. 145–9.

49. *An Austrian Diplomat*, pp. 58–9.

50. Review of C. K. Webster's *Congress of Vienna* in *English Historical Review*, vol. XXXIV, no. 2 (1919), pp. 264–5.

51. *Guide*, vol. I, §1, p. 1; 'Peacemaking, old and new', in *Cambridge Historical Journal*, vol. I, no. 1 (1925), p. 23.

52. Review of J. A. R. Marriott's *Eastern Question* in *English Historical Review*, vol. XXXII, no. 3 (1917), p. 437.

53. The reference is to a facetious entry by Sir Henry Wotton (1568–1639) in an album of an Augsburg merchant (1568–1639): '*Legatus est vir bonus, peregre missus ad mentiendum Reipublicae causae*' ('An ambassador is an honest man, sent to lie abroad for the good of his country'), cf. I.Walton, *Lives* (London, 1825 (first edn 1651)), pp. 122–5; A. W. Ward, *Sir Henry Wotton: A Biographical Sketch* (London, 1898), pp. 75–7.

54. Satow, *An Austrian Diplomat*, op.cit., p. 9 ff.; *Guide*, op.cit., vol. I, §200, pp. 168 ff.

55. *Guide*, vol. I, §139, pp. 119–121.

56. *Mutual Relations*, p.2.

57. *Guide*, vol. I, §206, p. 174.

58. Ibid., pp. 121–2, and §160, pp.142–3.

59. Ibid., §167, p. 145.

60. Ibid., §224, pp. 183–4.

61. Ibid., §1, p. 1; 'Peacemaking', p. 23.

62. *An Austrian Diplomat*, p. 8; 'Peacemaking', pp. 23 and 60; 'Reorganization,' pp. 1–4; Satow to L. F. L. Oppenheim, 22 March 1919 (copy), PRO 30/33/13/7.

63. *Guide*, vol. I, §139, pp. 121 and 125; '"Pacta sunt servanda"', pp.295–6.
64. Malmesbury to Lord Camden, 11 April 1813, in *Diaries and Correspondence of James Harris, First Earl of Malmesbury*, (4 vols, London, 2nd edn 1845), vol. iv, p.413, as quoted in: *Guide*, vol. I, §140, p. 129.
65. *Frederick the Great and the Silesian Loan*, p. 199.
66. *Guide*, §144, p. 132.
67. Cf. Satow diary, 10 January 1901, PRO 30/33/16/4.
68. *Neuf ans des souvenirs d'un ambassadeur d'Autriche à Paris sous le Second Empire, 1851–1859*, ed.by A. C. J. von Hübner (Paris, 1904), as quoted in: *An Austrian Diplomat*, p. 14.
69. 'Peacemaking', p. 23.
70. *Guide*, vol. I, §153, p. 136; cf. Satow's evidence to the Reay Committee in *Report of the Committee on Oriental Studies in London* (Cd. 4561), XXXV, Q 1914; C. O. Jan, 'The East Asian Diplomatic Service and the Observations of Sir Ernest Satow' (unpublished PhD thesis, University of Florida, 1976).
71. 'Peacemaking', p. 24; *Guide*, vol. I, §207, p. 175; cf. R. T. B. Langhorne, 'The development of international conferences, 1648–1830', in *Studies in History and Politics*, vol. I, no. 2 (1981–2), pp. 61–91.
72. *Mutual Relations*, p. 4; *International Congresses*, p. 2.
73. *Mutual Relations*, p. 4; cf. Satow to Oppenheim, 22 March 1919 (copy), PRO 30/33/13/7.
74. *International Congresses*, p. 2; *Guide*, vol. II, §439, p. 2.
75. *Guide*, p. 1.; cf. W. A. Phillips, 'Congress', in *Encyclopaedia Britannica*, 11th edn (London, 1911), vol. VI, pp. 937–8; F. von Holtzendorff, *Handbuch des Völkerrechts* 4 vols, (Leipzig, 1885–9), vol. III, §175, p. 679.
76. Marginal comment by Satow on Holtzendorff, *Handbuch des Völkerrechts*, PRO 30/33/22/4.; *Guide*, vol. II, §468, pp. 100–4.
77. 'Peacemaking', p. 24.
78. *Guide*, vol. II, §439, p. 2.
79. *International Congresses*, pp. 1 and 13.
80. Comte d'Angeberg, *Le Congrès de Vienne et les Traités de 1815* (Paris, 1864), p. 362, as quoted in: *Guide*, vol. II, p. 3.
81. *International Congresses*, pp. 2–3; 'Reorganisation of Europe', p. 4.
82. *International Congresses*, op.cit., pp. 9 ff.; *Guide*, op.cit., vol. II, §§440–67, pp. 3–99.
83. *International Congresses*, pp. 3–5; review of Webster's *Congress of Vienna*, p. 261; 'Reorganisation of Europe', pp. 4–5.
84. Review of Webster's *Congress of Vienna*, p. 261.
85. 'Peacemaking', pp. 23 and 60; 'Reorganisation', op.cit., pp. 4–5; H. W. V. Temperley to Satow, 4 November 1920, PRO 30/33/13/10.
86. *Mutual Relations*, p. 2; *An Austrian Ambassador*, p. 21.
87. *An Austrian Diplomat*, p. 56.
88. Review of Marriott's *Eastern Question*, p. 437.
89. *Guide*, vol. I, §159, p. 142.
90. Review of Webster's *Congress of Vienna*, p. 262.
91. 'Third Republic', p. 91.
92. *An Austrian Diplomat*, p. 57; 'Napoleonic literature', p. 440.
93. *An Austrian Diplomat*, p. 57.
94. *Guide*, vol. I, §§158–9, pp. 141–2.

95. Satow to Salisbury (private), 8 Oct.1900, Salisbury MSS, Hatfield House, A/106/34; Satow to Lansdowne (private), 28 Dec.1900, Lansdowne MSS, PRO, FO 800/119.
96. *Guide*, vol. I, §167, p. 145; review of P. J. Treat's *Early Diplomatic Relations between the United States and Japan* (1917), in *English Historical Review*, vol. XXXIII, no. 1 (1918), p. 130.
97. *Mutual Relations*, p. 5.
98. Ibid., p. 9; 'Reorganization', p. 20; 'Reply to Lord Avebury', p. 304.
99. *Austrian Diplomat*, pp. 57–8 (author's emphasis); cf.' "Pacta sunt servanda" ', pp. 307–310.
100. 'Napoleonic literature', pp. 440–1; *Austrian Diplomat*, pp. 56–9.
101. *Mutual Relations*, pp. 1–2; *Silesian Loan*, pp. 113–14.
102. 'Far East', p. 805.
103. Ibid., pp. 819–20 and 848–9; review of H. B. Morse's *International Relations of the Chinese Empire* (1918), in *English Historical Review*, vol. XXXIV, no. 1 (1919), p. 115.
104. *A Diplomat in Japan*, p. 63.
105. Ibid., p.82; 'Far East', pp. 846–7.
106. Satow to Sir Edward Grey (private), 31 March 1906, Grey MSS, PRO, FO 800/44; Satow diary, 3 July 1900, PRO 30/33/16/3.
107. *Mutual Relations*, pp. 5–6.
108. *Austrian Diplomat*, p. 14.
109. Review of Webster's *Congress of Vienna*, p. 262.
110. *Essays by the Late Marquess of Salisbury, K.G.* 2 vols, (London, 1905), vol. I, p. 11.
111. Cf. Nicolson, *Diplomacy*, p. 234; G. V. McClanahan, *Diplomatic Immunity: Principles, Practices, Problems* (New York, 1989), p. 161; E. Plischke, *Conduct of American Diplomacy*, 2nd edn (Princeton, NJ, 1961), p. 2.
112. Satow to Lord Reay, 6 July 1915, PRO, 30/33/11/17.
113. 'Reorganisation', pp. 4–5; 'Peacemaking', pp. 23 and 60.
114. *Mutual Relations*, p. 2; 'Peacemaking', p. 60; cf. C. Holbraad, *The Concert of Europe: a Study in German and British International Relations Theory, 1815–1914* (London, 1970).
115. *Austrian Diplomat*, pp. 56–7; *Mutual Relations*, p. 9; 'Reply to Lord Avebury', p. 304.

Further reading

Works by Satow

Sir Ernest Satow's most important book on diplomacy is *A Guide to Diplomatic Practice*, which was first published by Longmans, Green & Company of London in 1917. In 1922 he published a second edition in order to make corrections to the first and bring the work up to date. However, Satow died in 1929 and the three subsequent editions to appear were each revised by different persons recently retired from the Foreign Office. The third edition (1932) was produced by Hugh Ritchie, formerly a technical assistant in the Treaty Department; the fourth (1957) by Sir Nevile Bland, whose last post was ambassador at The Hague; and the fifth (1979) was revised, with great help from Desmond Packenham and, among others, the FO's legal advisers, by Lord Gore-Booth, who was permanent under-secretary at the Foreign Office in the second half of the 1960s. For students of Satow, therefore, the most valuable edition is the second (reprinted in vols VIII–IX of *The Collected Works*), while for professional diplomats the best one is obviously the most recent, that is the fifth, which has also been translated into Japanese and Chinese.

In addition, the following are valuable:

International Congresses (London, 1920).

A Diplomat in Japan (London, 1921).

The Collected Works of Ernest Mason Satow, 12 vols. (Bristol and Tokyo, 1998). vol. VII contains *Frederick the Great and the Silesian Loan.*

Historical background

Grenville, J. A. S., *Lord Salisbury and Foreign Policy: the Close of the Nineteenth Century* (London, 1964).

Kiernan, V. G., 'Diplomats in exile', in R. Hatton and M. S. Anderson (eds), *Studies in Diplomatic History* (London, 1970), pp. 301–21.

Lowe, P., *Britain and the Far East, 1819 to the Present Day* (London, 1981).

Nish, I. H., *The Anglo-Japanese Alliance* (London, 1966).

Steiner, Z. S., *The Foreign Office and Foreign Policy, 1898–1914* (Cambridge, 1969).

Steiner, Z. S., *The Times Survey of Foreign Ministries of the World* (London, 1982), ch. by Valerie Cromwell on the (British) Foreign Office.

Biography

Allen, B. M., *Sir Ernest Satow: a Memoir* (London, 1933). [Allen was related to Satow by marriage.]

Brailey, N., 'Sir Ernest Satow, Japan and Asia: the trials of a diplomat in the age of high imperialism', *Historical Journal*, 35, I (1992), pp. 115–50.

Kornicki, P. F., 'Ernest Mason Satow (1843–1929)', in Sir Hugh Cortazzi and Gordon Daniels (eds), *Britain and Japan, 1859–1991* (London and New York, 1991).

Ruxton, I. C. (ed.), *The Diaries and Letters of Sir Ernest Mason Satow: a Scholar-Diplomat in East Asia* (Lampeter, 1998).

Temperley, H. W. V., 'Sir Ernest Satow', in *Dictionary of National Biography 1921–30* (London, 1932).

General

Brailey, N. J., 'Sir Ernest Satow and his book *A Diplomat in Japan*', in *Proceedings of the Japan Society*, no. 131 (Summer 1998), pp. 56–69.

Lensen, G. A. (ed.), *Korea and Manchuria between Russia and Japan, 1895–1905: The Observations of Sir Ernest Satow* (Tallahassee, FL, 1966); see introduction.

8
Nicolson

T. G. Otte

Its literary tradition has proved to be one of the enduring peculiarities of the British diplomatic service. Although, as Harold Nicolson once observed, 'the man of letters has always been regarded with bewildered, although quite friendly, disdain' by his colleagues, successive generations of former diplomatists have found irresistible the temptations of pen and paper. [1] Like Satow, Nicolson wrote widely on various aspects of diplomatic history and diplomatic theory and practice. But unlike the more ponderous and scholarly Satow, Nicolson wrote with 'ease, fluency and wit', not surprisingly, perhaps, in a man whose *oeuvre* also comprised of literary work in the narrower sense, literary criticism and biographies and even two novels. [2] To some, indeed, he was 'the last of the great essayists in the classical manner'. [3]

Harold Nicolson, his biographer observed, 'probably never wrote a boring line in his life'; in the considered opinion of a recent critic, by contrast, Nicolson never wrote a profound line in his life either. [4] Such a view of Nicolson's work is not particularly new, nor, perhaps, particularly witty. Indeed, for most of his life Nicolson was said to view the world 'through the embassy window'. [5] In the misty eyes of a poet this might perhaps disqualify his work from serious consideration. But it is this very quality which renders it all the more interesting for the student of diplomacy. It is true, no doubt, that having left the diplomatic service Nicolson wrote for a living; and the heavy labour of hack work was not always conducive to producing consistently high quality. It is equally true that there is a not infrequent element of repetition in some of the minor articles; and not all of these were of lasting value. [6] Whatever the artistic merits of his other writings, his diplomatic *oeuvre* and his commentaries on contemporary and past politics were, and still are, stimulating rather than superficial, insightful and never insipid. In the words of Lewis Namier, he was 'one of the most articulate experts and best-informed writers on diplomacy'.[7] Yet, whilst a burgeoning 'Harold and Vita'-industry has shed light on almost every aspect of Nicolson's private and public life, the writer on diplomacy has been left lingering in undeserved obscurity.

Harold Nicolson was born in 1886 into a minor patrician family of Hiberno-Scottish descent with a well-established tradition of serving the crown in a military or civilian capacity.[8] Indeed, the ambassadorial and proconsular careers of members of his family provided role models for the young Nicolson. His father, Sir Arthur Nicolson, later Lord Carnock, had been ambassador at Madrid and St. Petersburg before becoming permanent under-secretary of the Foreign Office in 1910.[9] His much grander maternal uncle, the Irish magnate the Marquess of Dufferin and Ava, had been a minister under Palmerston and Gladstone, before serving as governor-general of Canada and viceroy of India as well as ambassador at St Petersburg, Constantinople, Rome and Paris.[10] No wonder, therefore, that the young Harold Nicolson turned to diplomacy as a career.

Educated at Wellington and Balliol, he entered the diplomatic service in 1909. After postings at Madrid and Constantinople he returned to the Foreign Office where he remained throughout the war years. He distinguished himself in 1918–19 when he was attached to the British delegation at the Paris Peace Conference. After the conference Nicolson was appointed private secretary to Sir Eric Drummond, the first secretary-general of the newly formed League of Nations.[11] His appointment was as much a reflection of the notable success of his conference work as of his strong pro-League leanings. At the time Nicolson was one of the few Wilsonian idealists in the British foreign service, men who regarded the League as a panacea for the ills of international politics rather than the pre-1914 'separatist alliances and combinations'.[12] This idealist preference for the League was coupled with a firm belief in the necessity of strong links with the United States.

His own experience of international politics in the immediate post-war years, however, soon had a disillusioning effect on Nicolson, who had been recalled to the Foreign Office in June 1920. But whilst his interest in the League waned, his interest in the American friendship remained unaltered.[13] Quite possibly under the strong influence of Sir Eyre Crowe, he became more sceptical of the efficacy of the League and returned to a more traditional concept of foreign policy, centred on the principle of the balance of power.[14] Equipped with a keen sense of irony, he later reflected that in 1919 President Wilson 'had sought to apply to international relations the principles of American democracy, [yet] the diplomatists continued undismayed to weave the old tapestry of alliances and combinations, of big or little *ententes*, of pacts and conventions'. [15] Whatever confidence in the League was left in him, was shattered in the mid-1920s when Nicolson was counsellor at the Tehran legation. [16] But the Persian experience was also an important turning point in another respect. In September 1926 Nicolson, acting as chargé d'affaires that summer, sent a despatch to the Foreign Office in which he criticized in no uncertain terms Britain's Persian policy and advocated its urgent revision. [17] On his recall to London in the summer of 1927 he was duly demoted to the rank of first secretary. He had always chafed under the constraints the diplomatic service placed upon its junior and middle-ranking members and under his own limited influence on policy decisions. [18] But now in despair at this turn in his career, which had left him 'strand[ed] in this bog in which I have wasted the best years of my life', and depressed at the prospect of having to execute a policy which he thought misguided, Nicolson began to consider leaving the service. [19] The final decision to quit diplomacy, however, was deferred until September 1929 when he accepted an offer to become a journalist for the Beaverbrook press. [20]

With the end of his diplomatic career Nicolson's public life began. It was not a step he took lightly; one, in fact, that he occasionally regretted. He remained attached to his old profession, longing to return to the 'orderly privacy of diplomacy' and 'to creep back into the F.O.'. [21] What finally induced him to leave diplomacy was a mixture of family and financial concerns. [22] But it seems that intrigues within the service, his disillusionment with the policy-makers and his own nascent political ambitions were equally potent considerations. [23] Ultimately, neither his political ambitions nor his hopes for a return to diplomacy were ever fully realized. But what was a source of constant disappointment for Harold Nicolson also provided him with a stimulus to turn his mind and intellectual energy to the study of diplomatic theory and practice.

Nicolson and Foreign Policy

Harold Nicolson's reputation as a writer on diplomacy has come to rest largely on his *Diplomacy* (1939) and the smaller treatise on *The Evolution of Diplomatic Method* (1954). Both are justly regarded as classics in their own right. Both, however, ought to be studied in conjunction with his other writings, his talks on the wireless and his speeches in the House of Commons between 1935 and 1945. [24] For, while his general political views may have been somewhat protean, his views on diplomacy and foreign policy remained consistent after the mid-1920s. [25]

The overall thematic link between these writings is the transformation of diplomatic practice in the aftermath of and in response to the Great War. Indeed, his continued efforts to examine diplomacy in its various forms may be seen as an attempt to render an *a posteriori* justification of his own conversion in the 1920s from a Wilsonian idealist to a more pragmatic realist. This form of enlightened scepticism informed Nicolson's entire diplomatic *oeuvre*, though the latter is without theoretical aspirations. It places him firmly within the 'Whig tradition' in diplomacy as the *via media* between radical (Cobdenite) non-interventionism and crude *Realpolitik* in its Bismarckian or Disraelian forms. [26]

Nicolson's approach to international politics embraced realist assumptions about the prevalence of power, whilst also acknowledging the moral dimension of politics. He was insistent that 'there must always remain certain principles which lie at the foundation of human society and which no man can repudiate without damage to his own individuality' – principles which sprang from the Graeco-Roman-Christian tradition, the bedrock of modern Western civilization. [27] This is not the place to examine in detail Nicolson's political outlook. Suffice it to say that it was shaped by an amalgam of elements of classical culture with its emphasis on moral and political rather than economic or technological terms, and the values of eighteenth-century rationalism: 'good sense, balance, moderation, order, intellectual truthfulness and tolerance.' [28] Nicolson is, perhaps, best described as a displaced liberal. *'Les principes de libéralisme'*, he observed in one of his wireless talks, *'conservent une validité éternelle'*. [29] Yet, like many a disenchanted patrician of his generation, reared moreover in the spirit of public service rather than party politics, he was politically somewhat disoriented, repeatedly changing his affiliations.

In matters of foreign policy, Nicolson was unable to transcend the tension between power and morality, inherent in his Whiggish outlook. [30] He accepted the need for 'certain principles of international conduct', but he was sceptical of the efficacy of international law. [31] Thus, he insisted that 'it is only upon the practicable or realistic that sound policy can be based'. [32] Foreign policy was shaped by geography, and by 'national self-interest expressing itself in terms of political expediency'. [33] Indeed, no foreign policy, he wrote, 'can ever be reliable unless it be based upon national egoism. The main difference between "good" and "bad" foreign policy is that, whereas the former is based upon enlightened egoism, the latter is based upon egoism of the "sacred" variety'. [34]

Regardless of its failure to function in July 1914, Nicolson regarded the 'balance of power' as the best method of preserving international peace. [35] He readily acknowledged the noble sentiments which led to the creation of the League of Nations and its successor the United Nations, but these were weak international instruments. [36] 'In a world in which no single country tried to impose its will by force the system of the balance of power would of course become unnecessary. But until we reach such a utopia we must realize that the only means of resisting violence is to oppose it with a greater balance of force.' [37] Such a conception of the balance of power inevitably was somewhat amoebian in character. Nicolson refuted the idea, as entertained, for instance, by Castlereagh, of 'an ideal equilibrium, calculated almost mathematically in terms of population and power'. He argued that 'any balance of power must be relative'. [38]

Perhaps nowhere is Nicolson's outlook on international affairs better expressed than in a private letter to Lionel Curtis in which he defended his 'realism' against the 'idealism' of the federalist movement:

> What always irritates me about the idealists is that they seek to arouse emotions in people by appealing to their fear of war.... Obviously the whole purpose of any international thought must be the avoidance of war.... I advocate physical prevention and you advocate spiritual prevention.... What the idealists always seem to forget is that wars always arise owing to the will-power on the other side.... One of the more practical lessons I have learnt in my life is that it is very easy to convince people that their own decent feelings can in some way be transferred to others. I am afraid I do not believe this and I think it a dangerous thing to do to suggest to people that violence can be controlled by anything except force. [39]

While Nicolson had no major theoretical aspirations, it would be erroneous to regard his writings on diplomacy and foreign policy as an attempt merely to chronicle the advent of new diplomacy. Nicolson's treatment of his chosen subject is both descriptive and analytical, combining biography, often in an impressionistic Stracheyesque manner, with historical narrative and analytical efforts to distil the essential and immutable principles of diplomacy. [40] That such essential principles existed and could be deduced, and that the advent of 'New Diplomacy' merely indicated a change in the methods employed in the conduct of diplomacy, is the underlying assumption of Nicolson's writings. [41]

The Concept of Diplomacy

Diplomacy, Nicolson approvingly quoted Satow's famous definition, 'is the application of intelligence and tact to the conduct of official relations between the governments of independent states.' [42] To Nicolson's mind, however, this was very much a minimalist definition. In consequence, he sought to develop a wider, though no less precise, definition of diplomacy. He offered various such definitions, of which the following would appear to be central: 'Diplomacy essentially is the organised system of negotiation between sovereign states' [43]; '... diplomacy is neither the invention or the pastime of some particular political system, but is an essential element in any reasonable relation between man and man and between nation and nation'; 'Diplomacy [is]... the ordered conduct of relations between one group of human beings and another group alien to themselves'; [44] '[D]iplomacy... designate[s] ... the art of negotiation' [45]; and 'The aim of sound diplomacy... is the maintenance of amicable relations between sovereign states. Once diplomacy is employed to provoke international animosity, it ceases to be diplomacy and becomes its opposite, namely war by another name.' [46]

These attempts at defining diplomatic practice allow for a series of inferences to be made, which illuminate further Nicolson's concept of diplomacy. First of all, they presuppose a certain element of alienation between different groups with established separate identities. Did such differences not exist, there would obviously be no need for a special method of conducting relations between these groups, for the latter would not regard themselves as distinct from each other. Nicolson did not elaborate further on this element of alienation or estrangement which lies at the core of diplomacy; and it was left to more recent writers to investigate diplomacy's prehistory. [47] But it was perhaps just as well that Nicolson refrained from indulging in mythological speculation, preferring instead, in his own ironical phrase, the 'surer and more reputable ground' of (recorded) history. [48]

A second inference which can be drawn from Nicolson's various definitions is that diplomacy is an inevitable and necessary element of the relations between different groups; furthermore, that for these relations to be sustainable, there has to be an agreed framework or a code of conduct to guarantee the 'ordered conduct of relations' [49]; and lastly that diplomacy, as the ordered conduct of relations, is essentially a system of negotiation. Negotiations, however, are impossible unless the parties involved recognize each other, at least in principle, as equals; hence Nicolson's observation that '[d]iplomacy... is the system of negotiation between sovereign states.' [50] As such it was historically evolved and subject to continuous change.

Old Diplomacy and New

The one historical change which affected diplomacy during Nicolson's professional career and which continued to occupy him as a writer on diplomacy was the aforementioned proclamation of a 'new diplomacy'. The revulsion at the carnage of the First World War, the first general war in Europe for almost a century, led to a search for its origins in which diplomatists were the readily identifiable main culprits. [51] The strong reaction against the pre-war aristocratic *internationale* of diplomatists, and particularly against what was called 'old' or 'secret diplomacy', was coupled with the advent of fully fledged mass democracies after the war. [52] 'New diplomacy' based, in Woodrow Wilson's famous phrase, on 'open covenants..., openly arrived at', was now widely accepted to be the best guarantee against the recrudescence of a major military conflict.

Nicolson was very much alive to the force and the impact of such arguments. Indeed, his career as a diplomatic writer and political commentator ought properly to be seen as an ongoing intellectual battle with the prophets of 'simpler' policies. Steeped in the history of European diplomacy, he never ceased to argue that the latter 'display[ed] no... sudden breaks in continuity'; and that, furthermore, the so-called 'new diplomacy' was not at all the paragon its advocates claimed it to be. [53] If diplomacy did indeed develop gradually, was talk of a 'new diplomacy' not mere hyperbole or even a facile act of political opportunism, an effort to appease the newly enfranchised masses? This would be the cynic's interpretation; and Nicolson, for all his scepticism, was not prone to cynicism. Above all, the problems of 'new diplomacy' were more complex.

The core element of diplomacy, in Nicolson's view, was that of negotiation within an organized and ordered framework, based on 'the element of representation – the essential necessity in any negotiator that he should be fully representative of his own sovereign at home'. [54] There was no doubt in Nicolson's mind that the professional diplomatist was the representative and servant of the sovereign authority of his state, whatever the latter's political form might be. [55] The very efficiency of a diplomatic service depended on the degree to which it was representative of its sovereign. 'Efficiency' and its 'representative' nature were the twin moving forces behind the development of modern diplomacy. With this in mind, Nicolson added a further aspect to his definition of diplomacy: 'Diplomacy... [is the] method of international procedure which commends itself to sensible persons of any given epoch, as the most "representative" and the most "efficient" for conducting negotiations between States.' [56]

Thus, diplomacy did not take place in a vacuum. Surveying the development of modern diplomacy, Nicolson argued that diplomatic practice, in its quest for exact 'representation', interacted unceasingly with domestic developments at home. To remain fully 'representative', and so efficient, diplomacy had to reflect the changing nature of political sovereignty. 'New diplomacy', therefore, was a mirage: 'the conflict between the "old" and the "new" diplomacy is... no sudden phenomenon, but a stage in this long process of adjustment.' [57] The changes which had occurred thus reflected a shift in the centre of power at home, but the essential principles of efficient diplomacy remained unaltered.

In the absolute monarchies of the seventeenth and eighteenth centuries, for example, the sovereign authority was identical with the person of the ruling prince. The 'conduct of foreign policy, the issues of war and peace' lay in his hands; and he it was whom the diplomatist had to represent and serve, and whose confidence he had to obtain. [58] In a modern democracy, by contrast, sovereignty had shifted from the princely few to the 'people'. The advent of the mass age, Nicolson admitted, had brought with it certain changes; but these were 'changes in the conduct of diplomacy' and not 'the abrupt severance between the ethical conceptions of one generation and those of the next'. [59]

It is true, entertaining 'a professional prejudice against sudden diplomacy', [60] Nicolson lamented the demise of 'the slow-moving, upper-class methods of the old diplomacy'. But he accepted as inevitable that in 'the age of the common man... international relations [had]... now [to] be conducted on democratic lines'. [61] What he resented, however, was the self-righteousness of the advocates of 'new diplomacy'. In his biography of his father, the first volume of his 'Studies in Modern Diplomacy' trilogy, he noted:

> The old diplomatist has not been fairly treated by his posterity. If he failed to foresee the war, he is, and with full justice, called a fool: if he did foresee the war, he is, quite unjustly, considered a knave.... What

was wrong was the civilization which they represented. But if we are tempted to regard our own state of mind as more humane and more enlightened, we should remember that we were taught our lesson by the death and mutilation of ten million young men. We have no cause to feel self-righteous when backed by so expensive an education. [62]

But this was more than just a plea for historical accuracy and fair historical judgement. For Nicolson, accepting the need for diplomacy to adjust to mass democracy did not mean wholeheartedly to approve of the concomitant changes in its conduct. Indeed, his own experience had heightened his awareness of the 'special disadvantages and illusions' to which he thought 'new diplomacy' was prone. [63] What changes, then, characterized the transition from old to 'new diplomacy' in so far as diplomatic practice is concerned? Two main areas can readily be identified in Nicolson's writings.

The first one of these concerns the impact of modern policy-making on diplomacy. Summarizing the nature of modern diplomacy in the age of democracy, Nicolson noted: 'The diplomatist, being a civil servant, is subject to the Foreign Secretary; the Foreign Secretary, being a member of the Cabinet, is subject to the majority in Parliament; and Parliament, being but a representative Assembly, is subject to the will of the sovereign people.' [64] The foreign policy-makers, on whose instructions the diplomatist managed the relations with another country, were therefore obliged to inform the sovereign electorate of their policy aims in an effort to obtain their approval. Thus, 'public opinion has now become a constant, rather than intermittent, factor in the conception and execution of foreign policy.' [65] But while the importance of public opinion was undeniable, Nicolson contended, its impact was not altogether beneficial. The public at large is inevitably less well informed about foreign affairs than are trained diplomatists. Easily swayed by emotions rather than rational calculation, it also lacks constancy and firmness. [66] But in Nicolson's experience, 'opinion in democratic countries moves slowly' whereas 'in foreign affairs events move rapidly'. [67] The most immediate danger lurking in this dichotomy was that the difficulty of inducing the people to think rapidly and correctly – the danger that their initial emotion may, although rapid, be incorrect – tempts the modern negotiator to avoid those problems which are likely to prove unpopular and to concentrate on secondary issues which will be more comprehensible and therefore more welcome, to the popular mind. [68]

The public, in Nicolson's estimation, readily understood the under-lying principles of foreign policy but it did not understand tactical manoeuvres. This particular circumstance rendered democratic diplo-macy cautious and slow-moving; and it circumscribed the freedom of action of the government. Nicolson accepted that the increased influ-ence of public opinion on foreign policy was irreversible. What was required, however, of the political élite was an effort at educating the public in matters of foreign policy, lest the latter became 'subservient to, and guided by, waves of popular emotion'. [69] His advice to political leaders was 'to refrain from policies which are difficult to explain openly and in detail. [...] . . . a foreign policy based upon ascertainable and avowable principles is more likely to command the ordinary citizen's consent'. [70]

Such a course demanded a fine political balancing act on the part of the policy-makers. Under the conditions of modern mass democracy the latter were in constant danger of succumbing to whatever was politically expedient in the short term. Nicolson elaborated on the main distinc-tion between the methods of the new and those of the old diplomacy in the concluding volume of his diplomatic trilogy:

> the former aims at satisfying the *immediate* wishes of the electorate, whereas the latter was concerned only with the *ultimate* interests of the nation. It is, very largely, a difference in time available. The old diplomatist, negotiating as an expert with fellow experts, was able to approach his problems in a scientific spirit, with due deliberation, and without regard to immediate popular support. Such a system was obviously open to abuse and danger. Yet democratic diplomacy is exposed to its own peculiar maladies which, in that they are less apparent, are even more insidious. In the desire to conciliate popular feeling it is apt to subordinate to expediency, to substitute the inde-finite for the precise, to prefer in place of the central problem . . . sub-sidiary issues upon which immediate agreement, and therefore popular approval can be attained. [71]

Nicolson was well aware that the temptation to obtain a sensational diplomatic triumph by means of premature and indiscreet publicity might prove irresistible. But, even though such sensational results might yield profit at the ballot box, they were in diplomatic terms, at best ephemeral, at worst, merely the prelude to future complications. [72] Success, he warned, 'is never, either in diplomacy or foreign policy, an ultimate justification'. [73] Diplomatic negotiations, after all, were not a 'football match ... in which one side scores against the other amid the cheers or hoots of the spectators.... diplomatic victories are invariably bad; a good diplomatic arrangement is one in which each party feels it has acquired benefits...'. [74]

Constant reference to the state of public opinion at home with a view to short-term political gains was only one aspect of the politicization of diplomacy under the auspices of 'new diplomacy'. The transition from the old diplomacy also inaugurated diplomacy by personal contact, not between diplomatists and the governments to which they are accredited, but between political leaders. [75] On the occasion of Foreign Secretary Lord Halifax's visit to Berlin and Berchtesgaden for talks with Hitler in November 1937, Nicolson reflected on the distinct disadvantages of the 'heart-to-heart method' of fireside chats. In his view the preference for the direct, or amateur, method was rooted in a profound ignorance of the function and principles of the practice of diplomacy. Face-to-face talks among foreign statesmen evaded and often violated the fundamental principles of sound diplomacy: patience, precision and discretion.

The personal visit of a statesman to a foreign capital placed severe time constraints upon the visitor. The talks with the foreign government, the avowed object of the visit, had to be pursued unceasingly and relentlessly. Under such circumstances there was 'no opportunity for that most vital solvent – the ordinary adjournment'. A personal visit allowed no time for deliberation and consultation with the government at home. Calm cogitation, however, was not the only casualty of personal diplomacy. The necessity to transact diplomatic business with the utmost economy of time also risked sacrificing precision for obtaining a 'result'. Diplomacy, Nicolson insisted, 'is negotiation by the exchange of written documents: it is not the art of conversation'. [76] The main purpose of diplomacy was negotiation of agreements 'in a ratifiable and dependable form'. [77] The danger of fireside talks was that 'all too often such talks turn into woodland rambles, on the return from which one side remembers only the bracken and the other side can only remember the trees.' And lastly, the amateur diplomacy of personal visits was irreconcilable with the principle of discretion. The visit of a Cabinet minister to a foreign capital inevitably gave rise to 'speculations, insinuations and imaginations' in the press. In consequence, as Nicolson knew only too well from his own experience, one of the parties involved might be tempted 'to disclose a wholly one-sided version of what passed'. Conversely, when both sides resisted such temptations, the impression was invariably conveyed 'that [they had] something abominable to hide'. [78]

Nicolson regarded the relative displacement of the professional diplomatist by the personal diplomacy of amateurs with dismay. He defined the function of the diplomatic service, in general terms, as that of

> a filter in the turgid stream of international affairs. Direct contact between British and foreign statesmen dispenses with that filter. I admit that the rush of water is thereby rendered more potent and more immediate: yet the conduct of foreign policy requires no gush or rush; it requires deliberation, experience and detachment. [79]

Echoing Lord Salisbury's famous metaphor he described foreign policy 'as a slow but majestic river, flowing sedately in a uniform direction, requiring merely, at moments of crisis, a glib but scrupulous rectification of the banks'. [80] In his biography of the American financier and diplomatist Dwight Morrow, the pendant to his modern diplomacy trilogy, he contrasted the values of old:

> the hurried imprecisions of democratic diplomacy are but frivolous factors in the stream of progressive evolution, and . . . effective agreements bearing upon concrete points are more valuable to mankind than any ineffective idealism however righteous or comprehensive these may seem. [81]

Political Guidance

Harold Nicolson's conception of diplomacy, however, was by no means confined to a narrow professionalism, as the above quote might suggest. On the contrary, he was acutely aware of the complex, and often uneasy relationship between diplomacy and foreign policy. It is true, he considered it a dangerous innovation in diplomatic practice to allow politicians to take a personal part in international negotiations. Yet he was equally adamant that the professional diplomatist could not carry out his tasks without political guidance. The idiosyncrasies and inconsistencies of his political masters might be a considerable irritant, as Nicolson knew only too well from personal experience, but the diplomatist was first and foremost a servant. [82]

The wider political context of diplomacy is vital for Nicolson's understanding of his old profession. Diplomacy to him was a lubricant which guaranteed the smooth conduct of international affairs, 'the art of creating and expanding confidence'. [83] Both foreign policy and diplomacy aimed at adjusting national to international interests. But Nicolson insisted that the dividing line between the two ought not to be blurred:

> Foreign policy is based upon a general conception of national requirements; and this conception derives from the need of self-preservation, the constantly changing shapes of economic and strategic advantage and the condition of public opinion as affected at the time ... Diplomacy ... is not an end but a means; not a purpose but a method. It seeks, by the use of reason, conciliation on and the exchange of interests, to prevent major conflicts arising between sovereign States. It is the agency through which foreign policy seeks to attain its purposes by agreement rather than by war. [84]

Foreign policy, however, as Nicolson never ceased to emphasize, is a distinct branch of politics, subject to its own rules and constraints. It was important 'to realise that foreign affairs are *foreign* affairs, that they are relations with foreigners'; and it was a cardinal error to assume that foreign policy could be formulated and then executed in the same manner as domestic legislation could be framed and executed. [85] Not surprisingly, Nicolson was highly critical of Neville Chamberlain's attempt to apply 'business methods to diplomacy'. [86] Those charged with the responsibility of foreign policy-making had to give consideration to the rights and interests of other countries as well as those of their own country. [87] They had 'to take into account not merely the needs, not merely the interests, not merely the ambitions, not merely the history of foreign Powers, but also their frame of mind and their habits of thought'. [88] It was here that the services of the professional diplomatist are required: it was his function to provide the necessary information and to assist in the process of adjusting different interests. [89]

Yet, no diplomatist, however astute or competent, could judge adequately the relevance of the information he gathered unless he was acquainted with the principles and the aims of the foreign policy of his own government. [90] Political guidance therefore was a quintessential precondition of successful diplomacy.

Like Satow before him, Nicolson expected policy-makers to have a firm grasp of the underlying principles and a clear idea of the elements of the foreign policy to be pursued. [91] Firmness in matters of principle, however, had to be combined with a degree of flexibility in questions of detail. Nicolson derided those who thought 'that there can be such a thing as an ideal British foreign policy and that this ideal can be furthered by the adoption of a single set of formulas applicable to any combination of circumstances which may arise.'[92] Still, he was above all a realist; he knew that his was an exacting standard, and that both professional diplomatists and politicians rarely lived up to it. Citing the conduct of Ramsay MacDonald, his old political patron, at the Stresa Conference in 1935, Nicolson observed that all too often basic principles were mistakenly identified as a detail of policy. His realism, however, was informed by a humane, classic view of the foibles of human nature:

> The problem of principle and detail is ... complicated by the desire for "improved relations", an inevitable and not at all discreditable tendency to which all diplomatists and statesmen are prone. Man is by nature a sociable animal and he finds an atmosphere of unabated discord and bickering uncongenial. He seeks to mitigate by concession in detail the animosities which he may rightly cherish in principle.[93]

The ideal statesman, Nicolson argued, was able to shift the dividing line between detail and principle without abandoning the latter; but he readily conceded 'that so few statesmen are either strong or wise'.[94] His own experience of some twenty years in the diplomatic service had taught him that 'Cabinets and Cabinet ministers came and went'; but what remained were '[t]he facts ... of any given case. The files, the previous papers, the figures, the precedents, above all the sharp distinction which exists between the desirable and the practicable'.[95] This sharp distinction is a question of political judgement.

As general foreign policy guidelines, however, Nicolson suggested four principles:

(1) The first of these applied de Callières's advice to diplomatists to the wider field of foreign policy. 'Foreign policy should always be straightforward, open and precise.'[96] Nicolson had always deprecated the all too common confusion between 'foreign policy' and 'diplomacy'.[97] No government, he argued, should give secret pledges or conclude secret treaties. In this sense, foreign policy should never be secret and covenants had always to be open. But he warned that it was 'ignorant to contend that they should be openly arrived at.... The endeavour to establish "open diplomacy" has led delegates to make propaganda speeches in public and conduct serious negotiations in the privacy of hotel bedrooms – which leads to waste of time and farce'.[98]

(2) The second principle is a corollary of the first: 'No Government should make promises which they cannot perform.'

(3) Since a country's responsibilities had to be commensurate with its strength, the government was required to 'have a clear conception of [the country's] relative strength'. [99]

(4) Nicolson identified 'self-preservation [as] the most permanent of human desires'. [100] The maintenance of national security is therefore the fourth general principle of foreign policy. [101] Thus, foreign policy 'should never be influenced by such emotions as prestige, party prejudice, sentiment of adventure'. [102]

For Nicolson these four principles furnished the basis of sound foreign policy. General principles, however, were one thing, the reality of diplomatic practice very often quite another. Much as he emphasized the immutable and universal essence of diplomacy and the continuity in its practice, he was equally insistent on '*the* national character of foreign policy'. [103] His own encounters with foreign diplomatists and ministers as well as his studies of diplomatic history strengthened his conviction that there were marked differences in the diplomatic styles of different powers. This is one of the underlying themes of his writings, which he later developed into a 'typology' of European diplomacy. [104] For Nicolson foreign affairs were not only foreign affairs in the sense that different countries had different interests and consequently pursued different political goals. It was a fallacy, he insisted, to assume that the foreigners with whom diplomatists had to negotiate, entertained the same notion of the art of negotiation. [105] Thus, foreign policy and its main instrument, diplomacy, could only be successful if they recognize these distinctions. [106]

Portrait of an Ideal Diplomatist

Most writers on diplomacy have devoted a considerable part of their efforts to the discussion of the qualities necessary for the ideal diplomatist. Nicolson's works are no exception. He was by no means oblivious to the prevailing popular misperceptions of the diplomatist's role. In the interwar years, however, the zenith of Nicolson's official and public career, the diplomatic profession had fallen into particular disrepute. Not surprisingly, Nicolson was anxious to restore the professional diplomatist's good reputation. Far from possessing the loathsome qualities attributed to them in popular mythology, diplomacy required from its practitioners 'a combination of certain qualities which are not always found in the ordinary politician, nor even in the ordinary man'. [107] Like Satow, Nicolson largely followed the precepts of François de Callières's early eighteenth-century manual on diplomatic practice. In his estimation, 'no other writer... has given so clear, so complete, or so unanswerable a definition of good diplomatic method'. [108] For Nicolson, deeply imbued with the spirit of the enlightenment, there was no need to go beyond that great Frenchman. He accepted in particular de Callières's emphasis on moral integrity as the foremost quality of the successful diplomatist. In one of the most often quoted paragraphs in *Diplomacy* Nicolson summarized the qualities of the ideal diplomatist as:

> Truth, accuracy, calm, patience, good temper, modesty and loyalty. They are also the qualities of ideal diplomacy. "But", the reader may object, "you have forgotten intelligence, knowledge, discernment, prudence, hospitality, charm, industry, courage and even tact." I have not forgotten them. I have taken them for granted. [109]

Nicolson dedicated his handbook on diplomacy to Sir Horace Rumbold, his erstwhile chief at the Berlin embassy in the late 1920s, describing him as 'an ideal diplomatist'. The following eulogy on Rumbold bears quoting *in extenso* as it illustrates further Nicolson's catalogue of the necessary qualities and capacities:

> [H]e was able to represent unerringly those qualities of truthfulness, tolerance and good sense which form the foundations of all sound diplomacy. He was self-confident without being self-assertive, proud but not vain, inflexible rather than rigid, shrewd but not cunning. He applied simple standards of decent conduct to the intricate problems with which he had to deal; he was so trustworthy that he enlarged the areas of trust; he was so respected that he made the most tortuous characters behave respectably. He was a man in whom there was no guile. [110]

Harold Nicolson was an unceasing and vociferous advocate of veracity as a virtue and a necessity in diplomacy. [111] The gentlemanly qualities of a firm character, civility in manner and address, good temper and imperturbability apart, [112] Nicolson placed great emphasis on the diplomatist's gift of discernment. Perspicacity and a shrewd grasp of a developing situation were at the very core of the diplomatist's craft. This alone was a difficult enough achievement, as Nicolson observed in a Foreign Office memorandum:

> any forecast of diplomatic development must inevitably deal, not with concentric forces, but with eccentric tendencies; such data as

are available emerge only from a mass of heterogeneous phenomena, mutually conflicting, mutually overlapping, and striving each towards some distinct and often incompatible solution. [113]

In general terms, Nicolson argued, '[t]he business of the diplomatist is to represent his own government in a foreign country.' [114] But to do so successfully, he had to understand the country to which he is posted; he had to be able to discern its ambitions and interests, and possible threats to the interests of his own government: he had to be a man of sound judgement, free of distorting 'affectations and prejudices'. But he did not need to be a local expert; nor, for that matter, did he need to be able to speak a difficult local language. [115] For translations or advice on details of local conditions he could turn to his staff of permanent officials 'whose business it is to advise and inform'. The ambassador's role, however, was 'to judge and decide' with a view to advising his government as to the policy best suited for a particular situation; and he had to perform this task by means of 'a meticulous though tolerant investigation of basic facts rather than by any adjustments of current political and economic theories'. [116] This unbiased approach to foreign affairs, this reverence for '[t]he facts ... of any given case', coupled with a firm understanding of the basic principles of the country's foreign policy was one of the hallmarks of what Nicolson termed the 'Foreign Office mind'. [117] The latter provided a framework or common outlook which in turn enhanced the efficiency and coherence of the diplomatic service. [118] Hence Nicolson's advocacy of a foreign service staff college, on the analogy of the army staff college at Sandhurst. [119] Such a mind-set had to be inculcated in budding diplomatists over a lengthy period of time. It could not be acquired with immediate effect by amateurs, as Nicolson observed of Neville Chamberlain's much-maligned adviser, the Treasury official Sir Horace Wilson, who had 'stepped into diplomacy with the high faithfulness of two curates entering a pub for the first time'. [120]

Expert knowledge, of course, was an essential ingredient of sound judgement; but without prudence, discernment and intelligence, without the 'Foreign Office mind' it was an almost dispensable commodity.

Diplomacy by Conference

One of the most significant innovations in diplomatic practice under the auspices of 'new diplomacy' was inaugurated at the Paris Peace Conference in 1919: diplomacy by conference. As a means to conduct diplomatic negotiations it was, of course, not new. But in the aftermath of the First World War special importance was afforded to this instrument, as the best means to settle difficult international issues. Few contemporary observers doubted that 'diplomacy by conference has come to stay'. [121] Nicolson was no exception. He considered international round-table gatherings to be among the main innovations introduced into diplomatic practice after 1918–19; but he was far more doubtful of its benefits than most contemporary commentators.

Nicolson himself had attended three major international conferences, two of these, the 1919 Paris Peace Conference and the Lausanne Conference in 1923, in an official capacity. In 1946 he covered the abortive Peace Conference at Paris for the BBC. A considerable part of his diplomatic writings was devoted to international conferences as functions of post-1919 diplomacy. 'Diplomacy by conference', therefore deserves to be treated separately.

Nicolson, perhaps because of his own painful conversion from Wilsonianism, remained a never tiring warner of the dangers of diplomacy by conference – 'perhaps the most unfortunate diplomatic method ever conceived'. [122] He did not query the seemingly undeniable advantages of this method. The fact that the policy-makers themselves were involved in the negotiations meant a considerable saving of time. Frequent meetings of heads of government, he conceded, allowed for 'absolute frankness in discussion', but it also heightened the importance of their personal relations. Nicolson himself had witnessed the altercation between Lord Curzon, Britain's foreign secretary, and the French premier Raymond Poincaré in September 1922, in the aftermath of the Chanak crisis. [123] The personal relations between the two men, at times strained to breaking point, did not assist the difficult negotiations before the Lausanne Conference in the following year. Such animosity was perhaps rare. But even when personal contact bred friendliness, the negotiations in hand were not necessarily facilitated. Conference diplomacy, in Nicolson's view, tended to magnify the adverse effects of private diplomacy. Like the fireside chats the foreign secretaries of his time had come to prefer to the more strenuous methods of the old diplomacy, conferences led to imprecision, the main enemy of sound diplomacy. Reflecting on his own experience at Paris and Lausanne, Nicolson noted, perhaps somewhat mischievously: 'The affability inseparable from any conversation between Foreign Ministers produces allusiveness, compromises and high intentions. Diplomacy, if it is ever to be effective, should be a disagreeable business. And one recorded in hard print.' [124] Nicolson, however, knew that there was no turning back to the days of old diplomacy, though after Munich he seems to have assumed that conferences had become transitory phenomena in international politics. [125] Ambassadorial conferences had become an important feature in diplomacy in the course of the nineteenth century [126]; and Nicolson conceded the necessity, on exceptional occasions, such as the conclusion of a peace treaty, for a major international conference:

> [T]here are occasions when international agreement can only be achieved by oral discussion between plenipotentiaries. There are occasions, also, when issues are so vital and immediate that 'policy' as well as 'negotiation' is involved. On such occasions the negotiators must be identical with the framers of policy, and the resultant congresses and conferences must be attended by the Prime Ministers or Foreign Secretaries of the several Powers. [127]

It was not simply a professional diplomatist's chagrin at the diminution of his tasks implicit in diplomacy by conference, which made Nicolson wary of this unwieldy instrument of international politics. His personal experience at Paris in 1919 confirmed Satow's earlier observations on 'the necessity of (a) some previous agreement as to the ends in view, and (b) a definite and rigid programme'. [128] Neither the inter-Allied London discussions prior to the conference proper, nor President Wilson's famous 'Fourteen Points' furnished an accepted basis for the ensuing negotiations; in the absence of a clear programme the negotiating parties were soon lost 'in mists of exhaustion, disability, suspicion and despair'; [129] and the failure of the conference to live up to its own high principles, Nicolson concurred with Keynes, had produced 'that web of sophistry and Jesuitical exegesis that was finally to clothe with insincerity the language and substance of the whole Treaty'. [130]

Almost a quarter of a century later, towards the end of the Second World War, he offered further reflections on the main lessons of past peace conferences. He stipulated that the victorious powers in particular had 'to agree in advance upon their general aims and principles: they must also agree as to the means by which these aims shall be secured and these principles be established'. The main complications at Paris in 1919, he observed, originated in a clash of interests and principles amongst the victorious Allies. It was important to remember 'that conflicts regarding means which entail action are more frequent and more obstinate than conflicts regarding ends which only imply theory'. [131] As to the need for an agreed programme he reiterated:

This is not a minor point; it is major point. The difficulty of all good peacemaking is time-pressure; hurry entails over-work and over-work entails imprecision. Time must be rationed in advance upon the sensible principle that the most important problems must be taken first. [132]

Nicolson insisted on a further weakness of the conference system as inaugurated after the Great War. The war had precipitated the final collapse of the established Great Power system, the 'Concert of Europe', which had formed the basis of diplomacy in the nineteenth century. In Nicolson's analysis, the emergence of the United States as a new Great Power and the rise of smaller nations had undermined the foundations of the existing international system without replacing it with a functioning new framework. In consequence, 'new diplomacy' found itself caught between two conflicting formulae: 'The first was the Roman, or aristo-cratic, formula of *authority*. The second was the American, or democratic, formula of *consent*.' [133] Nicolson's argument is incontestable. The innova-tions in diplomatic practice after 1919 exacerbated the underlying tension, inherent in the post-Westphalian system, between the reality of power and the principle of the equality of sovereign states. While the Great Powers continued to dominate international politics in the inter-war years, they were notionally equal with the smaller nations whose fate they shaped. Nicolson accepted this antinomy of modern international relations as a matter of fact, resignedly observing that the Great Powers had 'always striven to escape from this nasty conflict and to resort to all forms of cowardice, procrastination, hypocrisy and downright untruth-fulness rather than face this issue'. [134]

In his last diplomatic writings, after the Second World War, Nicolson reiterated his criticism of the permanent conference system introduced under the aegis of 'international tribunals', such as the League of Nations and the United Nations. The principle of one-state-one-vote, as enshrined in the UN Charter, did not alter the fact that '[t]he major decisions in this world are taken by those who possess power and are prepared to exercise it. The substitution of consent, or votes, for force has given the United Nations a certain unreality and has hampered its authority'. [135] The device of voting *in pleno* had been introduced as an innovation of diplomatic practice at the abortive Paris Peace Conference in 1946. With the rifts within the wartime Grand Alliance becoming ever wider and ever more apparent, however, the votes merely served to emphasize the divisions between the emerging 'Soviet bloc' and the Western nations. [136] These divisions were laid bare further by the introduction of 'open negotiations'. As a result, the conference degenerated into a 'succession of propaganda speeches which took no account of the merits of the issue under discussion, which committed the several delegations to positions from which it would be difficult to retreat, which aroused resentment, and which filled the assembled delegates with weariness and despair'. [137] In a BBC broadcast from the Paris conference he reminded his listeners that: *'La diplomatie, comme Callières l'a bien defini au dix-septième siècle, est l'art de négocier des accords durables entre états souverains. On ne peut pas négocier devant le microphone.'* [138]

The experience of the 1946 Paris conference confirmed Nicolson in his insistence on open policies and confidential negotiations. [139] The permanent state of conference at the UN had the same defects as that other version of 'open diplomacy', the personal diplomacy of politicians:

> These conferences . . . do much to diminish the utility of professional diplomatists and, in that they entail much publicity, many rumours, and wide speculation, – in that they tempt politicians to achieve quick, spectacular and often fictitious results, – they tend to promote rather than allay suspicion, and to create those very states of uncertainty which it is the purpose of good diplomatic method to prevent. [140]

Conclusion

Harold Nicolson's entire diplomatic *oeuvre* was written in the shadow of 'new diplomacy'. His modern diplomacy trilogy together with its American pendant was a first attempt to charter the course of events which had transformed the conduct of international relations in the first half of this century. But Nicolson was never a mere chronicler, a collector of diplomatic curios. Too little has been made of his writings on diplomatic theory and practice. His slightly quixotic professional career and his ultimately unfulfilled political ambitions have relegated him to the fringes of twentieth-century history; and it has been too tempting for some to dismiss his writings as intellectually lightweight because of their accessibility and the absence of any theoretical pretensions. [141] None of this is deserved.

Nicolson never climbed to the 'top of the greasy pole', but he was one of the best informed, most intelligent and forthright speakers on foreign affairs in the 'long parliament' of 1935. [142] The early and consistent warner of the dangers of appeasing the dictators cannot easily be written off as a political lightweight. Indeed, for some contemporary observers and foreign diplomatists Nicolson would have made an excellent foreign secretary. [143]

His expositions of diplomacy were graceful in style, but more importantly he brought to his task considerable professional experience, practical wisdom, enlightened realism and a humane scepticism. It is true, his attitude towards the changes in diplomatic practice in the aftermath of the Great War appears ambivalent. He accepted this transformation as irreversible whilst simultaneously deprecating 'new diplomacy'. Yet this seems an instance more of moral courage and less of intellectual ambivalence. True also that Nicolson's judgement was, on occasions, somewhat clouded. To anyone at the threshold of the twenty-first century his contention that women were ill-adapted to the tasks of diplomacy must appear singularly misguided. [144] Similarly his scepticism of 'new diplomacy' may have been a reflection of his social and political sentiments. Nicolson was indeed in many ways 'a nineteenth-century character... living an eighteenth-century life in the midst of the twentieth century'. [145] Yet his criticism of post-1919 diplomacy and his warnings of its illusions were consistently based on reasoned arguments, derived from professional experience and informed by a shrewd grasp of past and contemporary international politics; and as such they cannot be ignored. There is no doubt that Nicolson preferred the certainties of the old diplomacy to the vagaries of the new. But this was not blinkered nostalgia. He was well aware of the dangers of the pre-1914 diplomacy [146]; and nothing, except the ideological perversions of the twentieth century, was more objectionable to him than Palmerston's mistaken preference for blustering demagoguery over sound diplomacy. [147]

Nicolson was unable, nor did he attempt, to solve in conceptual terms the tension between power and morality in modern international politics. But his main ambition was to render an objective account of the nature of diplomacy and to establish its immutable essential elements, and not to engage in metaphysical speculation. This in itself was no mean achievement and much more intellectually honest than the soft-centred sentimentalities of 'idealism' and the cruder versions of hard-nosed 'realism'. For these reasons alone Harold Nicolson's diplomatic writings ought to receive due attention.

Notes

1. H. G. Nicolson, *The Evolution of Diplomatic Method* (London, 1954), p. 57. (Unless otherwise noted all works referred to in this chapter are by Nicolson.)
2. J. Lees-Milne, 'Sir Harold George Nicolson (1886–1968), in *Dictionary of National Biography, 1961–1970* (Oxford, 1981), p. 796.

3. N. Lawson, 'Spectator Notebook', in *Spectator* (3 May 1968), p. 592; D. W. Brogan, 'The Sage of Sissinghurst', ibid. (17 May 1968), p. 668.
4. Lees-Milne, 'Nicolson', p. 796; D. Cannadine, *Aspects of Aristocracy: Grandeur and Decline in Modern Britain* (London, 1995 (pb)), p. 221.
5. E. Wilson, 'Through the Embassy Window', in *New Yorker* (1 Jan.1944), pp.63–7; H. Trevor-Roper, 'Lord Cranfield as he wasn't', in *Spectator* (6 Sept.1968), pp.327–8; cf. Nicolson diary, 21 Feb. 1944, in N. Nicolson (ed.), *Harold Nicolson: Diaries and Letters, 1930–1962*, 3 vols (London, 1966–8), vol. II, pp. 350–1.
6. The extremely fastidious Nicolson himself was perhaps his most severe critic, cf. Nicolson diary, 23 Nov.1933, *Diaries*, vol. I, p. 157.
7. L. B. Namier, *In the Margins of History* (London, 1939), p. 4.
8. D. Cannadine, *The Decline and Fall of the British Aristocracy* (New Haven, CT, 1990), pp. 285–6; L. Colley, *Britons: Forging the Nation, 1707–1837* (London, 1994(pb)), pp. 155–64.
9. Cf. *Sir Arthur Nicolson, Bart., Lord Carnock: A Study in Old Diplomacy* (London, 1930); also Z. S. Steiner, *The Foreign Office and Foreign Policy, 1898–1914* (London, repr.1986), pp. 121–53; K. Neilson, '"My beloved Russians": Sir Arthur Nicolson and Russia', in *International History Review*, vol. IX, no. 4 (1987), pp. 521–54.
10. *Helen's Tower* (London, 1937); Sir A. Lyall, *The Life of the Marquis of Dufferin and Ava*, 2 vols (London, 1905).
11. Drummond to Nicolson, 11 Nov. 1919, and Nicolson to Drummond, 12 Nov. 1919, Sissinghurst Mss.
12. Nicolson to Tilea, 9 Dec. 1919, Tilea Mss, Ratiu Family Charitable Foundation, London, box 67; cf. *Peacemaking 1919* (London, 1933), p. 209; J. Barros, *Office Without Power: Secretary-General Sir Eric Drummond, 1919–1933* (Oxford, 1979), p. 386; E. Maisel, *The Foreign Office and Foreign Policy, 1919–1926* (Brighton, 1994), pp. 58–9.
13. Nicolson to Evelyn Wrench, 18 Feb. 1928, Wrench MSS, British Library, Add.MSS.59543; 'World government', in H. J. Laski (ed.), *Programme for Victory: A Collection of Essays Prepared for the Fabian Society* (London, 1941), pp. 53–4; 'Britain – base for offense', in *Britain*, vol. II, no. 4 (1943), pp. 1–3; *The Future of the English Speaking World* (Glasgow, 1949).
14. Min. Nicolson, 27 Aug. 1924, Public Record Office, Kew, FO 371/9819/C13663/2048/18; memo.Nicolson, 20 Feb. 1925, *Documents of British Foreign Policy*, 1st ser. XXVII, no. 205; cf. Maisel, *Foreign Office*, p. 165.
15. *Evolution of Diplomatic Method*, pp. 88–9; 'What France means to England', in *Foreign Affairs*, vol. XVII, no. 2 (1939), p. 358.
16. It is not surprising that one of the many subplots in his novel *Public Faces* deals with the attempts by the Persian government to exploit the League in an effort to play off one great power against the other, *Public Faces* (London, 1932), pp. 225–7.
17. Nicolson to Chamberlain (no.486), 30 Sept.1926, *DBFP*, ser.Ia, ii.no.447; cf. Nicolson to Oliphant, 25 Jan. and 6 Nov. 1926, and Nicolson to Lord and Lady Carnock, 15 June 1926, Sissinghurst MSS.
18. Nicolson to Vita Sackville-West, 3 Aug. 1928 (copy), Rumbold MSS, Bodl., MS Rumbold dep. 44; Nicolson to Lord and Lady Carnock, 8 June 1926, Sissinghurst MSS.

19. Nicolson to O'Malley, 23 Aug.1927 (copy), and Nicolson to Lady Carnock, 20 Apr. 1927, Sissinghurst MSS.
20. Nicolson to Lord Beaverbrook, 1 Aug. 1929, and Beaverbrook to Nicolson, 10 Aug. 1929, Beaverbrook MSS, House of Lords Record Office, BBK.C/256; Ramsay MacDonald to Nicolson (private and confidential), 20 Sept. 1929, Sissinghurst MSS.
21. Nicolson diary, 9 Jan. 1932, in S. Olson (ed.), *Diaries and Letters, 1930–1962* (London, 1996), pp. 36–7. For an account of his public career cf. vol. II of Lees-Milne's biography, and L. Wolff, 'The public faces of Harold Nicolson: the Thirties', in *Biography* vol. V, no. 3 (1982), pp. 240–52.
22. Nicolson to Sybil Colefax, 14 Sept.1929, Colefax MSS, Bodl., MS.Eng.c.3166; N. Nicolson, *Portrait of a Marriage* (London, 1973; pb 1990), pp. 197–8.
23. Nicolson to Sibyl Colefax, 7 Sept. 1927, ibid.; Nicolson to Rumbold, 12 Sept. 1929, Rumbold MSS, Bodl., Ms. Rumbold dep. 37; Lord Gladwyn, *The Memoirs of Lord Gladwyn* (London, 1972), 25; Nigel Nicolson to the author, 29 Sept. 1996.
24. A comprehensive survey of Nicolson's major writings can be found in D. Drinkwater, 'Professional Amateur: Sir Harold Nicolson's Writings on Diplomacy' (unpublished BA thesis, University of Queensland, 1977).
25. In the opinion of J. C. C. Davidson, a senior Conservative minister in the 1930s, Nicolson 'may have been a nice man with the right views, but he was not reliable and had the outlook of a journalist', as quoted in J. Charmley, *Duff Cooper* (London, 1986), p. 148; Nicolson to Sibyl Colefax, 25 Feb. 1938, Colefax MSS, Bodl., Ms.Eng.c.3166.
26.. M. Wight, 'Western values in International Relations', in M. Wight and H. Butterfield (eds), *Diplomatic Investigations: Essays in the Theory of International Politics* (London, repr.1966), pp. 90–1.
27. 'Marginal Comment', in *The Spectator* (10 Mar. 1950), p. 304; 'Causes and purposes', in *Nineteenth Century*, vol. CXXVI, no. 752 (1939), pp. 391–2; 'The Values of Europe', in *The Listener* (2 Jan. 1958), pp. 11–12; 'Romanticism vs. Classicism', unpublished MS, Sissinghurst MSS.
28. 'Man and circumstance', in *Foreign Affairs*, vol. XXIII, no. 3 (1945), p. 283; Nicolson to Gilbert Murray, 1 Jan.1941, Murray MSS, Bodl., Mss Murray 89; *The Age of Reason, 1700–1789* (London, 1960), p. xxi; *Good Behaviour, being a Study of Certain Types of Civility* (London, 1955), pp. 1–2.
29. BBC European Service broadcast, 3 Aug. 1946, MS, Sissinghurst MSS, 1. In the mid-1930s he described himself somewhat anachronistically as an Asquithian Liberal, cf. *Politics in the Train* (London, 1936), pp. 8–9.
30. *The Meaning of Prestige* (Cambridge, 1937), pp. 30–6.
31. 'The Past Week', BBC broadcast, 15 Aug.1938, MS, Sissinghurst MSS, fol.6; *Hansard* (Commons), 5th ser. cccxlv (3 Apr.1939); '"Bilbao"', in *The [National Labour] News-Letter*, vol. X, no. 22 (31 July 1937), pp. 228–9.
32. Nicolson to Sir Alfred Zimmern, 30 Apr. 1936, Zimmern Mss, Bodl., MS Zimmern 39; *Comments, 1944–1948* (London, 1948), p. 12.
33. *Diplomacy* (London, 1939), p. 133; 'Marginal Comment', in *Spectator* (30 June 1950), p. 885; 'The Psychology of Anglo-French Relations in 1935', MS, Sissinghurst MSS, fol.1; *Why Britain Is At War* (Harmondsworth, 1939), p. 135.
34. 'A Man and a Crisis, being a sketch of Anthony Eden', MS, n.d.[1935], Sissinghurst MSS, fol.1.

35. 'Perspectives on peace: a discourse', in Carnegie Endowment for Peace (ed.), *Perspectives on Peace, 1910–1960* (London, 1960), pp. 33–4; 'Has Britain a policy?', in *Foreign Affairs*, vol. XIV, no. 4 (1936), p. 550; 'The origins and development of the Anglo-French entente', in *International Affairs*. vol. XXX, no. 4 (1954), pp. 415–16.
36. 'Collective Security', in *Christian Science Monitor* (24 June 1936), pp. 1–2; 'Balance of Power Up-to-Date: A Discussion', in *The Listener* (16 Mar.1938), pp. 570–3.
37. 'The Rough Island Story', part 4, BBC Television broadcast, 12 July 1939, MS, Sissinghurst Mss, fol.3.
38. *The Congress of Vienna: a Study in Allied Unity, 1812–1822* (London, 1946), p. 155.
39. Nicolson to Lionel Curtis, 16 Aug. 1949, Curtis Mss, Bodl., Mss Curtis 58; 'Marginal Comment', in *Spectator* (12 Aug.1949), p. 203.
40. 'How I Write Biography', in *Saturday Review of Literature* (26 May 1934), pp. 709–11; *The Development of English Biography* (London, repr.1959), pp. 150–1; Nicolson to Lytton Strachey, 22 Jan. 1922, Strachey Mss, BL, Add.Mss.60682. Unlike Strachey, however, Nicolson never sacrificed factual accuracy for a sparkling epigram.
41. *Peacemaking 1919*, pp. 4–5; 'Secret Diplomacy: Old and New', in *The News-Letter: The National Labour Fortnightly*, vol. XI, no. 5 (4 Dec. 1937), 69–71; 'Diplomacy then and now', in *Foreign Affairs*, vol. XL, no. 1 (1961), pp. 39–49.
42. 'The Foreign Service', in *The British Civil Servant* (London, 1937), p. 47. Earlier Nicolson had praised Satow as 'the greatest . . . authority upon diplomatic practice', *Peacemaking 1919*, p. 80.
43. *Peacemaking 1919*, p. 4.
44. *Diplomacy*, pp. 14, 16.
45. *Evolution of Diplomatic Method*, p. 2.
46. 'Marginal Comment', in *Spectator* (12 Jan. 1951), p. 43.
47. J. Der Derian, *On Diplomacy: a Genealogy of Western Estrangement* (Oxford, 1987), chs 2 and 4; A. Watson, *Diplomacy: the Dialogue between States* (London, 1982), pp. 14–21, 82–94.
48. *Diplomacy*, p. 20.
49. Ibid., p. 16.
50. *Peacemaking 1919*, p. 4.
51. A. J. P. Taylor, *The Troublemakers: Dissent over Foreign Policy, 1792–1939* (London, 1957), pp. 167–200.
52. In Nicolson's estimation the representatives of 'old diplomacy' were 'men of peace.[. . .] They represented all that was most wise, honourable and pacific in the Old Diplomacy; they formed a distinguished group', *George V: His Life and Reign* (London, 1952), p. 176.
53. *Curzon: The Last Phase, 1919–1925: a Study in Post-War Diplomacy*, new edn (London, 1937), p. 184.
54. *Peacemaking 1919*, p. 4.
55. *Diplomacy*, p. 80.
56. *Curzon*, p. 184; 'Lord Palmerston', in H. J. and H. Massingham (eds), *The Great Victorians* (London, s.a.[1932]), pp. 376–7.
57. *Curzon*, p. 184; 'Foreign Service', p. 48.

58. *Diplomacy*, pp. 60–1.
59. *Peacemaking 1919*, pp. 4–5; 'The Future of Diplomacy', lecture notes, n.d.[1933?], Sissinghurst Mss.
60. *Marginal Comments, January 6 – August 4, 1939* (London, 1939), pp. 125 and 162.
61. 'Perspectives on peace', p. 38.
62. *Sir Arthur Nicolson*, pp. ix–x; 'Europe and the Post-War Generation', unpublished MS, n.d., Sissinghurst Mss. Mr Derek Drinkwater argues that the 'Studies in Modern Diplomacy ought to be seen to be including Nicolson's biography of Dwight Morrow, thus forming a tetralogy', Drinkwater, 'Professional Amateur', pp. 29–30. Whether Nicolson himself conceived of the four volumes as a unit seems, however, doubtful, cf. *Diaries*, vol. I, p. 176.
63. 'Perspectives on peace', p. 38; *Peacemaking 1919*, ch. 8.
64. *Diplomacy*, p. 82.
65. 'Modern diplomacy and British public opinion', in *International Affairs*, vol. XIV, no. 5 (1935), p. 599; *Marginal Comments*, pp. 189–92; 'Little Man, What Now?', in *The [National Labour] News-Letter*, vol. VIII, no. 8 (4 Jan. 1936), pp. 125–7; *Public Faces*, p. 95.
66. 'Has Britain a policy?', p. 559; 'What France means to England', in *Foreign Affairs*, vol. XVII, no. 2 (1939), pp. 358–9.
67. 'Men and circumstance', in *Foreign Affairs*, vol. XXIII, no. 3 (1945), p. 484; 'Foreign Service', pp. 56–7.
68. *Curzon*, p. 185; 'Some Aspects of Democratic Diplomacy', lecture notes, n.d., Sissinghurst MSS.
69. 'Marginal Comment', in *The Spectator* (26 Nov. 1948), p. 693; 'What is imperialism?', in *England: Journal of the Royal Society of St George*, n.s., vol. II, no. 15 (1943), pp. 4, 10; 'Diplomacy then and now', p. 40; Nicolson to Sir Alfred Zimmern, 30 Apr. 1936, Zimmern Mss, Bodl., Ms Zimmern 39.
70. 'Man and circumstance', p. 484; 'A Case of Conscience', in *The [National Labour] News-Letter*, vol. VIII, no. 7 (21 Dec. 1935), pp. 104–5.
71. *Curzon*, pp. 185–6; 'Lord Palmerston', pp. 377–8.
72. 'Perspectives on peace', p. 38; *The Independent Member of Parliament* (London, 1946), p. 13; *Helen's Tower* (London, 1937), pp. 165–6; *Public Faces*, pp. 201–2.
73. *Congress of Vienna*, p. 165; 'Lord Palmerston', p. 374.
74. BBC Home Service broadcast, 7 Aug. 1946, MS, Sissinghurst MSS, fol.6.
75. 'The Past Week', in *The Listener* (29 Sept. 1938), p. 672.
76. 'Secret Diplomacy', p. 70; cf. 'Germany and the Colonies', in *Fortnightly Review*, vol. CXLII, no. 12 (1937), pp. 641–8.
77. 'The Foreign Service', p. 60.
78. 'Secret Diplomacy', pp. 70–1; *Diplomacy*, pp. 100–1; *Marginal Comment*, p. 196.
79. 'Modern diplomacy and British public opinion', p. 610.
80. *Public Faces*, p. 2. Lord Salisbury likened (British) foreign policy to 'float[ing] lazily downstream, occasionally putting out a diplomatic boat-hook to avoid collisions', Salisbury to Lord Lytton, 9 Mar. 1877, Lady G. Cecil, *Life of Robert, Marquis of Salisbury*, 4 vols, (London, 1921), vol. II, p. 130.
81. *Dwight Morrow* (London, 1937), p. vi.
82. *People and Things*, pp. 9–14; 'Lord Curzon', in *The Listener* (21 Apr. 1937), pp. 737–9; *Diplomacy*, pp. 80–2.

83. 'Marginal Comment', in *Spectator* (25 Aug. 1950), p. 239.
84. *Congress of Vienna*, p. 164.
85. *National Character and National Policy: the Montague Burton International Relations Lecture 1938* (Nottingham, 1938), p. 3; 'Man and circumstance', p. 483; 'Peace Pledge', in *The [National Labour] Newsletter*, vol. X, no. 22 (31 July 1937), p. 341.
86. *Comments, 1944–1948* (London, 1948), p. 114.
87. 'Treaty making 1946', in *Current Affairs*, vol. I, no. 2 (1946), p. 5.
88. *National Character*, pp. 3–4.
89. 'The origins and development of the Anglo-French entente', in *International Affairs*, vol. XXX, no. 4 (1954), pp. 416–17.
90. 'Diplomacy then and now', pp. 41–2.
91. 'Treaty Making 1946', p. 5; *English Speaking World*, pp. 17–19.
92. *Independent Member*, pp. 14–15.
93. 'Man and circumstance', p. 483; 'Marginal Comment', in *Spectator* (18 Mar. 1949), p. 357 and (17 Feb. 1950), p. 208. Much earlier Nicolson confessed that 'I was never...much of believer in "good relations" as an aim in themselves. They act as a useful lubricant: & bad relations paralyse all action', Nicolson to Lancelot Oliphant, 26 Jan. 1926, Sissinghurst MSS.
94. 'Man and circumstance', p. 483.
95. *Politics in the Train*, pp. 7–8; 'The Planners', BBC broadcast, 18 Dec. 1940, MS, Sissinghurst Mss, fol.4; Nicolson to Sir Alfred Zimmern, 30 Apr.1936, Zimmern Mss, Bodl, MS Zimmern 39.
96. 'Treaty making 1946', p. 9; 'The Spanish Crisis', in *The [National Labour] Newsletter*, vol. X, no. 8 (19 Dec.1936), pp. 116–17; 'Is war inevitable?', in *Nineteenth Century*, vol. CXXVI, no. 749 (1939), pp. 1–13; 'Marginal Comment', in *The Spectator* (25 Aug. 1950), p. 239.
97. 'Secret Diplomacy', p. 69.
98. 'Perspectives on peace', p. 37.
99. 'Treaty making 1946', p. 9; 'Limited or Unlimited Obligations? What Ought British Foreign Policy To Be?', in *Listener* (9 Dec. 1936), p. 1107; 'Our Treaty With France', ibid. (6 Mar. 1947), pp. 328–9.
100. 'Anglo-French entente', p. 416; 'What France means to England', p. 361; *Diplomacy*, p. 177; *Why Britain Is At War*, pp. 135–6.
101. 'War Aims and Peace Aims', in *The [National Labour] Newsletter*, vol. IV, no. 41 (1940), p. 12.
102. 'Treaty making 1946', p. 9.
103. *National Character*, pp. 1–2; *Meaning of Prestige*, pp. 20–1.
104. 'National Character and International Cooperation', lecture notes, n.d. [1933?], Sissinghurst MSS; *National Character*, pp. 12–13; 'After Munich', pp. 521–3; 'The colonial problem', in *Foreign Affairs*, vol. XVII, no. 1 (1938), pp. 38–9; *Diplomacy*, pp. 127–53; 'We Speak a Different Language', *Listener* (24 Oct. 1946), p. 547.
105. *Diplomacy*, 128; 'The diplomatic background', in H. A. L. Fisher (ed.), *The Background and Issues of the War* (Oxford, 1940), pp. 95–119.
106. *National Character*, p. 4.
107. *Diplomacy*, p. 105.
108. *Evolution of Diplomatic Method*, pp. 62–8.

109. *Diplomacy*, p. 126; *Public Faces*, p. 5. In the fictitious figure of the 'third Baron Bognor' Nicolson offered a different, though tongue-in-cheek portrait, cf. *Some People* (London, 1927), pp. 142–3.
110. 'Introduction', in Sir H. Rumbold, *The War Crisis in Berlin, July–August 1914* (London, 1944), pp. xix–xxxvii.
111. 'A Cautionary Tale', in *Listener* (27 Nov. 1935), p. 973; Gladwyn, *Memoirs*, p. 58.
112. *Good Behaviour*, pp. 184 et seq.; 'Allen Leeper', in *Nineteenth Century*, vol. CXVIII, no. 704 (1935), pp. 473–83.
113. Memo., 'Consideration of Future Political and Diplomatic Developments', 10 Mar. 1918, Sissinghurst Mss.
114. 'Diplomacy then and now', p. 43.
115. *National Character*, p. 4; *Evolution of Diplomatic Method*, pp. 76–7, 82; *Friday Mornings* (London, 1944), p. 175; *Helen's Tower*, pp. 227–30. Nicolson praised Horace Rumbold for never making 'any concessions to the foreign way in which the natives pronounced [their] languages', Rumbold, *War Crisis*, p. xxiv.
116. 'Diplomacy then and now', pp. 42–3; *Friday Mornings*, pp. 23–4; *Dwight Morrow*, p. vi.
117. *Politics in the Train*, p. 8; speech in the House of Commons, 5 Nov. 1938, here quoted from a copy in the Attlee Mss, Bodl., Ms Attlee dep.1; 'Marginal Comment', in *The Spectator* (9 June 1950), p. 787.
118. Nicolson's colleague Owen O'Malley spoke of the 'brotherhood', cf. O. O'Malley, *The Phantom Caravan* (London, 1954), p. 157.
119. 'Foreign Service', p. 63; 'The Reform of the Foreign Service', *Friday Mornings*, pp. 122–3.
120. *Why Britain Is At War*, p. 106.
121. Lord Hankey, *Diplomacy by Conference: Studies in Public Affairs, 1920–1946* (London, 1946), p. 38; cf. R. T. B. Langhorne, 'The development of international conferences, 1648–1830', in *Studies in History and Politics*, vol. I, no. 2 (1981–2), pp. 61–91; E. Goldstein, 'The origins of summit diplomacy', in D. H. Dunn (ed.), *Diplomacy at the Highest Level* (London, 1996), pp. 23–37.
122. *Curzon*, p. 397.
123. *Curzon*, pp. 272–4; also *Diplomacy*, pp. 157–8; *Marginal Comments*, pp. 128–9.
124. *Peacemaking 1919*, pp. 208–9.
125. *Diplomacy*, pp. 159–60.
126. *Lord Carnock*, pp. 170–99.
127. *Curzon*, p. 397; *Congress of Vienna*, p. 165; 'Treaty making 1946', pp. 5 and 9–10; BBC Overseas Broadcast, 2 Aug. 1946, MS, Sissinghurst Mss, 2.
128. *Peacemaking 1919*, pp. 80–1; BBC Home Service broadcast, 31 July 1946, MS, Sissinghurst Mss, fol.1; *Congress of Vienna*, pp. 135–6.
129. *Peacemaking 1919*, p. 87; 'Introduction 1943', in *Peacemaking 1919*, new edn (London, 1945), pp. xvii–xviii; 'Ce qu'on peut apprendre des Traités de 1919', in *Choix*, no. 5 (1944), pp. 36–8.
130. J. M. Keynes, *The Economic Consequences of the Peace* (London, 1920), p. 47, as quoted in *Peacemaking 1919*, p. 88.
131. 'Introduction 1943', pp. x–xii; 'Treaty making 1946', p. 10; *Marginal Comments*, pp. 126–7; cf. diary, 12 June 1943, *Diaries*, vol. II, p. 301.
132. 'Introduction 1943', p. xxi; *Why Britain Is At War*, pp. 148–9.

133. *Curzon*, pp. 68 and 152–6.
134. BBC Home Service broadcast, 31 July 1946, MS, Sissinghurst Mss, fol.3.
135. 'Diplomacy then and now', p. 48; 'Introduction 1943', p. xix; 'A National View of Foreign Policy', in *The [National Labour] News-Letter*, vol. XI, no. 1 (9 Oct.1937), pp. 5–8; 'Why Russia Distrusts Us', in *Listener* (5 Sept. 1946), p. 311.
136. 'Peacemaking at Paris', pp. 196–7; BBC Home Service broadcast, 18 Oct. 1946, MS, Sissinghurst Mss, fol.3; cf. *Congress of Vienna*, p. 262.
137. 'Peacemaking at Paris', p. 197; 'The Paris Conference', *Comments*, pp. 196–200.
138. BBC European Service broadcast, 12 Oct.1946, MS, Sissinghurst Mss, fols.1–2; also 'Marginal Comment', in *Spectator* (22 Oct. 1948), p. 524.
139. 'Peacemaking at Paris', pp. 197–8.
140. *Evolution of Diplomatic Method*, p. 89.
141. Cannadine, *Aspects*, pp. 220–4.
142. For a contemporary view cf."Watchman", *Right Honourable Gentlemen* (London, 1940), pp. 209–12.
143. Min.Viorel Tilea, n.d. [May 1968?], Tilea Mss, Ratiu Foundation, file Nicolson.
144. *Friday Mornings*, pp. 124–7; cf. also the ambiguous character of Jane Campbell in *Public Faces*.
145. J. Sparrow, *Harold Nicolson and Vita Sackville-West: An Address Delivered . . . At A Memorial Services At St. James's, Piccadilly, 16 May 1968* (s.loc., 1968), p. 6.
146. *Curzon*, pp. 185–86.
147. 'Lord Palmerston', pp. 372, 378.

Further reading

Works by Nicolson

The 'Studies in Modern Diplomacy' trilogy:

1 *Sir Arthur Nicolson, Bart., First Lord Carnock: a Study in the Old Diplomacy* (London, 1930); publ. in the USA as *Portrait of a Diplomatist* (Boston and New York, 1930).
2 *Peacemaking 1919* (London, 1933).
3 *Curzon: the Last Phase, 1919–1925* (London, 1934); see especially the 'Terminal Essay'.

Diplomacy (London, 1939), subsequently revised in 1950 and again in 1963, and reprinted by the Institute for the Study of Diplomacy, Washington DC, in 1988.
The Congress of Vienna: a Study in Allied Unity, 1812–1822 (London, 1946).
The Evolution of Diplomatic Method (London, 1954); repr. by the Centre for the Study of Diplomacy in Leicester for the DSP in 1998.
Good Behaviour: Being a Study of Certain Types of Civility (London, 1955).

Historical background

Anderson, M. S., *The Rise of Modern Diplomacy, 1450–1919* (London, 1993).
Craig, G. A. and F. Gilbert (eds), *The Diplomats, 1919–1939* (Princeton, NJ, 1953).
Mayer, A. J., *Political Origins of the New Diplomacy, 1917–1918* (New Haven, 1959).

Osiander, A., *The States System of Europe, 1640–1990: Peacemaking and the Conditions of International Stability* (Oxford, 1994), ch. 5.
Sharp, A., *The Versailles Settlement: Peacemaking at Paris, 1919* (London, 1991).

Biography

Lees-Milne, J., *Harold Nicolson: a Biography, 1886–1968*, 2 vols (London, 1980–1).
Nicolson, N., *Portrait of a Marriage* (London, 1973).
Nicolson, N. (ed.), *Diaries and Letters of Harold Nicolson, 1930–1962*, 3 vols (London, 1966–8).

General

Bozeman, Adda B., *Politics and Culture in International History*, 2nd edn (New Brunswick, 1994).
Butterfield, H. and M. Wight, *Diplomatic Investigations: Essays in the Theory of International Politics* (London, 1966), ch. 9 (Butterfield, 'The new diplomacy and historical diplomacy').
Craig, Gordon A. and Alexander L. George, *Force and Statecraft: Diplomatic Problems of Our Time* (New York and Oxford, 1983), part I.
Hill, D. J., *A History of Diplomacy in the International Development of Europe*, 2 vols (London, 1921).
Morgenthau, Hans J., *Politics Among Nations*, 5th edn rev. (New York, 1978), pp. 535–41.
Mowat, R. B., *Diplomacy and Peace* (New York, 1936).

9
Kissinger

T. G. Otte

'But what of the amazing Dr Kissinger...'. [1]

Henry Kissinger has had a chequered history, exalted and reviled in equal measure. To his many detractors he is a ruthless, unprincipled and self-advertising 'Born-Again' Bismarck from Bavaria, transplanted into the heart of America's East Coast foreign policy establishment. To his admirers, of whom there are perhaps fewer, he 'is of course a superstar', a virtuoso of diplomacy who brought a much-needed dose of common sense and realism to the conduct of American diplomacy. [2] Such differences undoubtedly reflect Kissinger's position as an outsider. His academic provenance had set him apart already at Harvard. His gloomy Teutonic pessimism with its overtly Spenglerian overtones and his advocacy of political realism stood in contrast to much that was fashionable intellectually in the United States after 1945. At Harvard his colleagues were almost exclusively Kennedy Democrats; whereas he was a Rockefeller Republican – that in itself a minority position. In his academic writings and his policies he showed himself equally averse to the liberal Wilsonian idealism espoused by many Democrats and to the isolationist conservatism that has always prevailed in some circles of the Republican Party. Kissinger's intellectual provenance, his politics and his biographical background set him apart from mainstream America, and so made the Kissinger phenomenon more difficult to assess. [3]

It is not the purpose of this chapter to offer yet another assessment of Kissinger's term in office. The subject of investigation is Kissinger's approach to the framing and executing of foreign policy and his contribution to the evolution of modern diplomatic practice. This task is facilitated by Kissinger's avowedly conceptual approach to international relations. This search for a grand design, as a former senior British diplomat once noted, was 'the sort of idea that is apt to make . . . British [policy-makers] wince'. [4] But it makes Kissinger all the more fascinating a subject for the student of diplomacy.

Alfred Heinz Kissinger, as he then was, was born in 1923 in Fürth, Germany, into a comfortable, middle-class, orthodox Jewish family. The security of his early years was shattered by the rise to power of Adolf Hitler and his Nazi movement. Life in Germany became increasingly difficult under the Nuremberg racial laws of 1935. In August 1938, the Kissinger family left Germany, to settle in London before eventually moving on to Manhattan's Washington Heights. Here young Henry attended George Washington High School and the City College of New York before being drafted into the US Army on being naturalized in 1943. [5] It was in the army intelligence corps that Kissinger was 'Americanized', ironically under the aegis of another German refugee, Fritz Kraemer. His war-time work gave him a first taste of lecturing and administrative duties. Following demobilization Kissinger entered Harvard in 1947, where he studied under William Yandall Elliott and Carl Joachim Friedrich. He remained at Harvard for postgraduate studies and became executive director of the Harvard International Seminar (1952–69), which brought to the university budding politicians and diplomats from abroad, and so enabled Kissinger to build up contacts which would stand him in good stead during his years in public office. [6] In 1952, Kissinger became founder-editor of *Confluence*, an interdisciplinary journal with frequent disquisitions on international politics, though none of them by Kissinger himself. Whether intended or not, *Confluence* brought Kissinger to the attention of America's foreign affairs community. [7] On completing his doctoral thesis on great power relations in the immediate post-Napoleonic period, published later under the title *A World Restored*, he joined the Council on Foreign Relations in New York in 1954. Here he was involved in the work of a Council study group on the Eisenhower administration's controversial nuclear doctrine of 'Massive Retaliation'. The investigations resulted in Kissinger's next book, *Nuclear Weapons and Foreign Policy* (1957). [8]

The book helped his breakthrough. Returning to Harvard as associate director of the Center for European Studies, he also became a frequent contributor to *Foreign Affairs*. More importantly, he now carved out a niche for himself on the fringes of power, becoming an influential foreign policy adviser to Nelson A. Rockefeller during his bid for the Republican presidential nomination, while also being consulted, in a private capacity, by the Democrats' Advisory Committee on Foreign Policy. [9] In the 1960s Kissinger continued his work on nuclear issues in

The Necessity for Choice (1961) and in his study on the Atlantic alliance, published in 1965 as *The Troubled Partnership*. Throughout this period he maintained his contacts in the White House, most notably with President Kennedy's National Security Advisor and former Harvard colleague McGeorge Bundy. By 1968, with Rockefeller's renewed bid for the presidency aborted, Kissinger, it seems, had given up all expectations of a government post. However, in a surprise move, President-elect Richard Nixon made the protegé of his erstwhile rival for the Republican nomination and outspoken critic of himself his new head of the National Security Council. [10] Kissinger served in this capacity from January 1969 until November 1975. After Nixon's fall in the wake of Watergate, Kissinger was appointed the 56th United States Secretary of State in September 1973, America's first foreign-born and Jewish foreign minister. He remained at 'Foggy Bottom' until the end of the Ford presidency in January 1977. This is not the place to give a detailed account of Kissinger's time in both offices. The nature of his achievements and the extent of his influence on US foreign policy will remain the subject of academic controversies. His contribution to superpower détente and the opening to China as well as his crucial role in negotiating an end to the Vietnam War, for which he was awarded the 1973 Nobel Peace Prize jointly with his North Vietnamese counterpart Le Duc Tho, however, are indisputable. Even after the end of his official career Henry Kissinger has remained a much-sought-after adviser and commentator on international affairs, serving on bipartisan and presidential commissions in the 1980s and early 1990s. Apart from his three weighty tomes of memoirs (1979–99), he also published *Diplomacy* (1994), a history of post-Westphalian international politics to the end of the cold war.

The Presence of the Past: Politics and History

The convictions politicians form before they reach office, Kissinger noted in his memoirs, 'are the intellectual capital they will consume as long as they continue in office'. [11] No doubt, Kissinger himself consciously drew from the intellectual capital he had amassed during his academic career. One of the most remarkable features of his political and intellectual career is the consistency of his political thought. Not only the substance, but often the very phrasing of his ideas has remained unaltered. Kissinger's academic writings reflect his politico-philosophical beliefs, and are thus an important source for a more thorough understanding of his conceptual approach to international relations. Indeed, at least one writer identified Kissinger's 1951 Harvard honours dissertation, a complex and rather unorthodox study of the philosophy of history, as, 'in fact, a kind of personal testament'. [12] Yet another analyst observed that in his writings Kissinger had 'turned scholarship into projective biography'; that he prescribed his actions as a decision-maker in his academic writings. [13] Both observations are perhaps somewhat overstated. Nonetheless, there is a clearly discernible tendency in his historical studies and his strategic writings to distil the immutable essence of politics from the historical and contemporary cases under analysis and to derive general conclusions from them. The practical application of these lessons of history to political action characterizes his work both as an academic and as a statesman. His Harvard friend and fellow academic John Stoessinger described Kissinger's diplomacy as 'a virtual transplant from the world of thought into the world of power... a unique experiment in the application of scholarship to statesmanship, of history to statecraft'. [14]

Kissinger's approach to foreign affairs centres on two core insights: one is historical, the other philosophical in nature. [15] Kissinger has been described as a historian, though this may be somewhat misleading. None of his historical works are based on archival research, and some historians have therefore been tempted to dismiss his writings as 'amateurish'. [16] This, too, seems unjustified. Rather, his academic work is firmly rooted in the classical tradition of grand, historically saturated political theory.

For Kissinger the present is historically grown. Present politics is therefore shaped by the past. The latter, indeed, 'represents the most inexorable necessity with which we live'. [17] Its most distinguishing feature is its 'pitilessness'. [18] In terms of international politics, the foreign policies of individual nations reflect their physical environment and their natural resources; but above all they are firmly rooted in the soil of history. Thus, writing of America's European NATO allies in the early 1960s, he noted that they were not merely parts of the West's security machinery 'but... expressions of a historical experience'. Nations are therefore no abstract entities. A nation's aspirations, its 'sense of identity' and its 'memories' are not merely the result of a 'morbid obsession with the past'. Rather they constitute the essence of nationhood, for, as Kissinger observed in his study of the Vienna system, 'societies exist in time more than in space. [...] [A state] achieves identity through the consciousness of a common history. [...] History is the memory of states.' [19] More importantly for practical politics, every policy choice 'is not an isolated act but an accumulation of previous decisions reflecting history or tradition and values as well as... immediate pressures'. Each single decision is thus not only historically conditioned; it also circumscribes the range of possible future policy options. [20] Still, in Kissinger's understanding, history is constantly evolving. Present politics is thus fluid to an extent. Whilst it is historically derived, it is not irrevocably predetermined by the past. History, Kissinger asserted, 'is the foe of permanence'. [21] Its innermost principle is movement and development. No political entity is 'immune to change. No country has ever maintained an unaltered social structure. But the nature of the transformation is by no means foreordained'. [22] The implications for the student of diplomacy and its practitioner alike are obvious: international relations cannot be treated in the abstract, nor do they lend themselves to assumptions of unfettered policy choices. 'To plan policy on the assumption of equal possibility of all contingencies is to confuse statesmanship with mathematics. Since it is impossible to be prepared for all eventualities, the assumption of the opponent's perfect flexibility leads to paralysis of action.' [23] To understand, indeed for the statesman to survive international affairs, a thorough understanding of the historical context is indispensable. In light of history's fluid and contingent nature, the lessons derived from the past for the benefit of practical politics can, however, only ever be contingent themselves. History, Kissinger warned, is not 'a cookbook offering pretested recipes. It teaches by analogy, not by maxims'; and its lessons can therefore never be 'automatic'. [24] What guidelines for current politics can be distilled from the past, are confined to 'the consequences of certain actions'; but left to each generation is 'the task of determining which situations are comparable.' '[W]hatever meaning history has', he argued, 'is derived from the convictions of the generation which shapes it.' [25]

The second core insight which is central to Kissinger's conceptual approach is philosophical, though once again historically informed. His writings on history and international politics are underpinned by an assumption of a 'tragic' dimension of the *conditio humana*, what he called, perhaps somewhat laboriously and in overtly Spenglerian tones, 'the fatedness of existence'. [26] Reviewing Castlereagh's policy at the close of the Napoleonic Wars, Kissinger observed that 'in any political situation there are factors which are not amenable to will and which cannot be changed in one lifetime. This is the guise Necessity assumes for the statesman, and in that struggle with it resides his tragic quality'. On an another occasion Kissinger specified the tragic aspect of policy-making as lying 'precisely in its unavoidable component of conjecture'. [27] To some extent such pessimism seems to reflect parts of Kissinger's own early biography, as Bruce Mazlish noted. Indeed, it seems that for Kissinger the need for the policy-makers to acquiesce in external circumstances constitutes tragedy. [28] Yet, tragedy can be overcome by means of a creative act. History, Kissinger asserted, is a tale of civilizations, 'centuries of great achievements punctuated by catastrophic upheaval...but...each tragedy was followed by a new burst of creativity'. [29] Ultimately, however, his innate pessimism shines through. The creative act can overcome tragedy, but tends to sow the seeds of further tragedy, as he demonstrated in his assessment of Bismarck's achievements:

> His very success committed Germany to a permanent tour de force. It created conditions that could be dealt with only by extraordinary leaders. Their emergence in turn was thwarted by the colossus [i.e.Bismarck] who dominated his country for nearly a generation. Bismarck's tragedy was that he left a heritage of unassimilated greatness. [30]

In a 1974 interview with the *New York Times* Kissinger claimed that as a policy-maker he was 'conscious of the fact that every civilization that has ever existed has ultimately collapsed'. Still, there is an element of hope in Kissinger's tragic conception of human life. The decline of a civilization, he pointed out, 'is usually traceable to a loss of creativity and inspiration and therefore avoidable.' [31] To maintain the creative momentum and to provide inspiration, however, is the function of statesmanship.

Intuition *vs* Bureaucracy: Kissinger's Paradigm of Statesmanship

Unlike most writers on politics, Kissinger prefers to use the term 'statesman' when discussing the role of decision-makers. This preference reflects to some extent his conservative tastes. But it also indicates a higher standard which he applies to political leadership. This standard is derived from his philosophico-historical principles. The main yardstick by which a statesman is measured is his willingness and ability to confront reality. The past, Kissinger wrote in his 1951 thesis, 'sets the framework' which a statesman has to transcend. The statesman, in the Kissingerian conception, is a lonely, indeed an heroic figure – a 'lone cowboy' as he once incautiously suggested in a soon-to-be-regretted interview. [32]

'The usual fate of leaders is to inherit some intractable problem or commitment that has its own momentum', he reflected after he left office. Ordinary leaders tend to act in accordance with the prevailing political consensus, even though the latter 'often runs counter to the necessities of history'. They confine their actions to the amelioration of present circumstances. But in 'riding with the trend [they] will soon become irrelevant'. [33] The true statesman, by contrast, is prepared to grapple with the circumstances, to wrench politics from the tight fist of the past, in order to reshape reality. It is his 'responsibility to struggle against transitoriness and not to insist he be paid in the coin of eternity'. Kissinger's ideal statesman is thus endowed with extraordinary gifts. He must possess charisma, perseverance, the capacity for sober analysis as well as an intuitive understanding of the given situation and the forces at work within it. Intuition is of particular importance. For politics denies absolute certainty and the statesman needs 'to peer into darkness' while acting in 'a margin between necessity and accident'. To accept objective conditions, Kissinger argued, is an act of prudence, but 'to hide behind historical inevitability is tantamount to moral abdication'. [34] Political action, however, is a question of choices; and these choices are not guided by 'facts' but by their interpretation. In words that echo Max Weber's ideal type of political leadership, Kissinger asserted that every political choice is, therefore, 'essentially a moral act: an *estimate* which depend[s] for its validity on a conception of goals as much as an understanding of the available material'. The mark of true statesmanship, he concluded, is strategic vision, the 'ability to recognize the real relationship of forces and to make this knowledge serve [one's] ends'. [35] If a political leader possesses this vital intuitive insight into the trend of the main historical currents, and if he is equipped with a shrewd sense of timing, history will not overwhelm him but will be amenable to his creativity. Statesmanship requires, as he reflected in his memoirs, 'a knowledge of what could not be changed as well as an understanding of the scope available for creativity'. [36]

True statesmanship, however, according to Kissinger's paradigm, is not only a question of strategic foresight, tactical shrewdness, and willpower. Obtaining popular support is the 'acid test of a policy'. The statesman has to go beyond the confines of the existing political consensus if circumstances make this imperative. But this does not render consensus dispensable. On the contrary, like reality, political consensus, which after all reflects reality, has to be reshaped and reconstituted continuously. All policies, therefore, require 'harmonizing...with the national experience'. Thus, the statesman is also an educator: 'he must bridge the gap between a people's experience and his vision, between a nation's tradition and its future.' He 'must be judged not only by [his] actions but also by [his] conception of alternatives.'[37] The margin of success, however, could not be narrower. The statesman's failure to transcend the limited experience of his nation would render all policies ineffectual; his failure to carry the people with him would sentence him to political impotence. Citing the two architects of the 'Vienna system' as classic examples of ultimately failed statesmanship, Kissinger argued that the cause of their relative failure was their inability to create a new consensus and to interpret the historical trend correctly. They had 'set themselves tasks beyond the capacity of their material'.[38] The true statesman, therefore, must possess courage and humility in equal measure, the audacity to mould reality combined with a recognition of limits. If any historical figure conforms to Kissinger's high standard of statesmanship it must be the revolutionary conservative, Otto von Bismarck. In Kissinger's assessment, Bismarck's genius lay in his conscientious use of power as 'an instrument of self-restraint'. A real statesman, he concluded, is one who 'can look destiny in the eye without flinching but also without attempting to play God'.[39]

A further, central factor in Kissinger's conception of modern politics is the role and impact of bureaucracy. Like the force of circumstances and the requirements of consensual politics, bureaucracy tends to fetter the conduct of politics. His assessment of the 'iron cage' of modern bureaucracy is once more reminiscent of Weberian analysis. When discussing the need to rally domestic support, Kissinger placed this requirement also within a bureaucratic context. Before wider public support can be won, a policy needs to be 'legitimiz[ed]...within the governmental apparatus, which is a problem of bureaucratic rationality.'[40] The statesman, then, has to educate not only the wider public but also the governmental élites. Kissinger's pronounced distaste for bureaucracy, both in his academic writings and when in office, undoubtedly reflected his own personality and style.[41] But above all it was based on observation and reasoned argument, his earlier experience as an outside consultant to the Kennedy administration being a formative experience. For Kissinger, the spirit of policy and that of bureaucracy are nearly irreconcilable opposites. Policy is contingent, creative, partly conjectural and involves a willingness to take risks; bureaucracy strives for safety, calculability, 'objectivity' and risk-avoidance. Its essence is instrumental rationality and administrative feasibility; it is not concerned with ultimate values.[42] Bureaucratic edifices thus tend to introduce an element of rigidity into the political process. The growth of vast administrative machineries in the course of the twentieth century, Kissinger argued, has generated a momentum of its own. The smooth administration of governmental business, however, is purchased at the price of diminished ability to take action in extraordinary circumstances which are not amenable to routine procedures:

> The purpose of bureaucracy is to devise a standard operating procedure which can cope effectively with most problems.... Bureaucracy becomes an obstacle when what it defines as routine does not address the most significant range of issues or when its prescribed mode of action proves irrelevant to the problem.

The obstructive power of bureaucracy stems from its institutionalized inertia and its narrow intellectual outlook. The main currents of historical development which the statesman can grasp intuitively and transcend by means of a creative act are beyond the grasp of the bureaucrat. Moreover, the often cumbersome *modus operandi* of large bureaucratic structures, usually based on a miasmic committee system, encourages the development of the wrong skills: verbal dexterity and 'salesmanship' rather than analytical reflection and strategic thinking.[43] Kissinger, however, concedes that the ever more complex modern society requires administrative organization. But he warned that

> [a] society owes its vitality to its ability to strike a balance between the requirement of organization and the need for inspiration. Too much stress on organization leads to bureaucratization and the withering of imagination. Excessive emphasis on inspiration produces a tour de force without continuity or organizational stability.[44]

As regards foreign policy, Kissinger unceasingly emphasized the need to curtail the influence of bureaucracy. The bureaucratization of external affairs, he warned, tends to foster a mindset preoccupied with technical problems. Foreign policy is thus likely to become 'a prisoner of events' and blind to opportunities.[45] In his memoirs he observed that a 'complex bureaucracy has an incentive to exaggerate technical complexity and minimize the scope of importance of political judgment...It seemed to me no accident that most great statesmen had been locked in permanent struggle with the experts in their foreign offices, for the statesman's conception challenges the inclination of the expert toward minimum risk.'[46] Ultimately, he argued, bureaucratization can lead to impasses which could only be overcome by 'essentially arbitrary decisions'.[47] A statesman can thus be effective only if he is not ensnared in the webs of bureaucracy. The relationship between political leadership and administrative machinery also serves Kissinger as the defining criterion for distinguishing between three different types of contemporary political leadership, once again applying Weberian concepts to post-war political developments. [48]

Kissinger's Theory of World Order

Kissinger described his approach to international politics as geopolitical and strategic, both perhaps euphemisms for what he regards as traditional European power politics. [49] He 'spoke of realist theory to provide academic justifications for policies tailored to political needs.' [50] Central to his whole conception of international politics is the assumption that states are its key actors; and that their actions are primarily motivated by concerns for their national security. [51] His principal concern, in his scholarly works as much as when in office, was with the stability of the international system and the need for order. Indeed, an early Kissinger observer noted his 'habit of mind impatient of moralistic rhetoric in foreign policy and convinced . . . of the fundamental contrast between a "stable" and a "revolutionary" international order.' [52] Many analyses of Kissinger speculate on the roots of his strong advocacy of order, and invariably offer his childhood in Nazi Germany as the formative experience. Though superficially perhaps persuasive, such explanations remain partial at best. [53] After all, as Kissinger wryly noted in the concluding volume of his memoirs, 'the Germany of my youth had a great deal of order and very little justice; it was not the sort of place likely to inspire devotion to order in the abstract.' [54] Stability and order do not represent values in themselves. His preoccupation with the need for order seems to stem partly from his philosophical beliefs, the pragmatic concerns of a policy-maker, striving for intellectual balance and coherence in foreign policy, and from his assessment of the impact of nuclear weapons technology on post-1945 international politics. Stoessinger recounted that during his Harvard *viva voce* Kissinger referred to Goethe's dictum that order was preferable to justice. This, admittedly anecdotal piece of evidence, is nonetheless enlightening. It goes to the very core of Kissinger's search for a stable and moderate international order, as it is linked to his concern for the establishment of limits and constraints in international politics. For Kissinger, once again following Goethe, the exercise of power implies the responsibility to accept the limits of self-restraint. [55]

Of equal importance is Kissinger's assessment of the significance of modern weapons technology. The excess of power of nuclear weaponry,

Kissinger argued, renders it usable in extreme circumstances only. At the same time, however, the inefficacy of these weapons also robs diplomacy of one of its means of exerting pressure, while at the same time permeating every international dispute. Diplomacy, therefore, had become the complement to war rather than remaining an alternative to it. [56] The incommensurability of atomic weapons to political ends puts a premium on maintaining international stability as instability brings with it the risk of nuclear annihilation.

That under the conditions of the nuclear age the attainment of peace had come to be seen as the principal object of international politics, is of no surprise to Kissinger. Still, he warns that there are no simple choices in foreign affairs. The desire for peace furnishes no guarantee of its attainment. In light of historical experience, he argued that the alleged dichotomy between morality and pragmatism is unreal: 'Pragmatism without a moral element leads to random activism, brutality and stagnation; moral conviction not tempered by a sense of reality leads to self-righteousness, fanaticism, and the erosion of all restraint.' Those possessed by firm ideological convictions, he pointed out, tend to 'drive societies as well as international systems beyond their capacities'. Pragmatic action and moral considerations can not be separated even if only because 'we cannot maintain our principles unless we survive'. [57] 'The active quest for peace, therefore, is not only unending but also least likely to achieve its destination. Historically, the most tranquil periods in international politics were those in which peace was not purposely sought.' Kissinger warned that '[w]henever peace . . . has been the primary objective of a power or group of powers, the international system has been at the mercy of the most ruthless member of the international community'. [58]

Central to Kissinger's concept of international stability is the assumption that it is anchored in the principle of 'legitimacy' and 'in the balance of forces and its expression, the equilibrium'. [59] Kissinger was careful not to confuse 'legitimacy' with justice. 'Legitimacy' is an agreed framework of the existing international order. It serves him as a short-hand for an accepted code of international conduct, sanctioning the permissible objectives and tools of foreign policy. Such an accepted framework does not prevent conflicts. It does, however, limit their scope and intensity. They will be waged '*in the name* of the existing structure and the peace which follows will be justified as a better expression of the "legitimate", general consensus'. [60]

In Kissinger's analysis, the cold war international system did not possess a 'legitimate' framework, and was in fact a 'revolutionary period'. International order may lack legitimacy for political or ideological reasons. Whenever the *status quo* and its legitimizing framework are perceived as oppressive and unjust by a state, such as Germany after the Versailles treaty of 1919, that state will aim at undermining the international order, as it cannot attain its goals within the given arrangements. It will become a 'revolutionary power'. [61] On the ideological plane, 'revolutionary fervour' gives priority to change over the requirements of international harmony because it rejects the domestic structure of other member-states of the system. International order, then, depends to no small degree on the 'reconciliation of different versions of [domestic] legitimacy'. [62] Of course, as Kissinger the historian unfailingly reminds his audience, 'change is the law of life'. [63] No arrangement can be expected to survive in the form in which it was first conceived. But within a 'legitimate' framework conflicts of interest can be settled in a mutually acceptable way by following internationally accepted procedures for resolving such matters. In a revolutionary period, by contrast, conflicts of interest are not at issue as such but the international system itself. Although adjustments are possible, Kissinger noted, these are invariably seen as preliminary steps to consolidate positions before the inevitable final conflict for the overthrow of the system ensues. [64] He argued that the *status quo* powers often succumb to the temptation to meet the challenge posed by a revolutionary power or group of powers by traditional means, suitable for dealing with grievances of non-revolutionary powers. Whether driven by offensive or defensive motivations, the characteristic feature of a revolutionary power, however, is that nothing can reassure it but 'absolute security'. This, in turn, can only be had at the price of the 'neutralization of the opponent'. Absolute security, therefore, means absolute insecurity for all others and can only be obtained by means of conquest. Ultimately it requires the creation of a world empire. [65] Once again, Kissinger counselled moderation. The price for stability is relative insecurity:

> An international system which is accepted and not imposed will...
> always appear *somewhat* unjust to any one of its components. Paradoxically, the generality of this dissatisfaction is a condition of stability, because were any one power *totally* satisfied, all other would have to be *totally* dissatisfied and a revolutionary situation would ensue. The foundation of a stable order is the *relative* security – and therefore the *relative* insecurity – of its members. Its stability reflects, not the absence of unsatisfied claim, but the absence of a grievance of such magnitude that redress will be sought in overturning the settlement. [66]

It was therefore not the tragedy of the twentieth century, he pointedly observed, that two devastating world wars were unleashed; the tragedy was that the art of concluding peace in a moderate and mutually acceptable way was allowed to be forgotten. [67]

Kissinger frequently criticized the idealistic search for absolute solutions. [68] According to him, the most efficacious means of maintaining international stability is a functioning 'balance of power'. For that reason he praised the wisdom of Castlereagh and Metternich in seeking 'stability, not perfection, and the balance of power is the classic expression of the lesson of history that no order is safe without physical safeguards against aggression'. Kissinger, however, was adamant that maintaining the equilibrium is not a mechanical question or a quasi-mathematical exercise: 'it is a psychological phenomenon; if an equality of power is perceived it will not be tested. Calculations must include potential as well as actual power, not only the possession of power but the will to bring it to bear.' [69] Nor did he accept the simple alternative of 'balance or hegemony', advanced by Ludwig Dehio. He dismissed the idea of an exact balance as 'chimerical'. Rough equality is nonetheless indispensable since too great a material preponderance by one power would undermine its self-restraint and might induce weaker powers to act irresponsibly. [70] Kissinger distinguished between two complementary kinds of equilibria: a general or over-all balance of power between the powers which acts as a deterrent against a general war; and a special equilibrium as a subsystem of the international system, defining the 'historical relation' among certain powers, usually within a particular region. For any balance of power to operate smoothly its creators need to treat individual states not as units of a security mechanism but as 'historical expressions'. No state, he observed, 'will submit to a settlement, however well-balanced and however "secure", which seems to deny its vision of itself.' Still, he had to concede that history showed that a stable international system is not always attainable. [71] The balance of power, then, is not an automatic mechanism, nor even a manual of world politics, but rather a complicated set of rules, a formula of classical political wisdom, based on an approximate equality between the powers. It is within a functioning equilibrium that diplomacy operates best. [72]

Kissinger and Diplomatic Practice

In Kissinger's conceptual approach to international politics diplomacy is very much the handmaiden of statecraft. Like statecraft it requires a degree of intuition to reach its full potential; like statecraft it operates in the realm of the contingent. Hence his characterization of diplomacy as an art. Kissinger offered several definitions of diplomacy, of which this is the perhaps most comprehensive: '[diplomacy is] the art of relating states to each other by agreement rather than by the exercise of force.'[73] Diplomacy, then, is the conduct of international relations by means short of war. It is an instrument with which powers accept the limits of self-restraint; it is 'the art of restraining the exercise of power, of keeping power potential'.[74] In light of Kissinger's search for stability and moderation, diplomacy is, therefore, a key element of modern international politics, and complementary to the principle of 'legitimacy' and the mechanism of the equilibrium. It functions best within a legitimate world order, 'when each major power accepts the legitimacy of the *existence* of the other'. Indeed, it presupposes 'prior agreement on fundamentals which diplomacy can adjust but not create'. In a legitimate order its principal function is 'to compromise disagreements in order to perpetuate the international system'.[75]

In a revolutionary order, Kissinger argued in one of his earlier works, diplomatic settlements of disagreements have to be seen as temporary and of largely tactical significance with a view to enhancing one's position 'for the next test of strength'.[76] During his term in office, however, this minimalist conception of diplomacy underwent a subtle change. He was, as he recorded in his memoirs, under no illusions about the nature and the ambitions of Soviet foreign policy. Its makers were shaped by the intense competition for power and positions within the Communist party system. Their outlook on world politics was shaped by an ideology based on the assumed paramountcy of 'material factors and the objective balance of forces', and that explicitly rejected the legitimacy of the existing international system. International politics was conceived of as a struggle for power. This, combined with a quest for absolute security, common to all revolutionary powers, rendered Soviet diplomacy unreceptive to conciliatory policies unless 'objective conditions require them'. In light of historical experience, he argued, it would be political folly to pretend that 'revolutionaries were really misunderstood legitimists'.[77] Thus, in Kissinger's assessment, the bipolar international order at the height of the cold war had made diplomacy rigid.[78]

But this did not mean that revolutionary powers could not be encouraged to behave in a 'legitimate' way. Kissinger's famed diplomatic strategy of 'linkage' arguably aimed at serving precisely that purpose. The principle of 'linkage' was synonymous with the Nixon-Kissinger geopolitical and strategic approach to foreign policy and was crucial to their attempts at superpower détente. For Kissinger, negotiations with the Soviet Union were no sign of weakness, but rather a device to improve America's strategic position. Diplomatic negotiations were intended to 'link' ostensibly discrete policy issues in an effort to ensure progress on a 'broad front'. Kissinger defended 'linkage' by arguing that the alternative was not feasible: 'to separate issues into distinct compartments would encourage the Soviet leaders to believe that they could use cooperation in one area as a safety valve while striving for unilateral advantages elsewhere.' [79] The creation of mutually advantageous networks was thus meant to enhance the stability of the international system, as Kissinger elaborated to the Senate Foreign Relations Committee in 1974: 'By acquiring a stake in this network of relationships with the West, the Soviet Union may become more conscious of what it would lose by a return to confrontation.' [80] Thus the promise of extended commercial and technological exchanges with the United States was intended as 'a carrot for restrained Soviet political behavior'. [81] Détente thus contained within it the essential elements of 'containment'; it combined firmness and flexibility. That the Soviets steadfastly refused to accept the principle of 'linkage'; that it could backfire if it involved interference in the internal affairs of the Soviet Union, as in the case of the emigration of Soviet Jews to Israel; and that, in fact, this 'network of relationships' on occasions acted to the detriment of US national interests and placed constraints on the United States, as in the case of the clandestine Soviet purchase of subsidized American grain, lies beyond the purpose of this chapter. [82] Similar attempts to introduce some form of 'linkage' into the Vietnam negotiations failed. The 'carrot' of economic aid met with total incomprehension by the North Vietnamese and vanished in a culture gap. [83] 'Linkage' diplomacy was Kissinger's attempt to respond constructively to the challenge to international stability inherent in the revolutionary character of Soviet foreign policy. While, therefore, diplomacy perhaps functions best in a legitimate order, it can be utilized to encourage legitimate behaviour in the absence of an agreed concept of legitimacy.

In addition to fostering such notions, diplomacy in a revolutionary environment can help to adjust and manipulate the global equilibrium. Maintaining the balance of power, Kissinger emphasized unceasingly, 'is a permanent undertaking, not an exertion that has a foreseeable end'. He insisted that détente, desirable though it was, could not replace the overall balance of power; that it was 'the result of equilibrium, not a substitute for it.' This was also the rationale for triangular diplomacy, the attempt by the Nixon administration permanently to improve relations with the second communist power, Mao Zedong's People's Republic of China. 'Equilibrium was the name of the game', Kissinger asserted. This was not a crude attempt to exploit the growing tensions between Beijing and Moscow. But improved relations with China, based on common US–Chinese interests, were seen as a means 'to curb Moscow's geopolitical ambitions' and in so doing to bring pressure to bear on the Kremlin to contribute to a general easing of tensions. [84] Of course, a breakthrough to Beijing was also meant to isolate Hanoi, and so increase US 'leverage' over Moscow. Still, the creation of a Sino-Soviet-American triangle, the triangularization of international politics, was designed to reshape the global equilibrium. The emerging new strategic triangle, it was hoped, would give the United States a 'balancing position', and both communist powers would develop a stronger interest in better relations with the United States, thus stabilizing the equilibrium between the major international powers. [85] It is not without interest that in trying to establish the United States as the pivotal state of the new geostrategic triangle, Kissinger pursued precisely the kind of policy for which he had praised Metternich and Bismarck in his earlier academic writings. [86]

It would, however, be misleading to assume that the role of diplomacy in a revolutionary environment was primarily to adjust relations between the three major, potentially antagonistic powers. The necessity to manage the global balance of power entailed the need to preserve regional alliances. Before he entered politics, Kissinger investigated the problems of alliance diplomacy under the conditions of the nuclear age at some length. At the core of his assessment of the structural problems of NATO in the 1960s was the assumption that these problems had not been caused primarily by external factors but rather by differences in the historical perspectives and geostrategic positions of its members. In view of the increased range and destructive powers of modern weaponry, he argued, much of the strategic dispute within NATO revolved around determining the geographic location of the theatre of war in the event of deterrence breaking down. Coalition diplomacy was thus turned into 'an extraordinarily delicate undertaking' which was not amenable to purely technical solutions. In his earlier studies Kissinger favoured the creation of some form of political structure within which a common Atlantic foreign policy could be formulated and strategy coordinated. [87] But when in office he arguably committed the same mistake for which he had chided previous American administrations. By focusing much of their attention on superpower détente and triangularization, Nixon and Kissinger neglected to take into consideration the different historical perspectives of America's European allies. When he later wrote that NATO had become so bogged down in internal disputes that it had turned into 'an accidental array of forces in search of a mission', it was to no small degree a reflection of the extent to which the progress in superpower arms control talks had threatened to undermine the principle of extended deterrence on which Europe's security depended. [88] Arguably, Kissinger's diplomacy towards the European NATO allies was rather confined to manipulating the special West European equilibrium as a subsystem of the cold war international order. Hence his support for Great Britain's renewed application for entry into the European Common Market. France's ongoing concern about a resurgent Germany had been reawakened by Willy Brandt's *Ostpolitik* as the specifically West German form of détente. Both the British and French governments saw Britain's entry as a useful means of counterbalancing and restraining Germany. The German government, in turn, actively supported British entry in order to allay fears that Brandt was leaning unduly towards the Eastern bloc. [89] It has all too often been too tempting for writers on international affairs to dismiss Kissingerian diplomacy as cynical and manipulative. But it ought to be borne in mind that he did not actively exploit differences between powers, and that the overall objective was to maintain the existing special and general equilibria.

Kissinger defined diplomacy as the conduct of relations between states short of war. This, however, does not mean that diplomacy is completely divorced from matters military. Indeed, as a historian Kissinger argued that in the course of history the political influence of nations has always been roughly correlative to their military power. The balance of power, thus, not only reflects the respective might of the major powers, the latter also circumscribes the manoeverability of their diplomacy. Diplomacy and military strategy, he argued, should therefore support each other. But in as much as diplomacy is to a degree dependent upon military power for its influence, it can also utilize military means to serve its objectives. So, for instance, Kissinger justified American bombing raids on Hanoi as a diplomatic signal to the Vietcong leadership that breaking off the ongoing negotiations would come at a price. The use of military means was, then, quite clearly seen as an instrument to enhance the American negotiating position *vis-à-vis* the North Vietnamese. [90]

Nonetheless, Kissinger was adamant that negotiations were the main instrument of diplomacy. He defined diplomacy as a series of steps, merging into a continuum. Step-by-step diplomacy, therefore, progresses through a series of interim agreements. Kissinger repeatedly urged moderation and pragmatism on the practitioners of diplomacy. This applied to the overall objectives and the means employed in equal measure: 'Those who grab for everything, who forget that politics is the art of the possible, in the end may lose all.'[91] Like the classic writers on diplomacy he counselled against yielding to the temptation to strive for a 'diplomatic victory' as counter-productive. A unilateral 'victory', he argued, cannot be maintained indefinitely, since no country will adhere for any prolonged period of time to an agreement that is against its interests. Ultimately, diplomatic victories 'mortgage the future' and ought therefore to be avoided in favour of 'quiet diplomacy'. Not surprisingly he also emphasized the importance of cultivating an impression of reliability in diplomatic negotiations as a major foreign policy asset. In words that echo Callières's plea for honesty in diplomatic dealings, Kissinger observed that 'in foreign policy crude tricks are almost always self-defeating'.[92]

In his memoirs, Kissinger offered practical advice on a whole range of issues involved in diplomatic negotiations. Contrary to received wisdom he developed a case against formulating fall-back positions at the commencement of negotiations as such positions would invariably undermine the tenacity with which the negotiators stick to their official positions.[93] That negotiations are 'about trading concessions' is the underlying assumption of Kissingerian diplomacy. To succeed in their endeavours the negotiating parties must strike 'a balance of mutual concessions'. The sequence in which these are made, therefore, is of crucial importance; and they have to be seen 'as part of a mosaic'.[94] Speed, he stipulated, is often essential. Negotiations develop a momentum of their own and will reach a psychological moment when a decision has to be taken which can be fatally delayed by bureaucratic inertia and cumbersome decision-making mechanism. The decision whether or not that moment has arrived is a matter of judgement. But crucially, the successful negotiator needs to have an acutely developed sense of timing.[95] If a sense of history is essential to foreign policy analysis, then it is equally important in the practice of diplomacy. The three volumes of Kissinger's memoirs contain numerous reflections on the formative influence of a nation's history on its negotiating style.[96] Ignorance of the negotiating partner's past can therefore hamper the progress of the negotiations. Closely linked to the need for mutually acceptable concession is the need for secrecy. Here again Kissinger echoed earlier writers on diplomacy. Secrecy and confidentiality allow the parties involved to negotiate on the basis of reciprocity without being subjected to domestic pressures. Secret negotiations, indeed the clandestine meetings that became a hallmark of Kissinger's diplomacy, also free the negotiators 'from the necessity of living up to criteria set beforehand by the media and critics'. [97]

If Kissinger is forthcoming in imparting advice as to the practical conduct of diplomacy, he is altogether more reticent in commenting upon its actors. Generally, he acknowledged the potential value of traditional diplomatic actors such as the resident ambassador. Improved telecommunication and the advent of the jet age, he reasoned, have seriously curtailed an ambassador's freedom as negotiator and his role is somewhat reduced to that of a 'diplomatic postman'. But ambassadors are still indispensable as political interpreters whose highly developed antennae pick up the signals of any change in the host country's policies. The main function of a modern embassy then is to gather facts, analyse them and, if necessary, to forewarn the home government before an emergency arises. In addition, it is the embassy's task to organize and manage the commercial, cultural and other exchanges that have become a prominent feature of modern bilateral relations, as well as supervising the operations of the intelligence services. Just as diplomacy is the tool of statecraft, so is the diplomat the servant of his government. Indeed, it seems that Kissinger did not expect diplomats to display any initiative, though on at least one occasion he praised a senior US Foreign Service Officer for having the nous to encourage the first tentative steps towards Sino-American 'ping-pong diplomacy'. [98]

Still, the central figure in a nation's diplomacy is the foreign minister as the chief negotiator, subject only to presidential or cabinet guidance. Kissinger's own diplomatic style followed the blueprint laid out in his 1968 paper on bureaucracy and foreign policy in which he argued that the 'extra-bureaucratic means of decision' were necessary. To free diplomatic agents from the dead hand of bureaucracy he advocated increased reliance on special or personal emissaries. In later years he reflected that the need for strict secrecy in negotiations also made it virtually impossible to create a consensus within the administrative machinery prior to major policy decisions without running the risk of leaks. [99]

Kissinger himself, of course, became just such a special emissary, acting on Nixon's behalf outside the existing State Department and Cabinet machineries. The use of such extra-bureaucratic envoys was not the only distinguishing characteristic of the Kissinger-Nixon style. In addition, a parallel machinery was set up, albeit on a smaller scale, to advise on policy matters and prepare negotiations. This shadow bureaucracy was part of an elaborate network of communication 'channels' which bypassed the State Department, thus concentrating decision-

making powers in the President's and Kissinger's hands. [100] The creation
of different 'backchannels' soon after Nixon's inauguration, linking the
White House directly with foreign leaders, was meant to leave the two
statesmen unconstrained by the cumbersome decision-making pro-
cesses and the bureaucratic politics of the State Department. The purpose of these 'backchannels' was not merely to open up new means of
communication with other governments, without having to go through
the State Department; nor were they meant completely to eclipse that
ministry. Central to the Nixon-Kissinger strategy was a twin track negotiating and decision-making process. As Kissinger elaborated in the
context of perhaps the most important of these new 'backchannels',
'the Channel' with Soviet ambassador Dobrynin:

> We would, informally, clarify the basic purposes of our governments
> and when our talks gave hope of specific agreements, the subject was
> moved to conventional diplomatic channels. If formal negotiations
> there reached a deadlock, the Channel would open up again....-
> Neither side was precluded from raising [an] issue formally because
> of adverse reactions from the other. But at least inadvertent confron-
> tations were prevented. It was a way to explore the terrain, to avoid
> major deadlocks. [101]

The utility of informal channels lay not only in expediting negotiations
and rendering diplomacy more flexible by feeding results achieved in
the 'backchannel' into the 'frontchannel' and vice versa. It also enabled
US diplomacy to establish contact with states with which there were no
formal diplomatic relations. The first tentative contacts with mainland
China, for example, were made informally between the US and Chinese
ambassadors to Poland. Earlier, Pakistani intermediaries had been used
to convey to Beijing 'our basic attitude in a low-key manner'. Similarly,
meetings at the United Nations served as useful channels of communication before the resumption of formal relations. [102]

The effort involved in maintaining the momentum behind the twin-
track process was enormous. It undoubtedly achieved the results Nixon
and Kissinger set out to achieve. But success also produced unintended
consequences. The small staff that ran the 'backchannels' was soon
overwhelmed by the sheer volume of complex, simultaneous negotiations and Kissinger had to have recourse to interdepartmental mechanisms whilst keeping the contents of the negotiations from the State
Department. [103] More significantly, the circumvention of established
procedures demoralized senior Foreign Service Officers and exacerbated

already strained relations between White House and State Department. 'Hell hath no fury like a bureaucrat scorned', Kissinger conceded in retirement. The insensitivity with which the Nixon-Kissinger duo bypassed established channels no doubt led to State Department efforts to sabotage at the implementation stage the settlements arrived at by Kissinger in secret negotiations. Nixon and his national security adviser had been anxious to free themselves from the shackles of excessive bureaucracy. Ironically, in so doing, they had also lost 'the usual bureaucratic safety net'. [104] Kissinger, indeed, made the same mistake as Bismarck: he failed to lay lasting foundations to underpin his diplomatic efforts and condemned himself and his successors to a *tour de force*. During Nixon's first term such an enormous effort was possible; under the unfavourable circumstances of the post-Watergate period it was perhaps already beyond the realm of practical politics.

Apart from practical problems in executing policy, the extreme secrecy entailed in 'backchannel' diplomacy could also backfire on the negotiations themselves. Kissinger's demand for strict secrecy aroused Chinese suspicions that it was merely a device to enable US diplomacy to reverse course quickly. Lack of trust in the reliability of the negotiating partner obviously does not facilitate the smooth progress of the talks. [105]

If Kissinger's dual channel diplomacy was a key feature of 'Nixingerism', the further development of summitry and Kissinger's own, very public 'shuttle diplomacy' were equally crucial to it. Summit meetings between heads of government are perhaps the only issue on which Kissinger changed his mind. In his earlier writings, possibly under the impression of the failed four-power conferences in the mid-1950s and certainly in a rather doctrinaire manner, he warned of the futility of such meetings in the absence of an agreed concept of legitimacy. [106] By contrast, during the Nixon presidency its two leading foreign policymakers agreed that summitry could aid superpower détente, though Kissinger insisted on its strictly instrumental value. Summit talks have to deal with specific issues 'rather than general atmospherics'. For talks to be meaningful they have to be well prepared: decisions to be taken at the summit have to be formulated in detail already in previous negotiations at subordinate levels. Reflecting on the preparations for Nixon's 1972 trip to China, Kissinger wrote:

> Heads of government have too much at stake to be principal negotiators. They usually are too busy to master the manifold details on which successful negotiations depend. They are too self-centred to

202 Diplomatic Theory from Machiavelli to Kissinger

submit gracefully to the inevitable pressures of a protracted negotiation. If there is a deadlock, there is no recourse. Summits are, moreover, too brief to permit the meticulous analysis that assures the
durability of an agreement. [107]

Still, even a well-prepared summit meeting can, of course, reach an
impasse. In such an event, Kissinger warned, heads of government
might be tempted to make dangerous concessions in order to save the
summit and so also fend off challenges to their domestic positions. [108] A
further potential danger of summitry is its emphasis on personal relations. Summit talks, he insisted, ought to be 'directed towards substance, not cosmetics'. [109]

Such warnings seem sensible enough. Still, Kissinger's emphasis on an
interest-based approach to the conduct of diplomacy can not disguise
the fact that he himself was a consummate manipulator of personal
relations and that this was also a key to his negotiating successes.
Yitzhak Rabin later recalled that Kissinger 'created a kind of personal
relationship that forced people to be committed to him'. [110] This was
most apparent during his 'shuttle diplomacy' to negotiate a Middle
Eastern ceasefire in 1973 with which his name will always be identified.
This 'blend of summitry, diplomacy by conference, travelling circus and
secret diplomacy', as one unfriendly commentator described it, hinged
to no small degree on personal relations. [111]

Conclusion

Henry Kissinger has never ceased to capture the imagination of scholars
and the general public alike. He was one of the major statesmen of the
second half of the twentieth century. In retrospect his period in office
between 1969 and 1977 may well be regarded as a significant turning
point in post-1945 US foreign policy. First as Nixon's all-too-visible
foreign policy wizard and then as Secretary of State, Kissinger played a
crucial role in shaping a new framework for post-Vietnam US foreign
policy. By the time Kissinger entered the government, the war in South
East Asia had destroyed America's cold war foreign policy consensus.
This provided a challenge as well as an opportunity for him. It enabled
him to bring his conceptual framework to bear on the new situation and
respond to it constructively. Superpower détente, the opening to China,
the Yom Kippur ceasefire, and the end to the Vietnam War – though here
he failed to secure peace with honour – these are testimony to his
achievements as statesman. Nonetheless, he failed conspicuously to

create a new foreign policy consensus. Perhaps this was beyond the capacity of any outsider, even one of Kissinger's stature. Ultimately, his open avowal of traditional European power politics sat too uneasily with the main tenets of American political culture.

The primacy of politics and the national interest are central to his consciously conceptual approach to foreign policy. Not surprisingly, he accords diplomacy a subservient role, subject to politico-strategic guidance by statesmen. Indeed, as one former diplomat observed, Kissinger is perhaps not noted for his diplomatic tact himself. [112] His contribution to the evolution of diplomatic theory and practice are somewhat ambivalent, too. Given his overwhelming concern with the realm of politics one might, indeed, wonder whether he is a diplomatic theorist at all. Yet, by highlighting the link between diplomacy and politics he very effectively circumscribed the potential of diplomacy as the main tool of international politics as well as its limits. His conception of this tool is firmly rooted in traditional European diplomacy, as, for instance his emphasis on the need for reliability and honesty demonstrates. Similarly, however much he was in the political limelight, in practice he relied on the classic usages of secrecy and patience in negotiations. His insistence on the need for thorough preparation of conferences and summit meetings also harks back to the precepts of classical diplomatic writers.

If Kissinger was traditional and conservative in his conceptualization of diplomacy, it stands in contrast to the innovations he wrought upon diplomatic practice. 'Backchannel' negotiations, the hallmark of Kissingerian diplomacy, may be criticized for taking traditional diplomatic secrecy to extremes. Yet, it was a constructive attempt to overcome the impasse in superpower relations and to leave behind the wasteland of late 1960s US foreign policy. The extrovert nature of his Middle Eastern 'shuttle diplomacy' has also been criticized by more traditional writers. It is easy to be deceived by the carefully cultivated image of the supersonic Secretary of State. Beneath the external haste and swirling dust lay quiet, concentrated and purposeful activity. Ultimately, Kissinger's innovations were geared towards achieving political results commensurate with US national interests and the maintenance of a global equilibrium. Nonetheless, these innovations entailed a tour de force that was difficult to sustain. That subsequent Secretaries of State have reverted to more traditional, slower and arguably more bureaucratic forms of diplomacy perhaps shows the greatness and the limitations of Henry Kissinger as diplomat and statesman.

Notes

1. G. McDermott, *The New Diplomacy and Its Apparatus* (London, 1973), p. 70.
2. W. F. Buckley jr, *United Nations Journal* (London, 1975), p. 53; H. J. Morgenthau, 'Henry Kissinger, Secretary of State: an evaluation', in *Encounter*, vol. XLIII, no. 5 (Nov. 1974), pp. 57–61.
3. J. Joffe, 'In defense of Henry Kissinger', in *Commentary*, vol. XCIV, no. 6 (1992), p. 51.
4. Sir N. Henderson, *Channels and Tunnels: Reflections on Britain and Abroad* (London, 1987), p. 78.
5. D. Ward, 'Kissinger: a psychohistory', in D. Caldwell (ed.), *Kissinger: His Personality and Policies* (Durham, NC, 1983), pp. 24–63; M. and B. Kalb, *Kissinger* (New York, 1975 (pb.)), pp. 42–9; W. Isaacson, *Kissinger: a Biography* (London, 1993), pp. 17–38.
6. R. Schulzinger, *Henry Kissinger: Doctor of Diplomacy* (New York, 1989), p. 11; H. Starr, *Henry Kissinger: Perception of World Politics* (Lexington, KT, 1983), p. 23.
7. For his critics, *Confluence* was a further example of Kissinger's courtier-like assiduity in cultivating contacts with influential people, cf.Isaacson, *Kissinger*, pp. 72–4.
8. Cf. L. Freedman, *The Evolution of Nuclear Strategy*, 2nd ed. (London, 1989), pp. 106–10; Isaacson, *Kissinger*, pp. 82–94.
9. Schulzinger, *Henry Kissinger*, p. 14; also, albeit hostile, S. M. Hersh, *The Price of Power: Kissinger in the Nixon White House* (New York, 1983), pp. 13–15.
10. H. A. Kissinger, *White House Years* (Boston and London, 1979), pp. 7–16; W. Bundy, *A Tangled Web: the Making of Foreign Policy in the Nixon Presidency* (London, 1998), pp. 52–3; J. Hoff, *Nixon Reconsidered* (New York, 1994), pp. 154–7.
11. *White House Years* (Boston, 1979), p. 54.
12. S. R. Graubard, *Kissinger: Portrait of a Mind* (New York, 1973), p. 6. The reference is to H. A. Kissinger, 'The Meaning of History: Reflections on Spengler, Toynbee and Kant' (unpublished BA thesis, Harvard University, 1951).
13. As quoted in B. Mazlish, *Kissinger: the European Mind in American Policy* (New York, 1973), p. 151.
14. J. G. Stoessinger, *Henry Kissinger: the Anguish of Power* (New York, 1976), pp. 7, 37; cf. also R. L. Beisner, 'History and Henry Kissinger', *Diplomatic History*, vol. XIV, no. 4 (1990), pp. 511–27.
15. A recent writer went further, arguing that Kissinger's perspective on politics is the result of 'a coherent philosophy of history', cf. G. Russell, 'Kissinger's philosophy of history and Kantian ethics', in *Diplomacy & Statecraft*, vol. 7, no. 1 (1996), p. 97.
16. Most famously, E. R. May, 'The "Great Men" Theory of Foreign Policy', *New York Times Book Review* (3 Apr. 1994), pp. 3 and 24; cf.Kissinger's reply in ibid. (24 Apr. 1994), p. 31. More favourable are G. A. Craig, 'Looking for Order', *New York Review of Books*, vol. XLI, no. 9 (12 May 1994), pp. 8–14, and H. Thomas, 'The Hard Lessons of History', *Times Literary Supplement*, no. 4767 (12 Aug. 1994), pp. 9–10.
17. 'The Meaning of History', as quoted in P. W. Dickson, *Kissinger and the Meaning of History* (New York, 1978), p. 70.

18. *Years of Upheaval* (Boston, 1982), p. 791.

19. *The Troubled Partnership: A Re-Appraisal of the Atlantic Alliance* (New York, 1965), pp. 24–5; 'An American view', in *Survival*, vol. III, no. 2 (1961), pp. 72–4; 'The Future of NATO: A Plan to Reshape NATO', in *Current*, no. 264 (1984), pp. 31–8.

20. 'Domestic structure and foreign policy', in *Daedalus*, vol. XCV, no. 2 (1966), p. 525.

21. *White House Years*, p. 55.

22. *Necessity for Choice* (New York, 1961), p. 300.

23. *A World Restored: Metternich, Castlereagh and the Problems of Peace, 1812–22* (London, 1957), p. 74.

24. *White House Years*, p. 54; *World Restored*, p. 331; cf. R.Weitz, 'Henry Kissinger's philosophy of international relations', in *Diplomacy & Statecraft*, vol. II, no. 1 (1991), p. 106.

25. *Troubled Partnership*, pp. 21 and 251; 'The lessons of the past: a conversation with Walter Laqueur', *Washington Quarterly*, vol. I, no. 1 (1978), p. 8; 'A statesman looks at the world', interview in *The Times* (1 June 1994).

26. 'Meaning of History', as quoted in Graubard, *Kissinger*, p. 8. There is an interesting parallel in Spengler's apparent influence on Hans Morgenthau, the founding father of American realism, cf. J. Farrenkopf, 'The challenge of Spenglerian pessimism to Ranke and political realism', in *Review of International Studies*, vol. XVII, no. 3 (1991), p. 269, fn.10.

27. *World Restored*, p. 186; *Necessity for Choice*, p. 355.

28. Mazlish, *Kissinger*, p. 188.

29. *Troubled Partnership*, p. 249.

30. 'The white revolutionary: reflections on Bismarck', *Daedalus*, vol. XCVII, no. 3 (1968), p. 890; *Diplomacy* (London–New York, 1994), pp. 134–5. Kissinger came to a virtually identical judgement of Metternich's policy, cf. *World Restored*, pp. 322–3.

31. *Department of State Bulletin*, no. 71 (11 Nov. 1974), as quoted in Russell, 'Kissinger's philosophy', p. 118.

32. 'Kissinger: an Interview with Oriana Fallaci', in *New Republic*, no. 167 (16 Dec. 1972), pp. 17–22; cf. *White House Years*, pp. 1409–10.

33. *Years of Upheaval*, pp. 5 and 1208.

34. *White House Years*, p. 55; *World Restored*, p. 329.

35. *World Restored*, p. 325; 'Clinton's shortsighted policy on Iraq', in *Jerusalem Post* (22 Mar.1998); cf. M. Weber, 'The profession and vocation of politics', in P. Lassman and R. Speirs (eds), *Max Weber: Political Writings* (Cambridge, 1994), pp. 309–69.

36. *Years of Upheaval*, p. 5; *White House Years*, pp. 597, 781.

37. *World Restored*, pp. 213, 329; 'Reflections on power and diplomacy', in E. A. J. Johnson (ed.), *The Dimensions of Diplomacy* (Baltimore, MD, 1964), p. 24.

38. *World Restored*, pp. 328–9.

39. 'White revolutionary', p. 890; *Diplomacy*, p. 167; *Years of Upheaval*, p. 1208.

40. *World Restored*, p. 326; cf. M. Weber, *Economy and Society*, 2 vols (Berkeley, CA, 1964), vol. II, ch.11.

41. Mazlish, *Kissinger*, p. 96; D. Landau, *Kissinger: the Uses of Power* (London, 1974), pp. 83–7.

42. *World Restored*, pp. 326–7.
43. 'Domestic structure', pp. 507, 510.
44. *Nuclear Weapons and Foreign Policy* (New York, 1957), p. 432; *Years of Renewal*, p. 1067.
45. *World Restored*, p. 327.
46. *White House Years*, p. 39.
47. As quoted in Beisner, 'History', p. 520.
48. Kissinger distinguished between 'bureaucratic-pragmatic', 'ideological', and 'revolutionary-charismatic' types of leadership, cf. 'Domestic structure', pp. 514–25; cf. Weber, *Economy and Society*, vol. I, ch. 3.
49. *White House Years*, p. 31.
50. Schulzinger, *Kissinger*, p. 5.
51. *White House Years*, p. 60; *Years of Upheaval*, p. 238; 'As the Cheers Fade', in *Newsweek* (21 June 1999), pp. 38–40.
52. A. Hartley, *American Foreign Policy in the Nixon Era* (London, 1975), p. 6 (*Adelphi Papers*, no. 110); cf. 'The search for stability', in *Foreign Affairs*, vol. XXXVI, no. 4 (1959), p. 54.
53. Cf. especially Mazlish, *Kissinger*, pp. 34–7; Stoessinger, *Kissinger*, p. 14; P. Schlafly and C. Ward, *Kissinger on the Couch* (New Rochelle, NY, 1975), p. 135.
54. *Years of Renewal*, p. 1078; 'Bosnia: Only Just Beginning . . .', in *Washington Post* (11 Sept. 1995); 'New World Disorder', in *Newsweek* (31 May 1999).
55. Stoessinger, *Kissinger*, p. 14. The quote is: 'I shall rather commit an injustice than tolerate disorder', J.W. von Goethe, 'Die Belagerung von Mainz', in *Goethes Werke*, 12 vols. (Leipzig, s.a.), vol. XI, p. 173; cf. W.Mommsen, *Die Politischen Anschauungen Goethes* (Stuttgart, 1948), p. 192, and Kissinger, 'Ansprache', in *Erlanger Universitätsreden*, 3rd ser., no. 31 (1990), p. 29.
56. *Nuclear Weapons and Foreign Policy*, pp. 4–5, 191; *Troubled Partnership: a Reappraisal of the Atlantic Alliance* (New York and London, 1965), pp. 18–19; 'Force and diplomacy in the nuclear age', in *Foreign Affairs*, vol. XXXIV, no. 3 (1956), pp. 352–4; 'NATO: evolution or decline', in M. D. Hancock and D. A. Rustow (eds), *American Foreign Policy in International Perspective* (Englewood Cliffs, NJ, 1971), p. 264.
57. *Years of Renewal*, p. 1076; 'Reflections on American diplomacy', in *Foreign Affairs*, vol. XXXV, no. 1 (1956), p. 42; 'Limits to what the US can do in Bosnia', in *Washington Post* (22 Sept. 1997).
58. *World Restored*, p. 1.
59. 'The Congress of Vienna: a reappraisal', in *World Politics*, vol. VIII, no. 2 (1956), p. 265.
60. *World Restored*, pp. 1–2.
61. *Diplomacy*, pp. 241–5; *World Restored*, pp. 1–2.
62. 'Congress of Vienna', p. 264; *Nuclear Weapons and Foreign Policy*, pp. 5, 317.
63. *Years of Renewal*, p. 1075.
64. *World Restored*, p. 2; 'White revolutionary', p. 900.
65. *World Restored*, p. 2; Weitz, 'Kissinger's philosophy', p. 105. Instructive is a comparison with the work of fellow emigré Eric Voegelin, cf. 'World empire and the unity of mankind', in *International Affairs*, vol. XXXVIII, no. 2 (1962), pp. 170–88.
66. 'Congress of Vienna', pp. 264–5; 'Search for stability', pp. 54–5.

67. *Die sechs Säulen der Weltordnung* (Berlin, 1992), pp. 8–9; 'Balance of Power Sustained', in G. Allison and G. T. Treverton (eds), *Rethinking American security* (New York, 1992), pp. 238–48.
68. *Nuclear Weapons and Foreign Policy*, p. 318; *Years of Renewal*, p. 1076; 'Europe Needs a Strong NATO, Not Utopian Gimmicks', in *International Herald Tribune* (22 Jan. 1994); 'The Dilution of NATO', in *Washington Post* (8 June 1997).
69. *World Restored*, pp. 317–18; *White House Years*, p. 115; cf. 'A Plan for Europe', in *Newsweek* (18 June 1990), pp. 32–7.
70. 'White Revolutionary', pp. 899–900; 'Congress of Vienna', p. 266; 'A Postwar Agenda', *Newsweek* (28 Jan.1991), pp. 41–7; cf. L. Dehio, *The Precarious Balance: The Politics of Power in Europe, 1494 to 1945* (London, 1962), pp. 7–8.
71. *World Restored*, pp. 146–7; 'Fuller Explanations', *New York Review of Books* (12 Feb. 1967), as quoted in Weitz, 'Kissinger's Philosophy', p. 105; 'Living with the Inevitable', *Newsweek* (4 Dec. 1989), pp. 51–8; 'A New Union in Europe', in *Washington Post* (12 May 1998).
72. 'The Limitations of Diplomacy', *New Republic* (9 May 1955), pp. 7–8.
73. *World Restored*, p. 326; 'Limitations of Diplomacy', p. 8; 'Search for Stability', pp. pp.543–4.
74. 'American Policy and the Prevention of War', *Yale Review*, vol. XLIV, no. 3 (1955), p. 333; 'Limits of Diplomacy', p. 8.
75. 'Congress of Vienna', p. 279; 'Limitations of Diplomacy', pp. 7–8; 'Reflections on American Diplomacy', *Foreign Affairs*, vol. XXXV, no. 1 (1956), pp. 45–6.
76. 'Reflections', p. 46.
77. *Years of Upheaval*, p. 245; *Troubled Partnership*, pp. 190–9; 'Domestic Structure', pp. 36–7; *Nuclear Weapons and Foreign Policy*, p. 360; 'Power and Diplomacy', p. 37.
78. *White House Years*, p. 67; 'Strategy and Organization', *Foreign Affairs*, vol. XXXV, no. 3 (1959), pp. 381–2; 'American Strategic Doctrine and Diplomacy', in M. Howard (ed.), *The Theory and Practice of War* (London, 1965), p. 273.
79. *White House Years*, pp. 1302 and 129. In its embryonic form this concept can already be found in 'Force and Diplomacy', p. 363.
80. *State Department Bulletin* (14 Oct. 1974), p. 508, as quoted in C. Bell, *The Diplomacy of Détente: The Kissinger Era* (London, 1977), p. 30.
81. *White House Years*, p. 1250.
82. *Diplomacy*, ch. 29; Bell, *Diplomacy of Détente*, p. 206; J. Hoff-Wilson, ' "Nixingerism, NATO, and Détente', *Diplomatic History*, vol. XIII, no. 4 (1989), p. 505. Kissinger implicitly acknowledged this in *White House Years*, p. 1254.
83. *Years of Renewal*, p. 37.
84. *White House Years*, pp. 115, 1143, 763–7; cf. 'The Realist', interview in the *Daily Telegraph* (10 June 1994); 'US Mediation Essential', *Washington Post* (19 July 1999).
85. *Diplomacy*, pp. 722–5; *White House Years*, pp. 191–3; 'A Constructive, Long-Term Chinese–US Relationship', *International Herald Tribune* (28 Mar. 1994).
86. *World Restored*, p. 247; 'White Revolutionary', pp. 912–13; 'Clinton and the World', *Newsweek* (1 Feb.1993), pp. 12–14.
87. 'Coalition Diplomacy in a Nuclear Age', *Foreign Affairs*, vol. XLII, no. 4 (1964), pp. 528–32, 536–42, 544; *Troubled Partnership*. pp. 23–8, 105–17, 140–59; 'NATO's Nuclear Dilemma', *The Reporter* (23 Mar. 1963), pp. 32–3.

88. T. Draper, *Present History* (New York, 1983), p. 81; cf. H. Schmidt, 'The 1977 Alistair Buchan Memorial Lecture', in W. F. Hanrieder (ed.), *Helmut Schmidt: Perspectives in Politics* (Boulder, CO, 1982), pp. 23–37.
89. *White House Years*, pp. 422–5; *Years of Upheaval*, pp. 146–53; 'After Victory: Defining an American Role in an Uncertain World', keynote conference address, 2 Mar. 1995, Nixon Centre press release.
90. *White House Years*, pp. 195, 1037–8; 'Current Problems in Anglo-American Military Relations', unpublished speech, Oct. 1960, Nitze Mss, Library of Congress, Washington, box 47, folder 2. I am grateful to Dr C. A. Pagedas for bringing this document to my attention.
91. *White House Years*, pp. 701, 1293, also 1280–1 and 1302.
92. Ibid., pp. 635, 140.
93. Ibid., p. 368.
94. *Diplomacy*, pp. 744–5; *White House Years*, p. 803.
95. *White House Years*, pp. 803, 818.
96. Cf. ibid, pp. 118, 259–60; *Years of Renewal*, pp. 194–6.
97. *White House Years*, pp. 803, 1124.
98. Ibid., pp. 139, 661, 672, 708, 1092–3.
99. 'Domestic structure', p. 511; *White House Years*, p. 805.
100. Bundy, *Tangled Web*, pp. 55–8; Hoff, *Nixon Reconsidered*, pp. 157–66; R. M. Nixon, *RN: The Memoirs of Richard Nixon* (New York, 1978), p. 340.
101. *White House Years*, p. 138, also pp. 28–30, 722–3, and 1289.
102. Ibid., pp. 181, 684, 786.
103. Ibid., p. 805.
104. *Diplomacy*, p. 744; *White House Years*, p. 806.
105. *White House Years*, pp. 724–5.
106. 'Limitations', p. 7; 'American policy and prevention of war', in *Yale Review* vol. XLIV, no. 3 (1955), pp. 321–2.
107. *White House Years*, pp. 128, 142, 769, 781. Abba Eban is more critical especially of the preparations for the 1972 meeting, *The New Diplomacy: International Affairs in the Modern Age* (London, 1983), p. 363.
108. Ibid., p. 552.
109. As quoted in McDermott, *New Diplomacy*, p. 32.
110. As quoted in Isaacson, *Kissinger*, p. 551. Rabin later used the same method against Kissinger to good effect, cf. M. Golan, *The Secret Negotiations of Henry Kissinger* (New York, 1976), p. 237.
111. Sir G. Jackson, *Concorde Diplomacy: the Ambassador's Role in the World Today* (London, 1981), p. 16; cf. *Years of Upheaval*, pp. 809–10.
112. C. Powell, 'No Diplomat', in *New Republic* (13 June 1994), pp. 63–5.

Further reading

Works by Kissinger

A World Restored: Metternich, Castlereagh and the Problems of Peace 1812–1822 (Boston, 1957).
Nuclear Weapons and Foreign Policy (New York, 1957).
The Necessity for Choice: Prospects of American Foreign Policy (New York, 1961).
The Troubled Partnership: a Re-appraisal of the Atlantic Alliance (New York, 1965).
American Foreign Policy (New York, 1969), subsequently revised in 1974 and 1977.

For the Record: Selected Statements 1977–1980 (London, 1981).
Diplomacy (London, 1994).
Memoirs:
1. *The White House Years* (Boston and London, 1979).
2. *Years of Upheaval* (London, 1982).
3. *Years of Renewal* (London, 1999).
Articles and chapters:
'Force and diplomacy in the nuclear age', *Foreign Affairs*, vol. 34, Apr. 1956, pp. 347–66.
'Reflections on American diplomacy', *Foreign Affairs*, vol. 35, Oct. 1956, pp. 37–56.
'Strategy and organization', *Foreign Affairs*, vol. 35, Apr. 1957, pp. 379–94.
'The search for stability', *Foreign Affairs*, vol. 37, July 1959, pp. 537–60.
'Reflections on power and diplomacy', in E. A. J. Johnson (ed.), *The Dimensions of Diplomacy* (Baltimore, 1964), pp. 1–32.
'Classical diplomacy', in J. G. Stoessinger and A. F. Westin (eds), *Power and Order: Six Cases in World Politics* (New York, 1964).
'Coalition diplomacy in the nuclear age', *Foreign Affairs*, vol. 42, July 1964, pp. 525–45.
'The white revolutionary: reflections on Bismarck', *Daedalus*, vol. 97, no. 3 (1968), pp. 888–923.

Historical background

Andrianopoulos, G. A., *Western Europe in Kissinger's Global Strategy* (New York, 1988).
Beisner, R. L., 'History and Henry Kissinger', *Diplomatic History*, vol. 14, no. 4 (1990).
Bell, C., *The Diplomacy of Detente: the Kissinger Era* (New York, 1977).
Bowker, M. and P. Williams, *Superpower Detente: a Reappraisal* (London, 1988).
Bundy, W. P., *A Tangled Web: the Making of Foreign Policy in the Nixon Presidency* (London, 1998).
Garthoff, R. L., *Detente and Confrontation: American-Soviet Relations from Nixon to Reagan* (Washington, 1994).
Hoff, J., *Nixon Reconsidered* (New York, 1994).
Kimball, J. P., *Nixon's Vietnam War* (Lawrence, KS, 1998).
Quandt, W. B., *Peace Process: American Diplomacy and the Arab–Israeli Conflict since 1967* (Washington and Berkeley, 1993), parts 2 and 3.
Stoessinger, J. G., *Henry Kissinger: the Anguish of Power* (New York, 1976).

Biography

Caldwell, D. (ed.), *Kissinger: His Personality and Policies* (Durham, NC, 1983).
Hersh, S. M., *Kissinger: The Price of Power – Henry Kissinger in the Nixon White House* (London and Boston, 1983).
Isaacson, W., *Kissinger: a Biography* (New York and London, 1992).
Kalb, M. and B. Kalb, *Kissinger* (New York, 1975).
Landau, D., *Kissinger: the Uses of Power* (London, 1974).
Mazlish, B., *Kissinger – The European Mind in American Policy* (New York, 1973).

Morris, R., *Uncertain Greatness: Henry Kissinger and American Foreign Policy* (New York and London, 1977).
Schulzinger, R., *Henry Kissinger: Doctor of Diplomacy* (New York, 1989).

General

Ball, G., *Diplomacy for a Crowded World* (London, 1976).
Craig, G. A. and A. L. George, *Force and Statecraft: Diplomatic Problems of Our Time*, 2nd edn (New York and Oxford, 1990).
Falk, R., *What's Wrong with Henry Kissinger's Foreign Policy* (1974).
Graubard, S. R., *Kissinger: Portrait of a Mind* (New York, 1973).
Hoffmann, S., *Primacy or World Order: American Foreign Policy since the Cold War* (New York and London, 1978).
Joffe, J., 'In defense of Henry Kissinger', *Commentary*, vol. 94, no. 6 (1992).
Morgenthau, H. J., 'Henry Kissinger, Secretary of State: an evaluation', *Encounter*, vol. 43, no. 5 (Nov. 1974), pp. 57–61.
Russell, G., 'Kissinger's philosophy of history and Kantian ethics', *Diplomacy & Statecraft*, vol. 7, no. 1 (1996).
Weitz, R., 'Henry Kissinger's philosophy of international relations', *Diplomacy & Statecraft*, vol. 2, no. 1 (1991).
Windsor, P., 'Henry Kissinger's scholarly contribution', *British Journal of International Studies*, Apr. 1975.

Index

Harvard Center for European
Studies 182
Harvard International Seminar 182
Hill, D. J. 128
Hill, Henry Bertram 73
history
consciousness of 184–7, 198
study of 131–2
Hitler, Adolf 161, 182
'honourable spies' 97–8, 117, 122
Hübner, Count von 135, 139

idealism 155, 172, 193
ideological convictions 191
implementation of agreements 41–2
independence of states 129
information-gathering by
diplomats 17–18, 74, 133–4, 199
international assemblies 135–6
international law 16, 56, 98, 115,
129–30, 136, 143–4, 154
international society 52
intuition 187, 194
Israel 195; *see also* Arab–Israeli conflict
'Italian method' of diplomacy 7,
34, 43
Italy 140

James I of England 51
Japan 126–7, 129, 142
Julius II, Pope 15, 19–20, 33, 35
just war 53

Kelsey, Francis W. 52
Keynes, J.M. 169
Kissinger, Henry 3–5, 38, 40–1,
181–203
Diplomacy 183
memoirs 183, 189–90, 198
The Necessity for Choice 183
*Nuclear Weapons and Foreign
Policy* 182
The Troubled Partnership 183
A World Restored 182
Kraemer, Fritz 182

language skills 135, 167
Lausanne Conference (1923) 168
Lauterpacht, H. 53

law of nations 54, 56–8, 61, 90–2, 98,
115, 117
Le Duc Tho 183
League of Nations 152, 155, 170
legation, right of 54
legitimacy 191–2, 194–5
Leo X, Pope 33
linkage, strategy of 194–5
'localitis' 37
Louis XII 9, 14, 20
Louis XIII 71–3, 76, 79
Louis XIV 106, 111, 115, 117–18,
120
Ludovico Sforza, Duke 35
Lyons, A. B. 59

Macaulay, T. Babington (Baron)
11, 131
MacDonald, Ramsay 164
Machiavelli, Niccolò 3–4, 7–24, 34–6,
38–9, 42, 51, 78, 89, 91, 100, 111,
115–16, 120
'Advice to Raffaello Girolami' 9,
16, 18–20
The Art of War 24
The Discourses 10, 13–14, 16, 20,
22, 24, 34
The History of Florence 10, 16, 23
Mandragola 11
the *Missions* 10, 15–16, 19–20, 22
The Prince 10, 12–15
Mahler, Gustav 125
Malmesbury, Earl of 134
Mao Zedong 196
Mattingly, Garrett 11, 34, 108–9
Maurice, Prince 50
Mazarin, Jules 88, 99, 111
Mazlish, Bruce 185
Medici, Marie de 71
Medici family 9, 33
Meinecke, Friedrich 7, 14, 42
Mendoza, Bernadino de 52
Metternich, Prince 137, 193, 196
'middle way' between weakness and
strength 10
military force 11–12, 23–4, 72, 99,
121, 130, 141–2, 144, 197
military service 23–4
'Mirror of Princes' 90

1488351R00121

Made in the USA
San Bernardino, CA
21 December 2012